SUPERMAN BATMAN

BIG NOISE

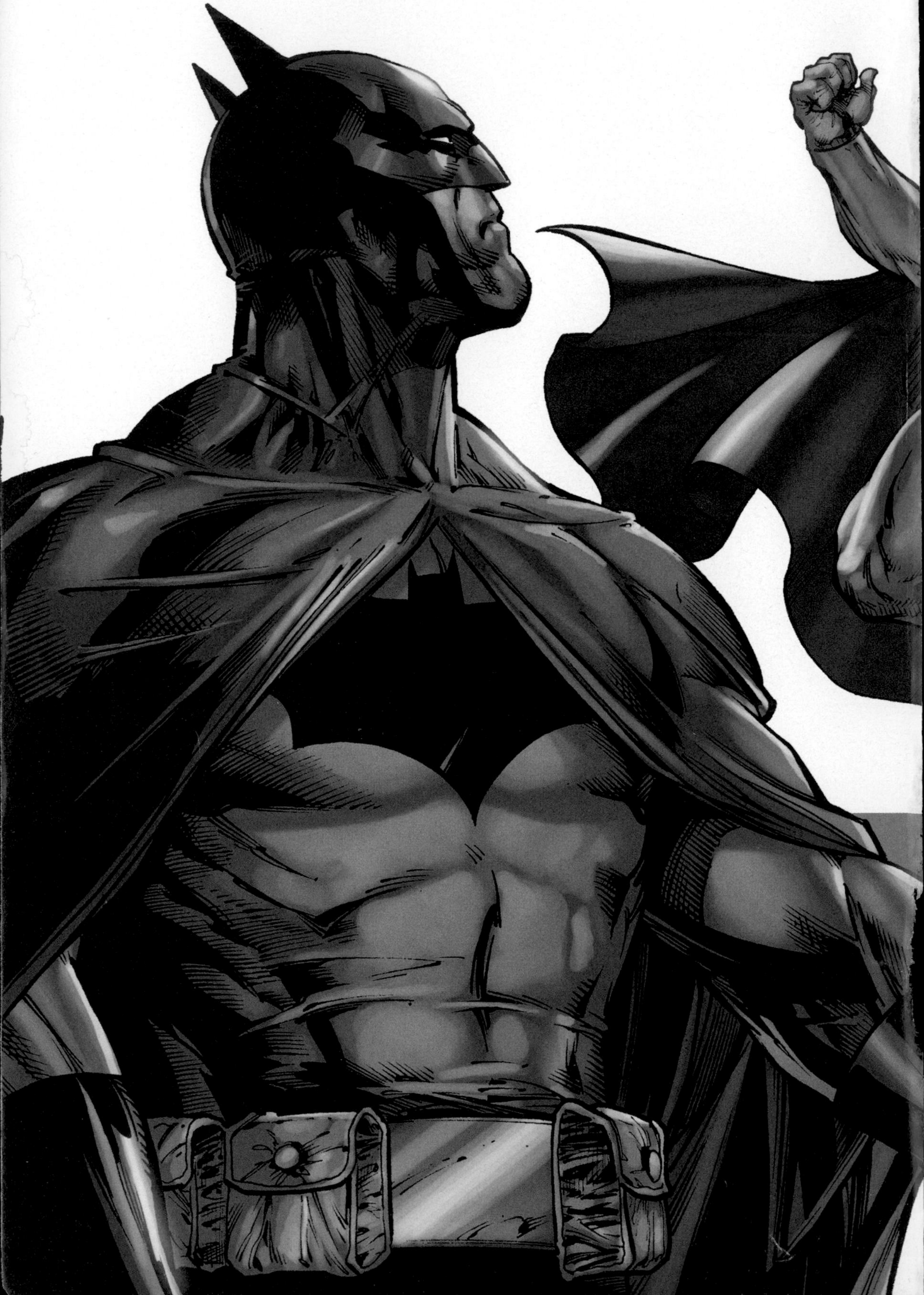

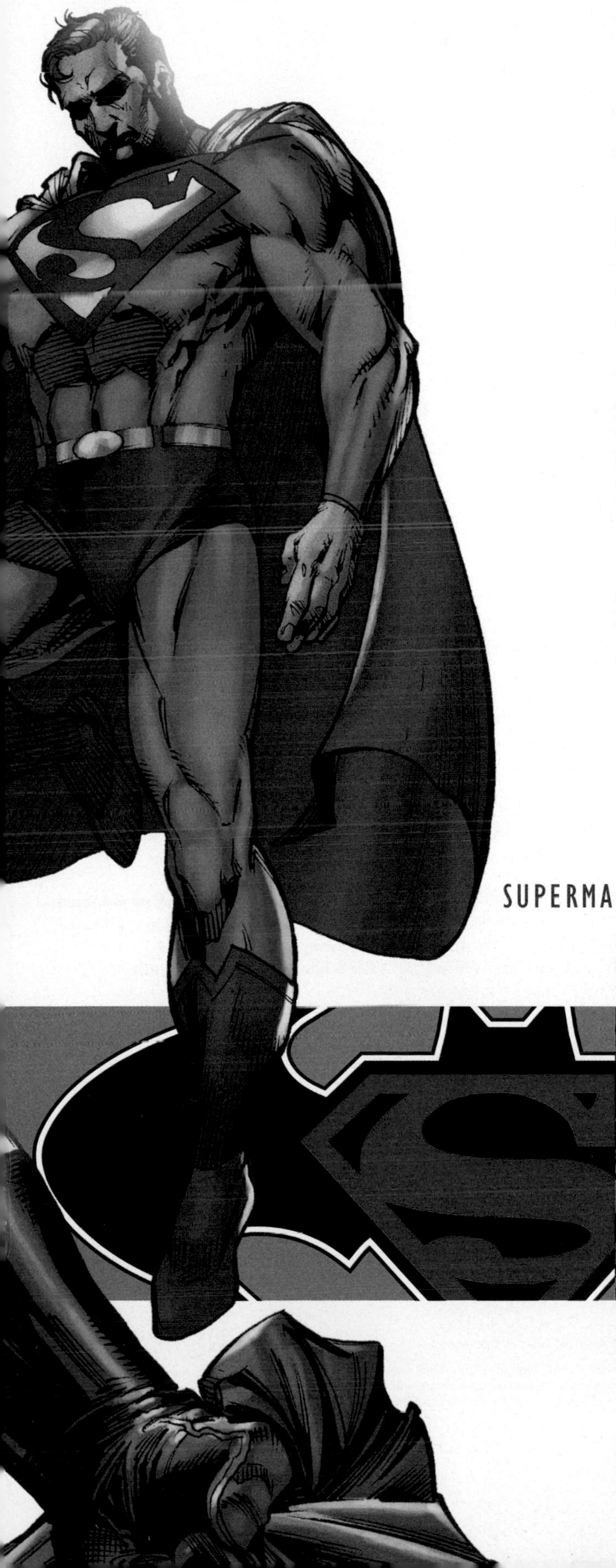

Joe Casey
Joshua Williamson (co-writer, Part 4)
Writers

Scott Kolins
Ardian Syaf
Jay Fabok
Pencillers

Scott Kolins
Vicente Cifuentes
David Enebral
Norm Rapmund
Marlo Alquiza
Prentis Rollins
Rebecca Buchman
Derek Fridolfs
Walden Wong
Inkers

Michael Atiyeh
Ulises Arreola
Pete Pantazis
Colorists

Rob Leigh
Letterer

SUPERMAN BATMAN

BIG NOISE

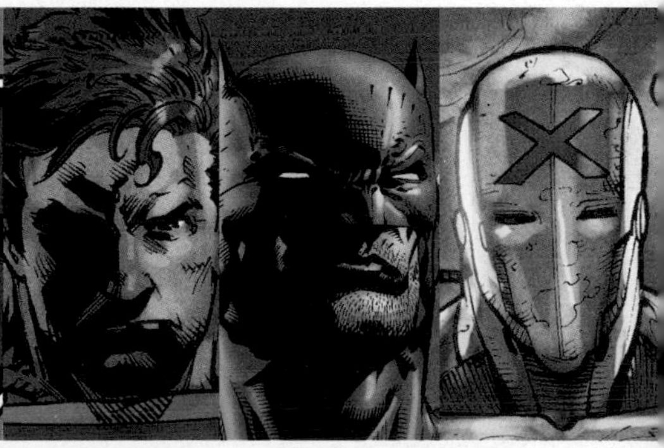

Ardian Syaf, Vicente Cifuentes and Ulises Arreola
Collection cover

Superman created by Jerry Siegel and Joe Shuster
Batman created by Bob Kane

EDDIE BERGANZA Editor-Original Series   ADAM SCHLAGMAN Associate Editor-Original Series   REX OGLE Assistant Editor-Original Series
BOB HARRAS Group Editor-Collected Editions   BOB JOY Editor   ROBBIN BROSTERMAN Design Director-Books   CURTIS KING JR. Senior Art Director

DC COMICS

DIANE NELSON President   DAN DIDIO and JIM LEE Co-Publishers   GEOFF JOHNS Chief Creative Officer   PATRICK CALDON EVP-Finance and Administration
JOHN ROOD EVP-Sales, Marketing and Business Development   AMY GENKINS SVP-Business and Legal Affairs   STEVE ROTTERDAM SVP-Sales and Marketing
JOHN CUNNINGHAM VP-Marketing   TERRI CUNNINGHAM VP-Managing Editor   ALISON GILL VP-Manufacturing   DAVID HYDE VP-Publicity
SUE POHJA VP-Book Trade Sales   ALYSSE SOLL VP-Advertising and Custom Publishing   BOB WAYNE VP-Sales   MARK CHIARELLO Art Director

SUPERMAN/BATMAN: BIG NOISE

Published by DC Comics. Cover, text and compilation Copyright © 2010 DC Comics. All Rights Reserved.

Originally published in single magazine form in SUPERMAN/BATMAN 64, 68-71. Copyright © 2009, 2010 DC Comics. All Rights Reserved.
All characters, their distinctive likenesses and related elements featured in this publication are trademarks of DC Comics. The stories,
characters and incidents featured in this publication are entirely fictional. DC Comics does not read or accept unsolicited submissions
of ideas, stories or artwork.

DC Comics, 1700 Broadway, New York, NY 10019
A Warner Bros. Entertainment Company
Printed by Quad/Graphics, Dubuque, IA, USA. 05/13/11. Second Printing.
ISBN: 978-1-4012-2914-6

SUSTAINABLE
FORESTRY
INITIATIVE
Certified Chain of Custody
Promoting Sustainable
Forest Management
www.sfiprogram.org

Fiber used in this product line meets the
sourcing requirements of the SFI program.
www.sfiprogram.org SGS-SFICOC-0130

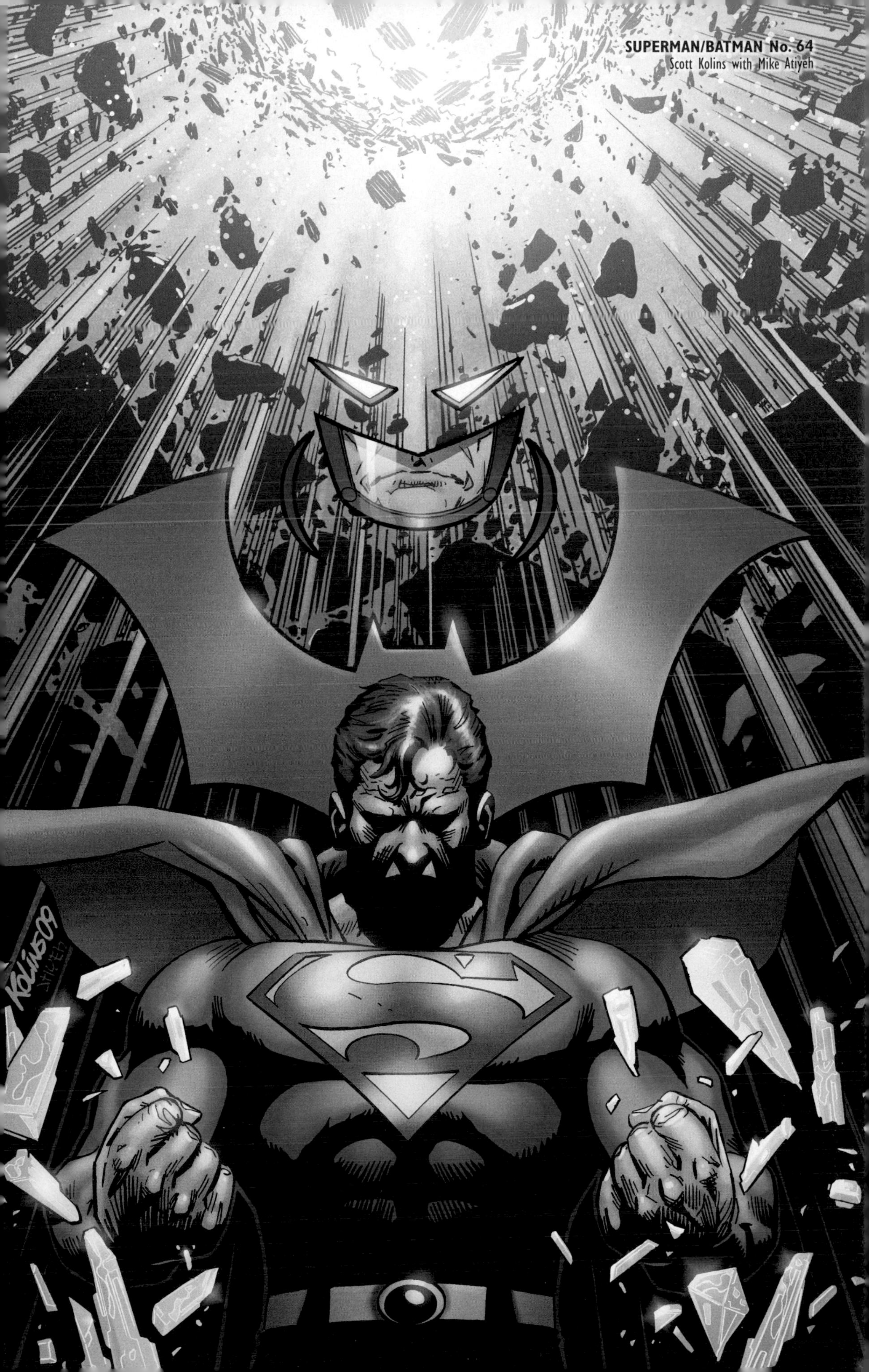

SUPERMAN/BATMAN No. 64
Scott Kolins with Mike Atiyeh

PRELUDE TO THE BIG NOISE: THREE MONTHS AWAY

Artist: Scott Kolins

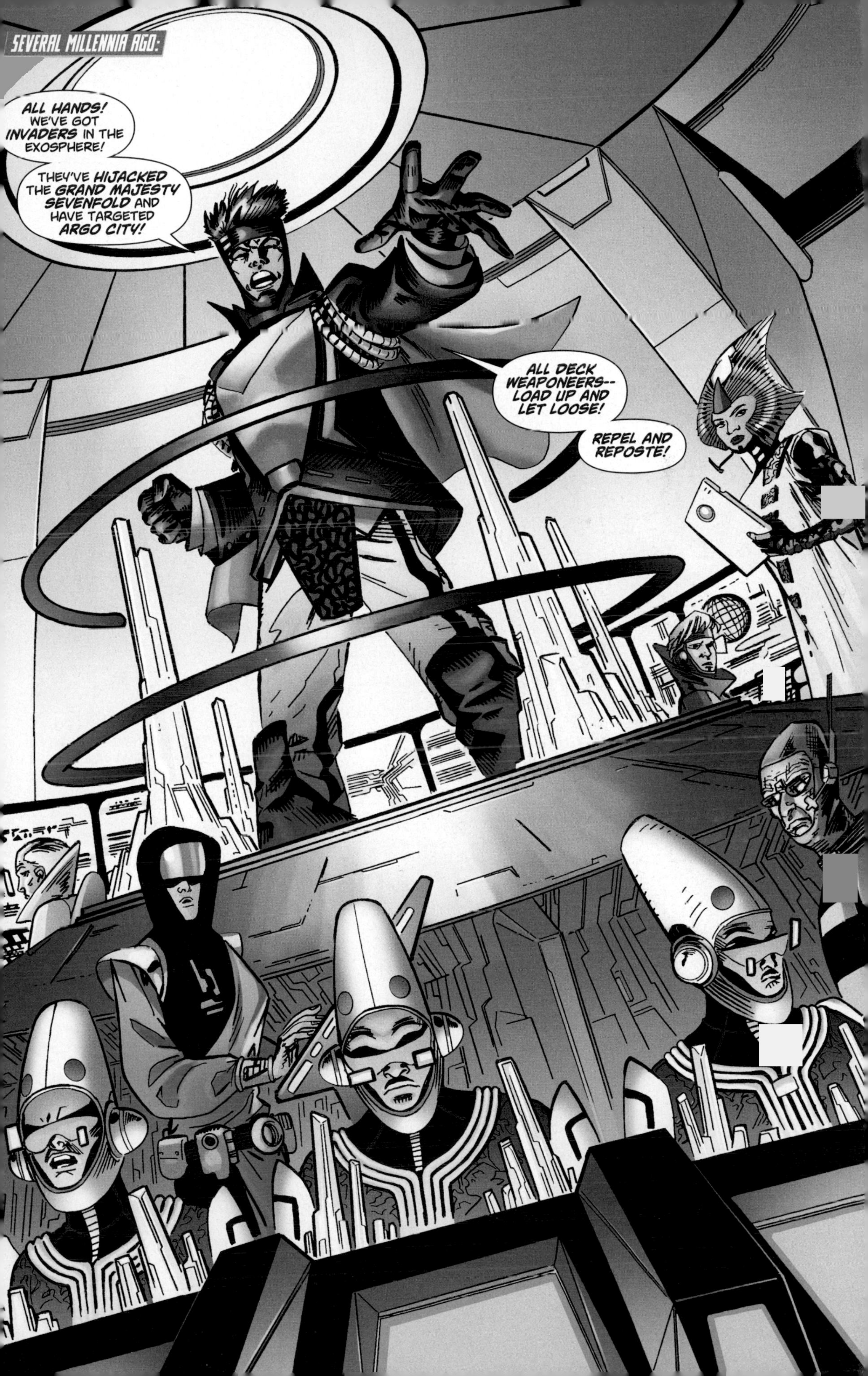
SEVERAL MILLENNIA AGO:
ALL HANDS! WE'VE GOT INVADERS IN THE EXOSPHERE!
THEY'VE HIJACKED THE GRAND MAJESTY SEVENFOLD AND HAVE TARGETED ARGO CITY!
ALL DECK WEAPONEERS-- LOAD UP AND LET LOOSE!
REPEL AND REPOSTE!

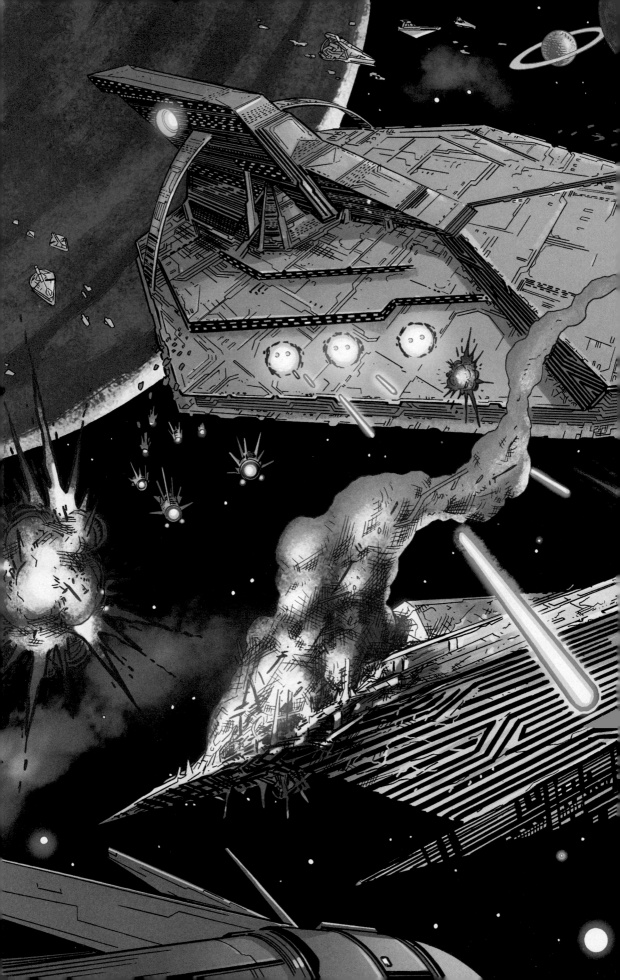

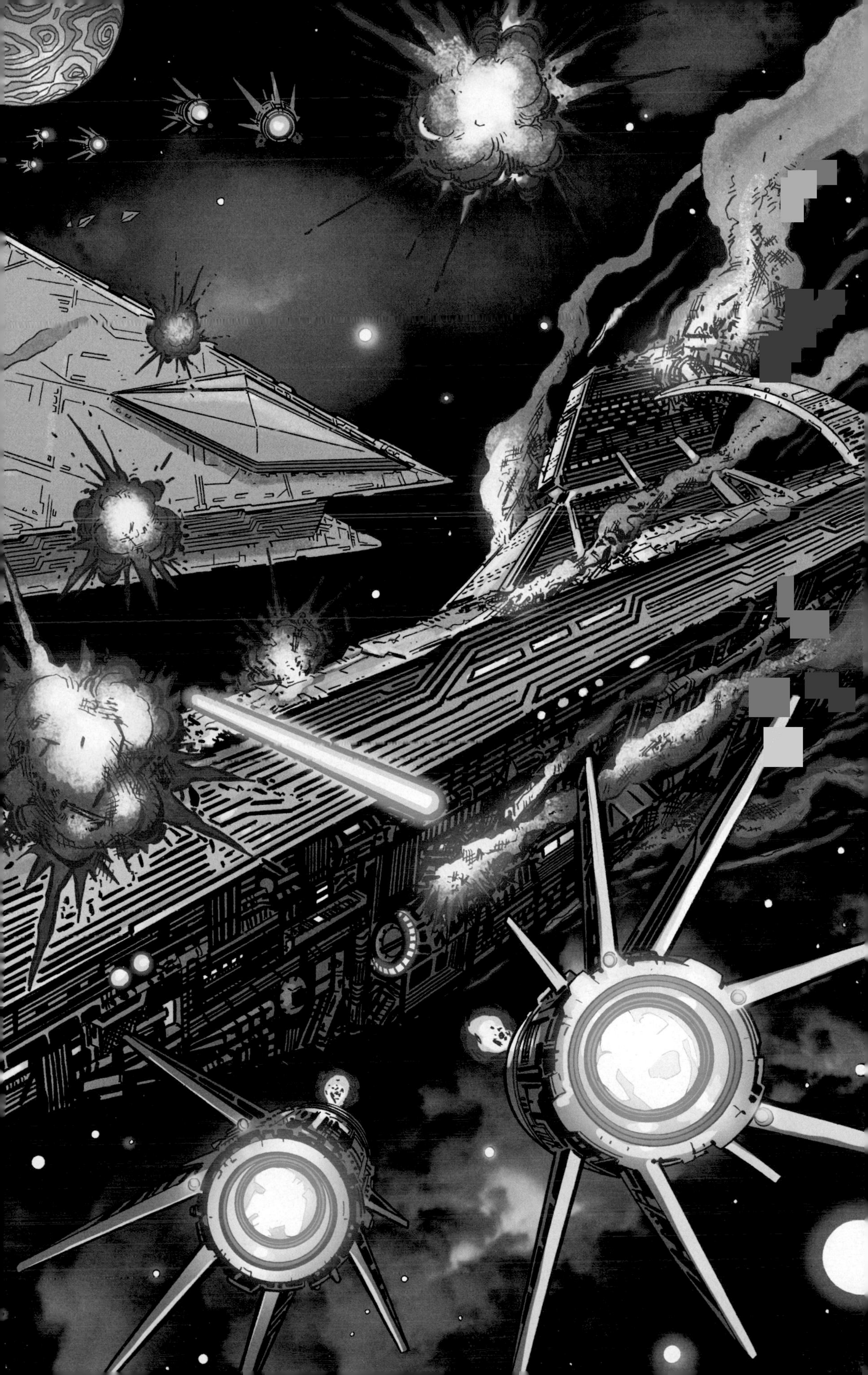

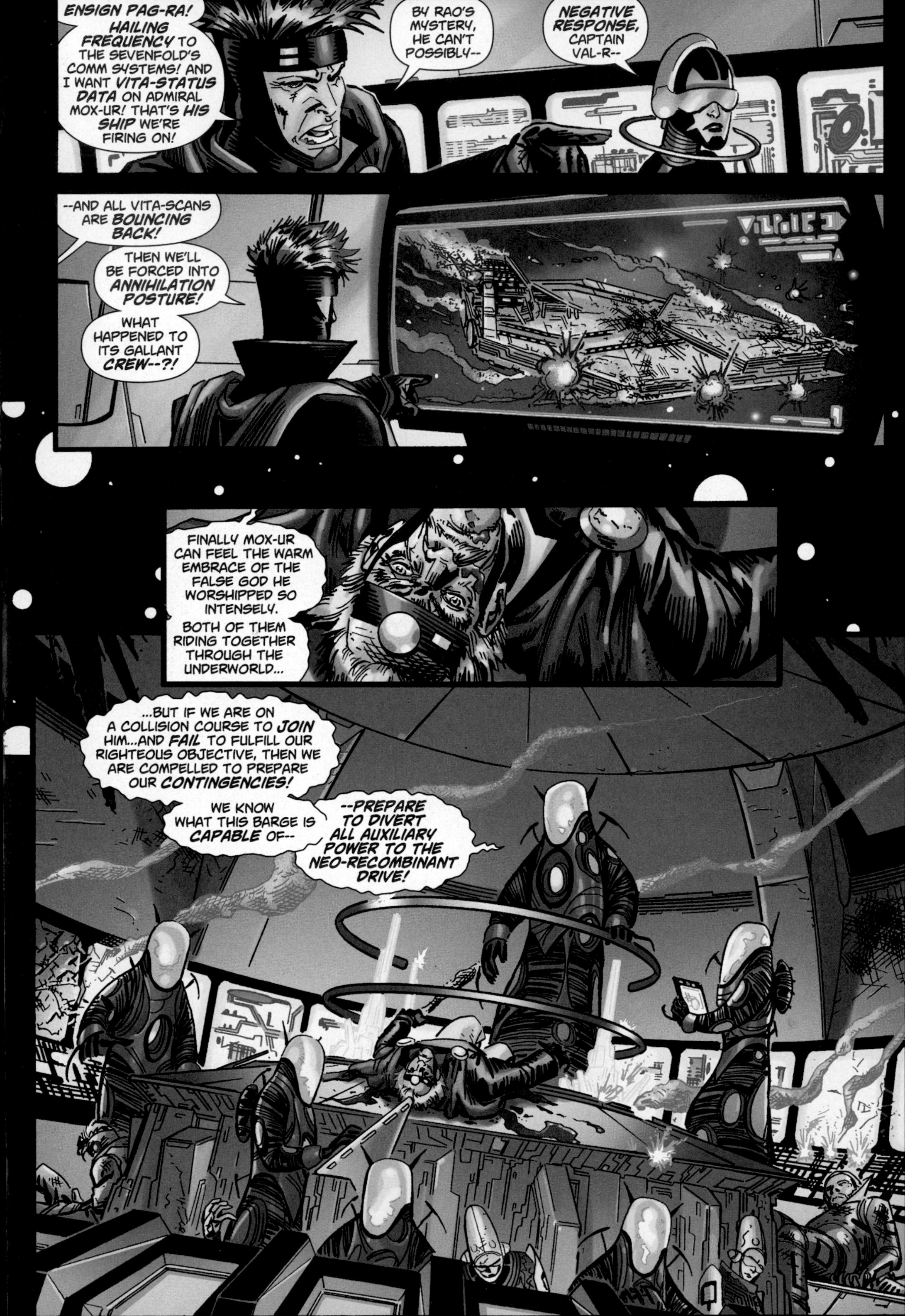
ENSIGN PAG-RA! HAILING FREQUENCY TO THE SEVENFOLD'S COMM SYSTEMS! AND I WANT VITA-STATUS DATA ON ADMIRAL MOX-UR! THAT'S HIS SHIP WE'RE FIRING ON!
BY RAO'S MYSTERY, HE CAN'T POSSIBLY--
NEGATIVE RESPONSE, CAPTAIN VAL-R--
--AND ALL VITA-SCANS ARE BOUNCING BACK!
THEN WE'LL BE FORCED INTO ANNIHILATION POSTURE!
WHAT HAPPENED TO ITS GALLANT CREW--?!
FINALLY MOX-UR CAN FEEL THE WARM EMBRACE OF THE FALSE GOD HE WORSHIPPED SO INTENSELY.
BOTH OF THEM RIDING TOGETHER THROUGH THE UNDERWORLD...
...BUT IF WE ARE ON A COLLISION COURSE TO JOIN HIM...AND FAIL TO FULFILL OUR RIGHTEOUS OBJECTIVE, THEN WE ARE COMPELLED TO PREPARE OUR CONTINGENCIES!
WE KNOW WHAT THIS BARGE IS CAPABLE OF--
--PREPARE TO DIVERT ALL AUXILIARY POWER TO THE NEO-RECOMBINANT DRIVE!

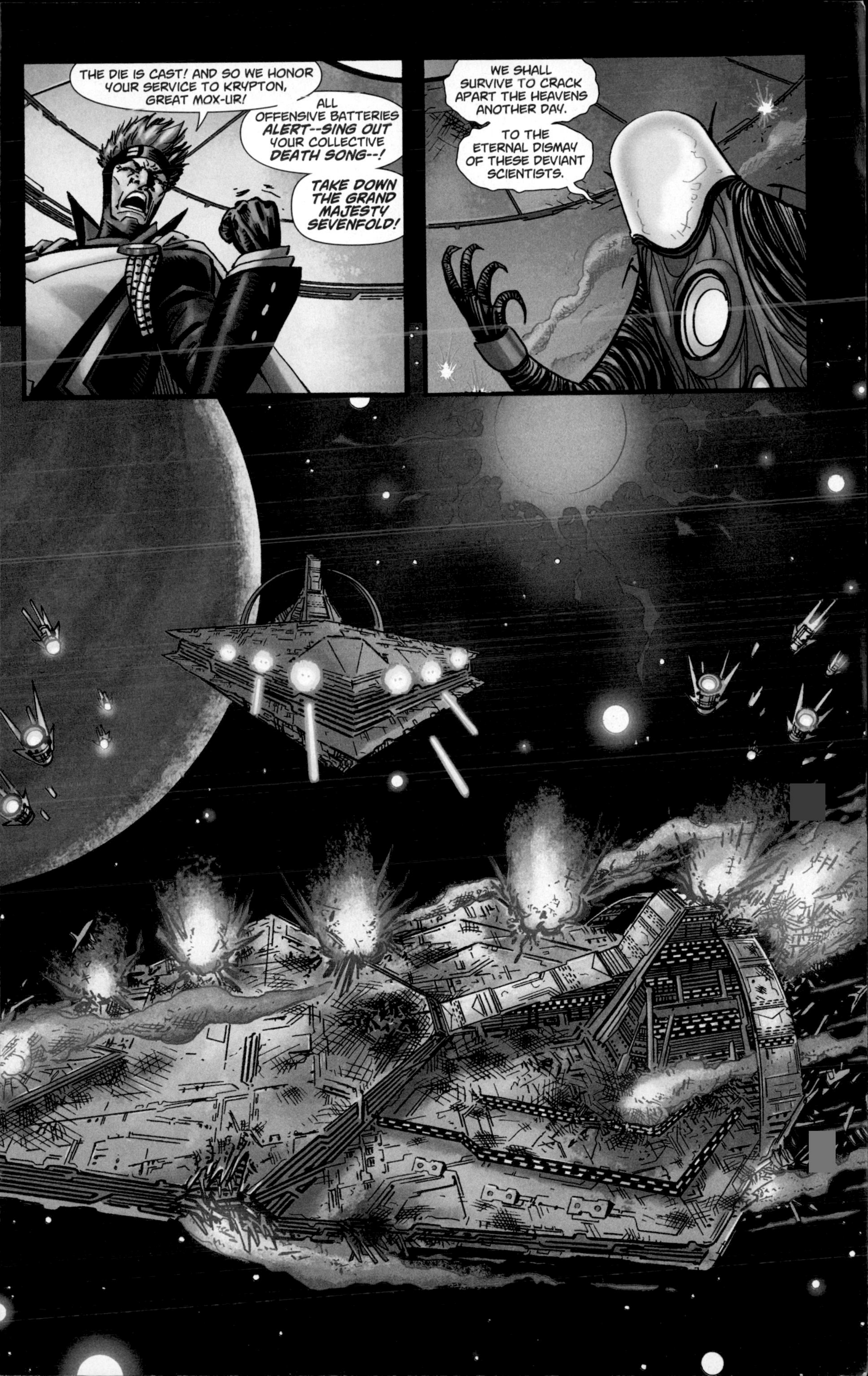
THE DIE IS CAST! AND SO WE HONOR YOUR SERVICE TO KRYPTON, GREAT MOX-UR!
ALL OFFENSIVE BATTERIES ALERT--SING OUT YOUR COLLECTIVE DEATH SONG--!
TAKE DOWN THE GRAND MAJESTY SEVENFOLD!
WE SHALL SURVIVE TO CRACK APART THE HEAVENS ANOTHER DAY.
TO THE ETERNAL DISMAY OF THESE DEVIANT SCIENTISTS.

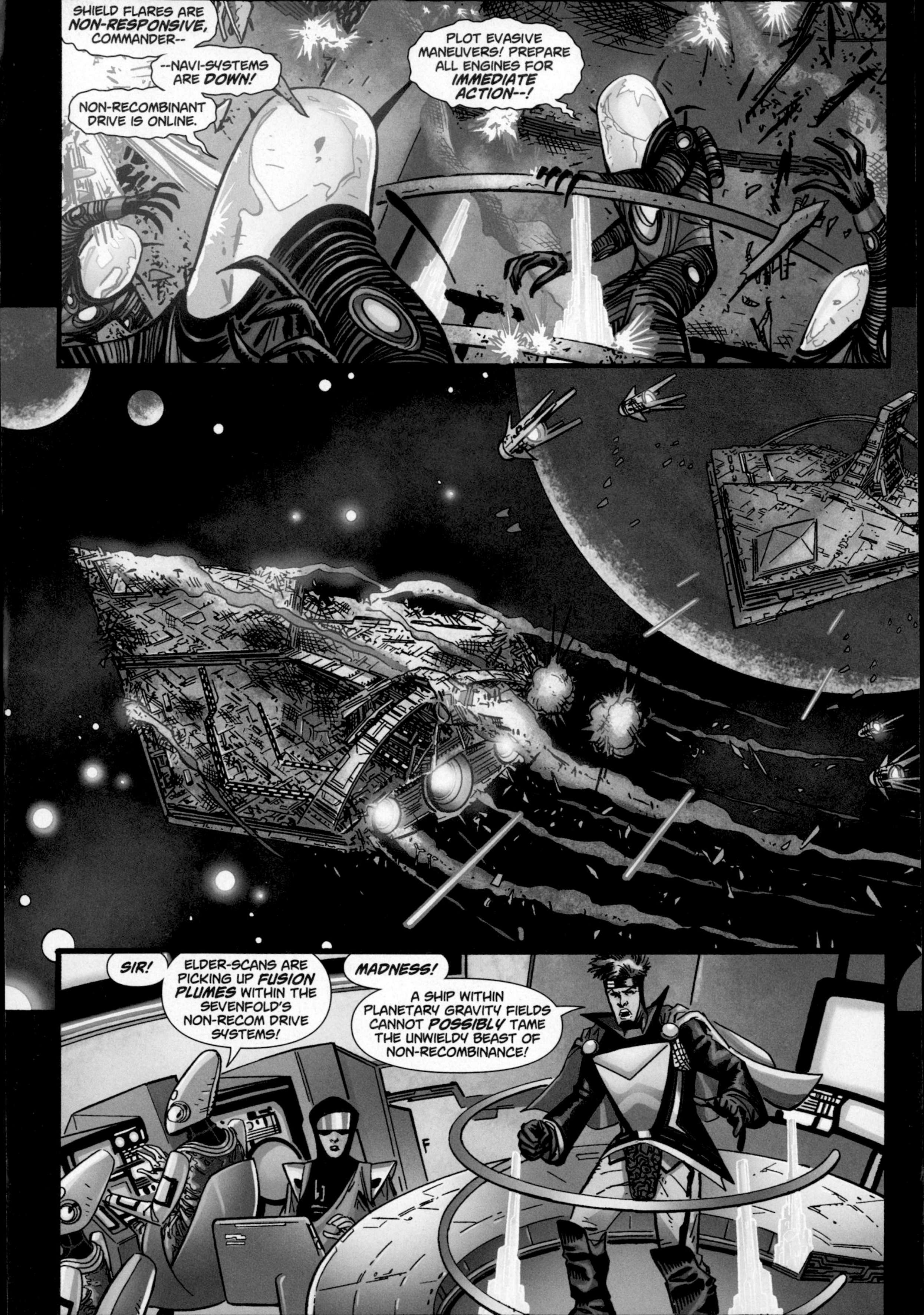
SHIELD FLARES ARE NON-RESPONSIVE, COMMANDER--
--NAVI-SYSTEMS ARE DOWN!
NON-RECOMBINANT DRIVE IS ONLINE.
PLOT EVASIVE MANEUVERS! PREPARE ALL ENGINES FOR IMMEDIATE ACTION--!
SIR!
ELDER-SCANS ARE PICKING UP FUSION PLUMES WITHIN THE SEVENFOLD'S NON-RECOM DRIVE SYSTEMS!
MADNESS!
A SHIP WITHIN PLANETARY GRAVITY FIELDS CANNOT POSSIBLY TAME THE UNWIELDY BEAST OF NON-RECOMBINANCE!

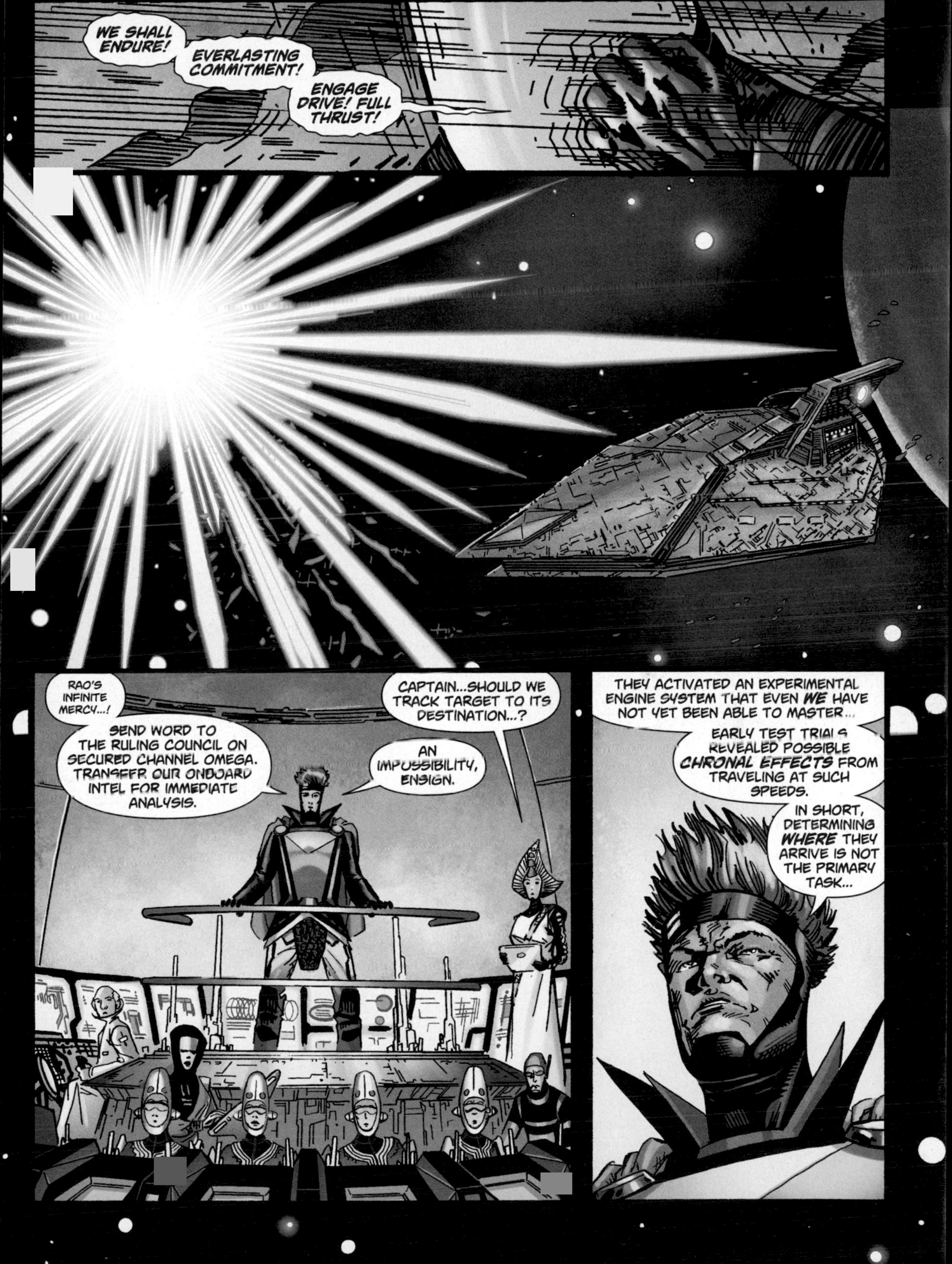

WE SHALL ENDURE!
EVERLASTING COMMITMENT!
ENGAGE DRIVE! FULL THRUST!
RAO'S INFINITE MERCY...!
SEND WORD TO THE RULING COUNCIL ON SECURED CHANNEL OMEGA. TRANSFER OUR ONBOARD INTEL FOR IMMEDIATE ANALYSIS.
CAPTAIN...SHOULD WE TRACK TARGET TO ITS DESTINATION...?
AN IMPOSSIBILITY, ENSIGN.
THEY ACTIVATED AN EXPERIMENTAL ENGINE SYSTEM THAT EVEN WE HAVE NOT YET BEEN ABLE TO MASTER...
EARLY TEST TRIALS REVEALED POSSIBLE CHRONAL EFFECTS FROM TRAVELING AT SUCH SPEEDS.
IN SHORT, DETERMINING WHERE THEY ARRIVE IS NOT THE PRIMARY TASK...

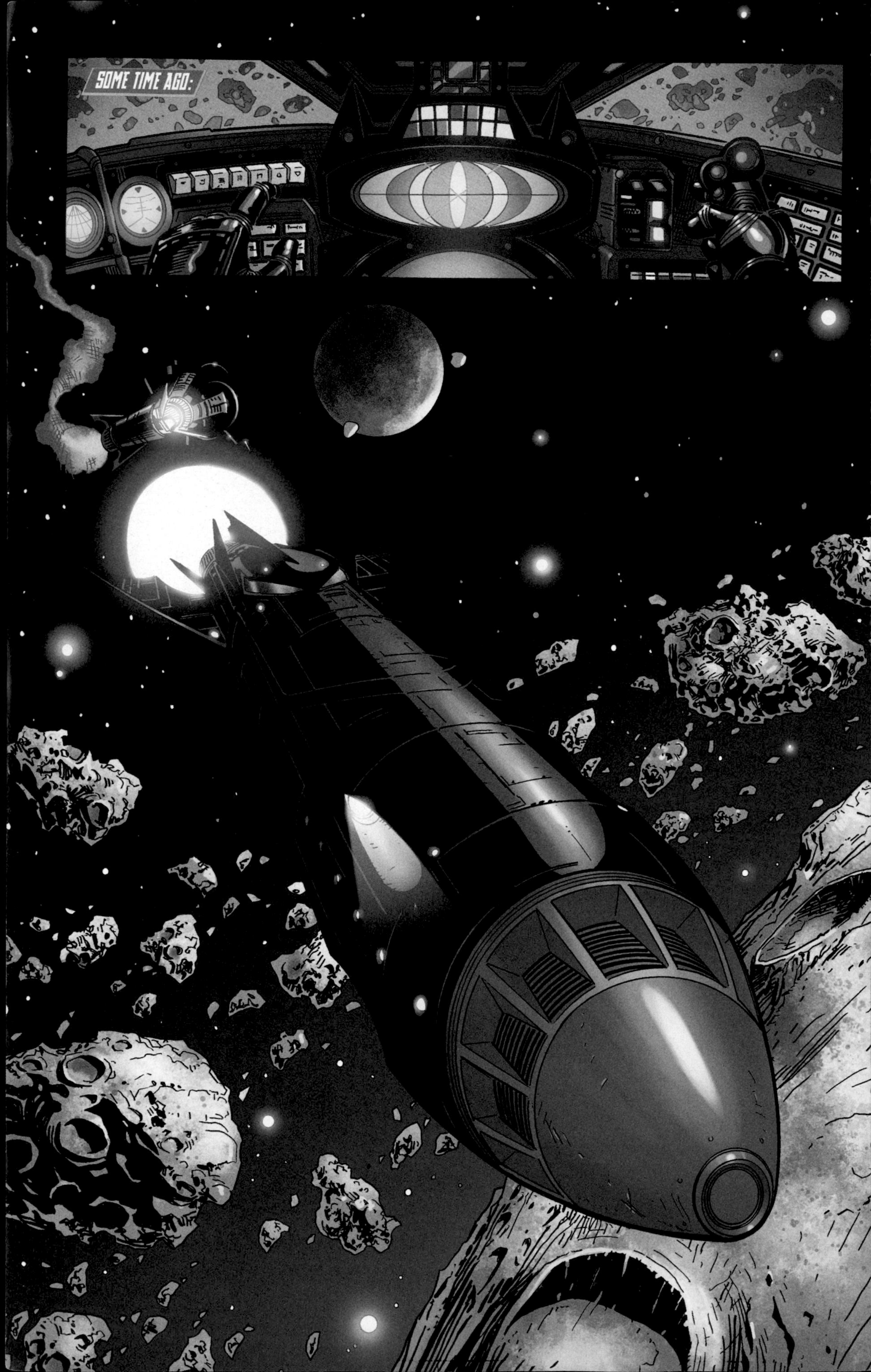
SOME TIME AGO:

OPEN GAMMA
CHANNEL. ONBOARD
COMMUNICATIONS
ACTIVE.

ENCRYPTION
ENABLED. BEGIN
RECORD—

ALFRED.
I'VE REACHED
THE TARGET. IN THE TIME IT
TAKES FOR THIS MESSAGE TO
REACH YOU, I'LL HAVE ALREADY
GONE EXTERIOR FOR FURTHER
INVESTIGATION.

THIS MAY BE NOTHING
BUT A RANDOM DERELICT.
REGARDLESS, THESE THINGS
DON'T JUST APPEAR OUT
OF *NOWHERE*.

CONTINUE RELAYING
ANY RELEVANT DATA
FROM THE CAVE TO MY
ONBOARDS HERE AND
I'LL BE IN TOUCH.

END
TRANSMISSION.

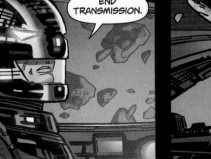

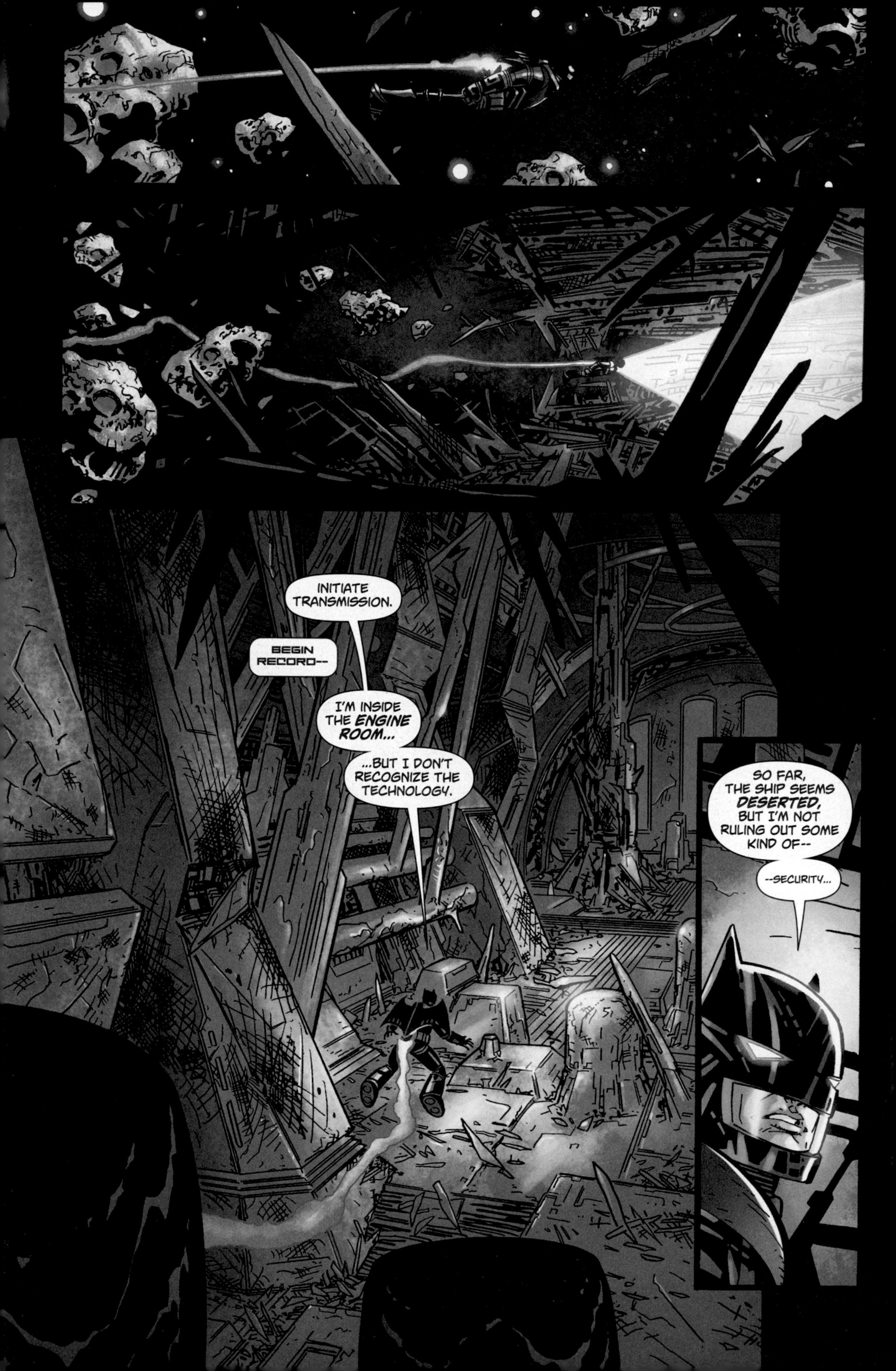

INITIATE TRANSMISSION.
BEGIN RECORD--
I'M INSIDE THE *ENGINE ROOM*...
...BUT I DON'T RECOGNIZE THE TECHNOLOGY.
SO FAR, THE SHIP SEEMS *DESERTED,* BUT I'M NOT RULING OUT SOME KIND OF--
--SECURITY...

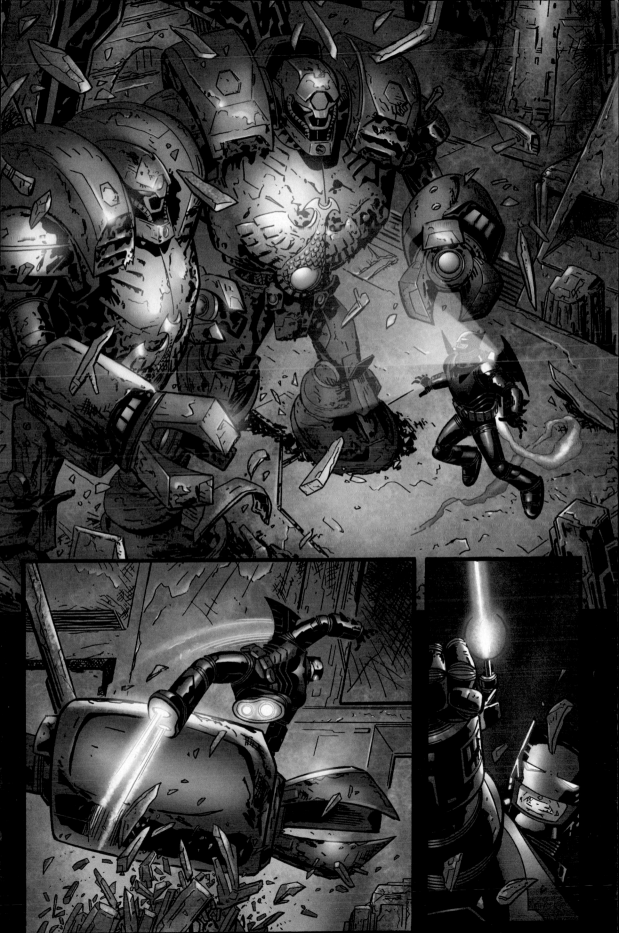

Hh.

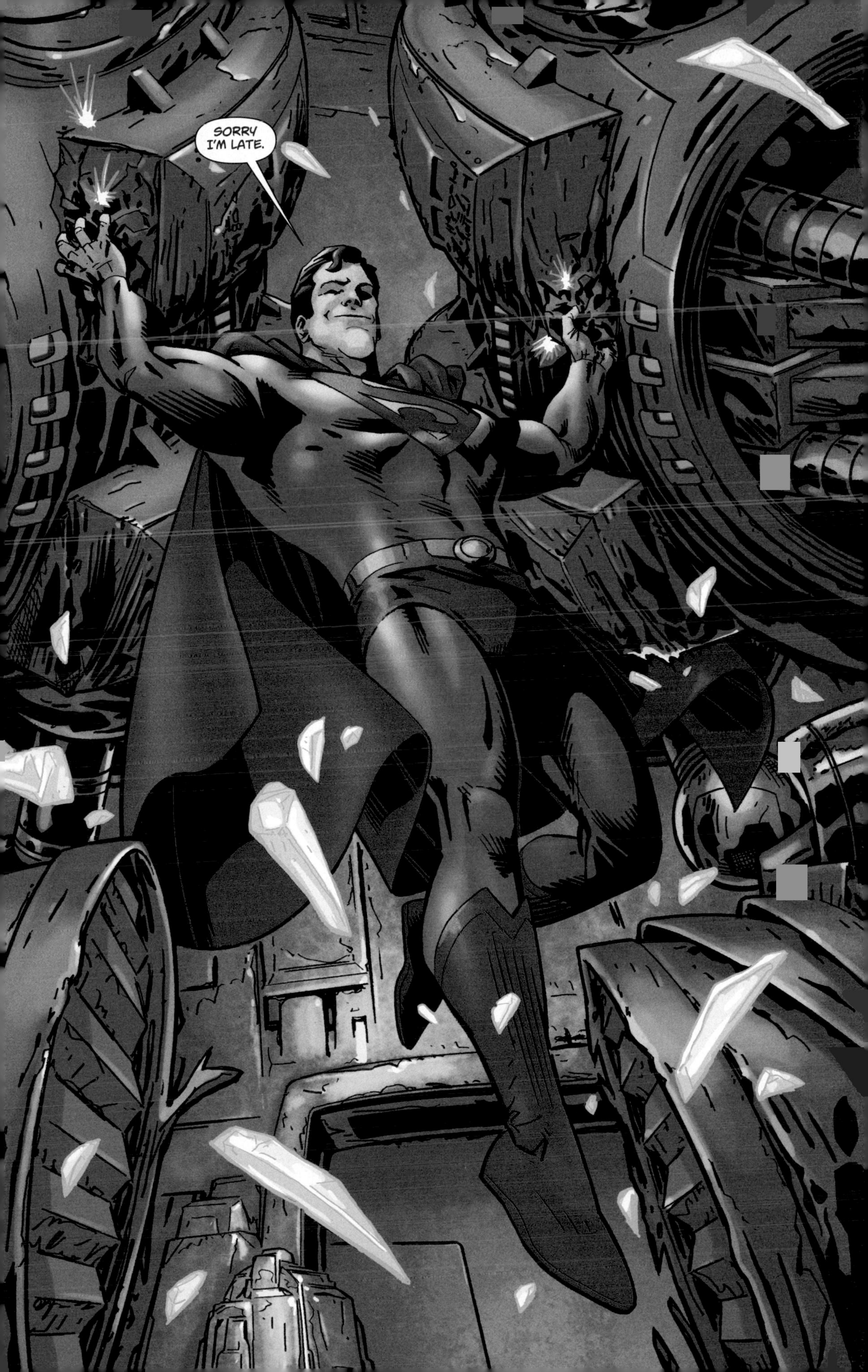
SORRY I'M LATE.

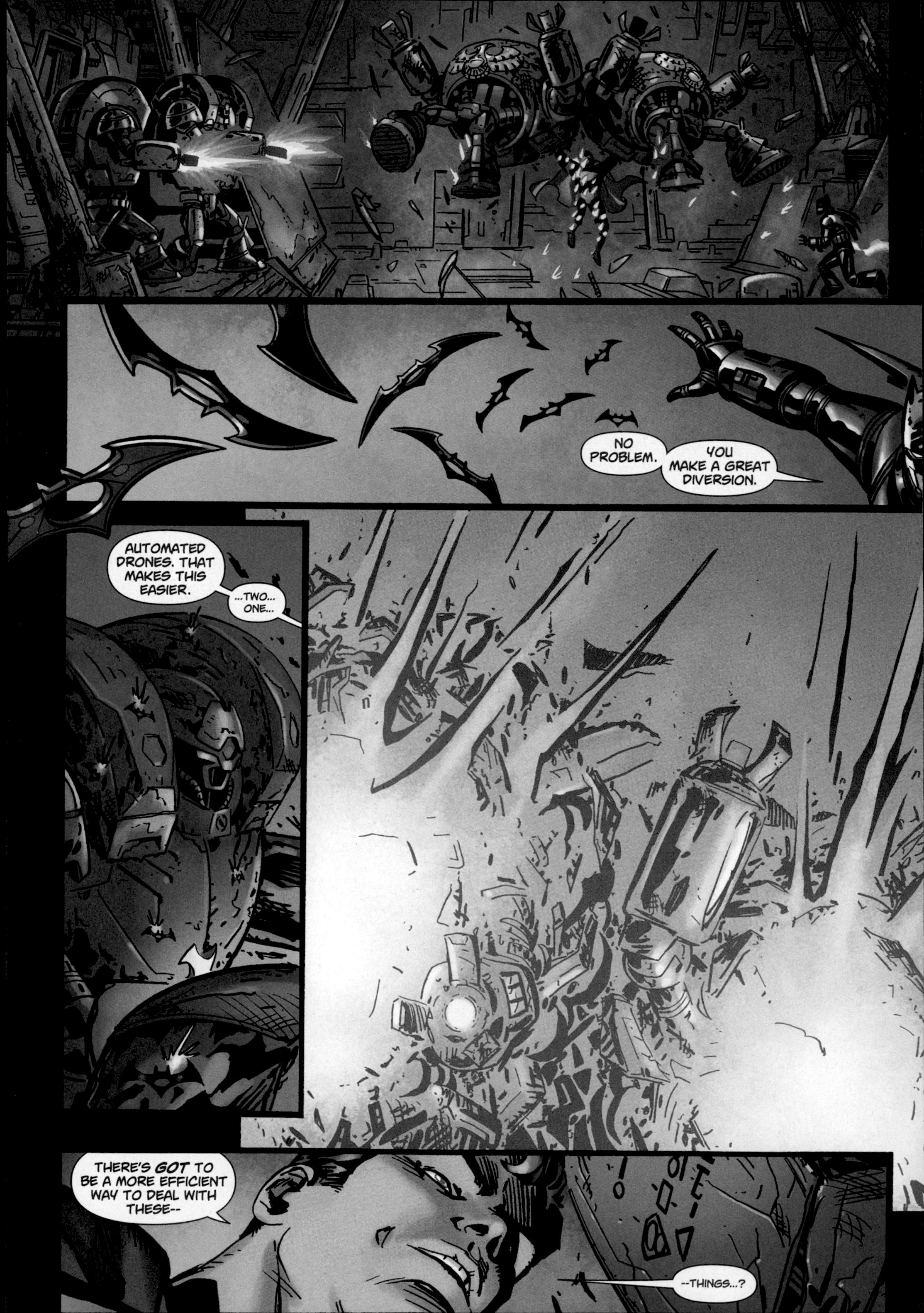
NO PROBLEM.
YOU MAKE A GREAT DIVERSION.
AUTOMATED DRONES. THAT MAKES THIS EASIER.
...TWO... ONE...
THERE'S GOT TO BE A MORE EFFICIENT WAY TO DEAL WITH THESE--
--THINGS...?

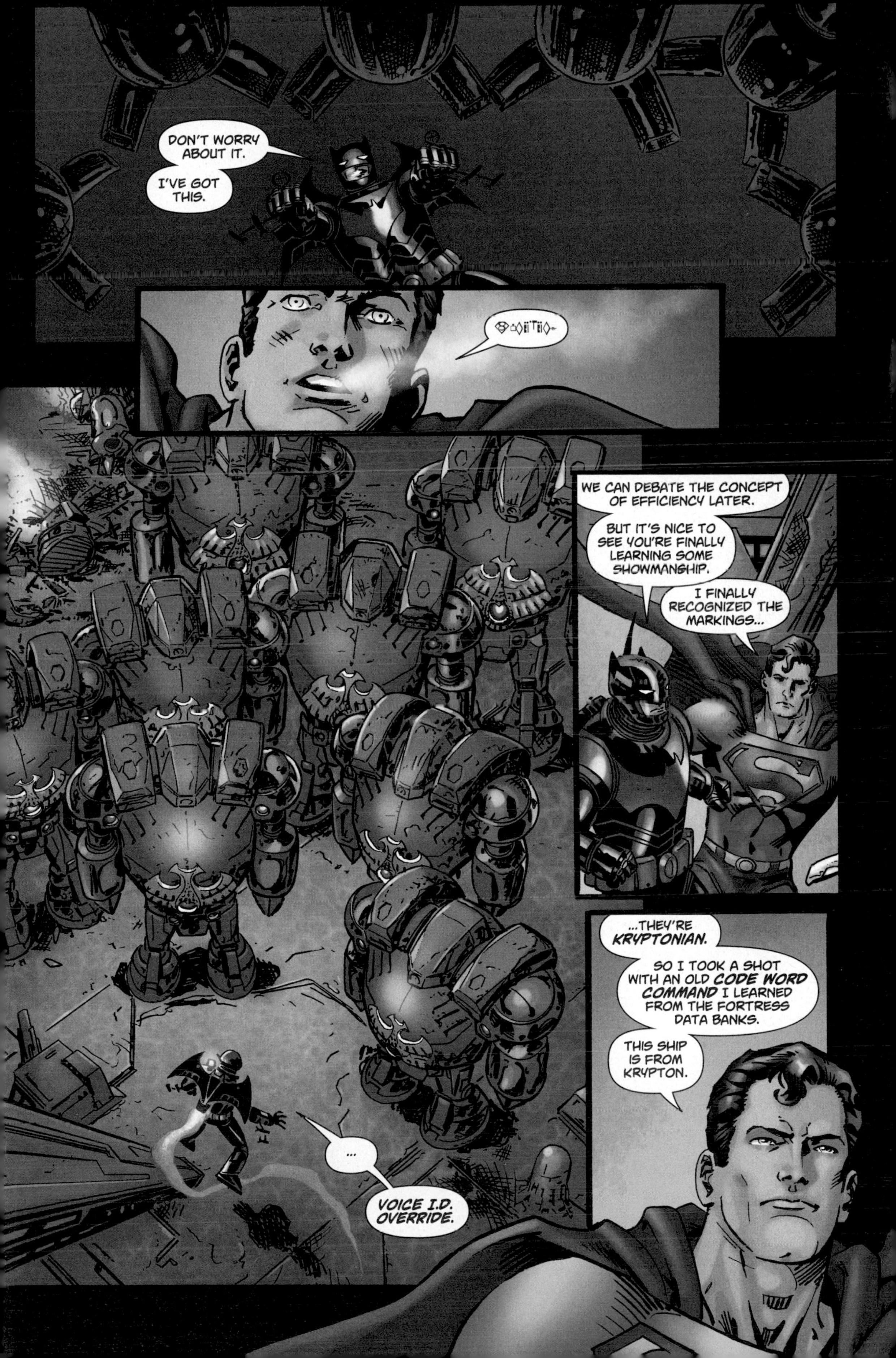
DON'T WORRY ABOUT IT.
I'VE GOT THIS.
...
VOICE I.D. OVERRIDE.
WE CAN DEBATE THE CONCEPT OF EFFICIENCY LATER.
BUT IT'S NICE TO SEE YOU'RE FINALLY LEARNING SOME SHOWMANSHIP.
I FINALLY RECOGNIZED THE MARKINGS...
...THEY'RE KRYPTONIAN.
SO I TOOK A SHOT WITH AN OLD CODE WORD COMMAND I LEARNED FROM THE FORTRESS DATA BANKS.
THIS SHIP IS FROM KRYPTON.

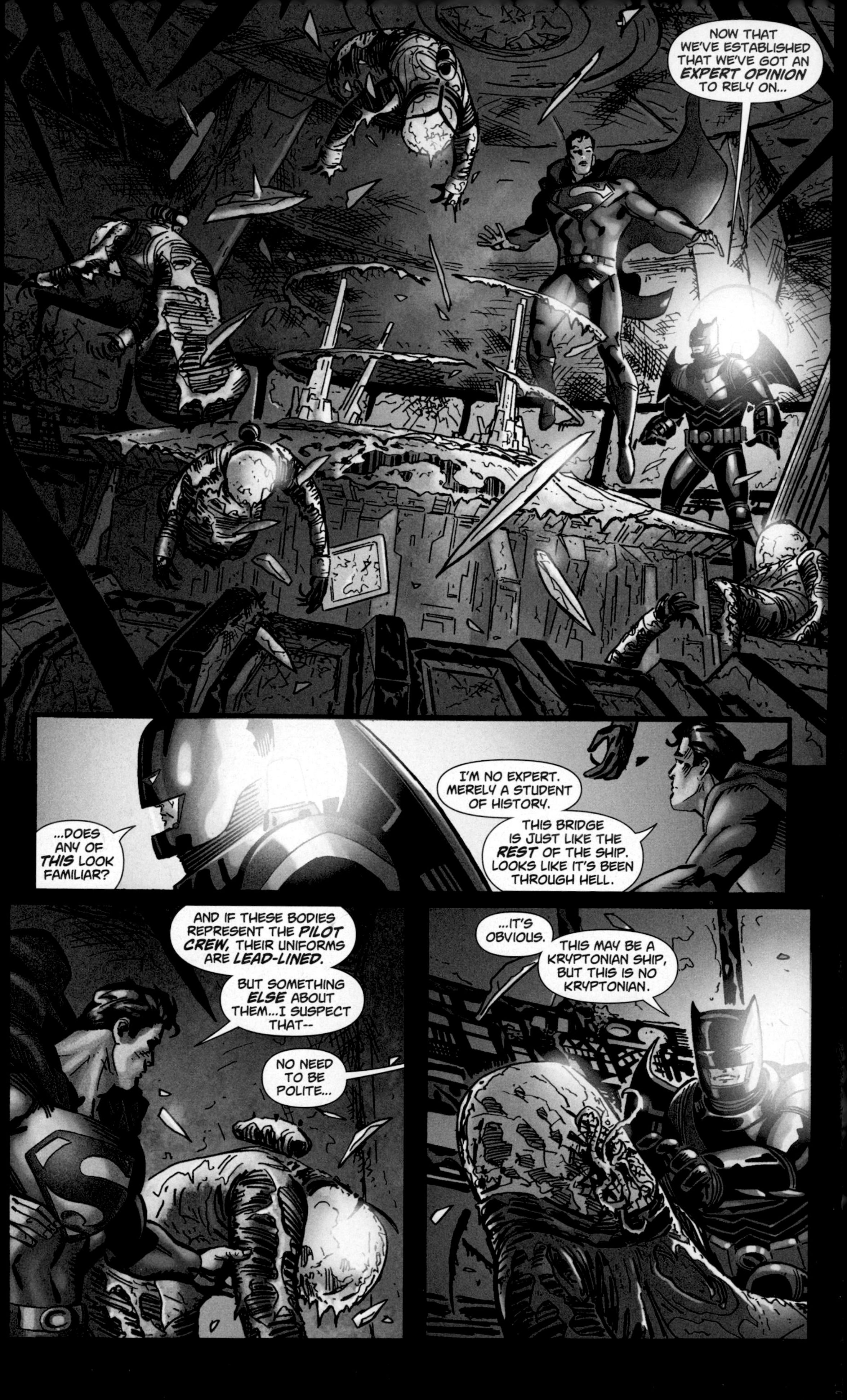
NOW THAT WE'VE ESTABLISHED THAT WE'VE GOT AN EXPERT OPINION TO RELY ON...
...DOES ANY OF THIS LOOK FAMILIAR?
I'M NO EXPERT. MERELY A STUDENT OF HISTORY.
THIS BRIDGE IS JUST LIKE THE REST OF THE SHIP. LOOKS LIKE IT'S BEEN THROUGH HELL.
AND IF THESE BODIES REPRESENT THE PILOT CREW, THEIR UNIFORMS ARE LEAD-LINED.
BUT SOMETHING ELSE ABOUT THEM...I SUSPECT THAT--
NO NEED TO BE POLITE...
...IT'S OBVIOUS.
THIS MAY BE A KRYPTONIAN SHIP, BUT THIS IS NO KRYPTONIAN.

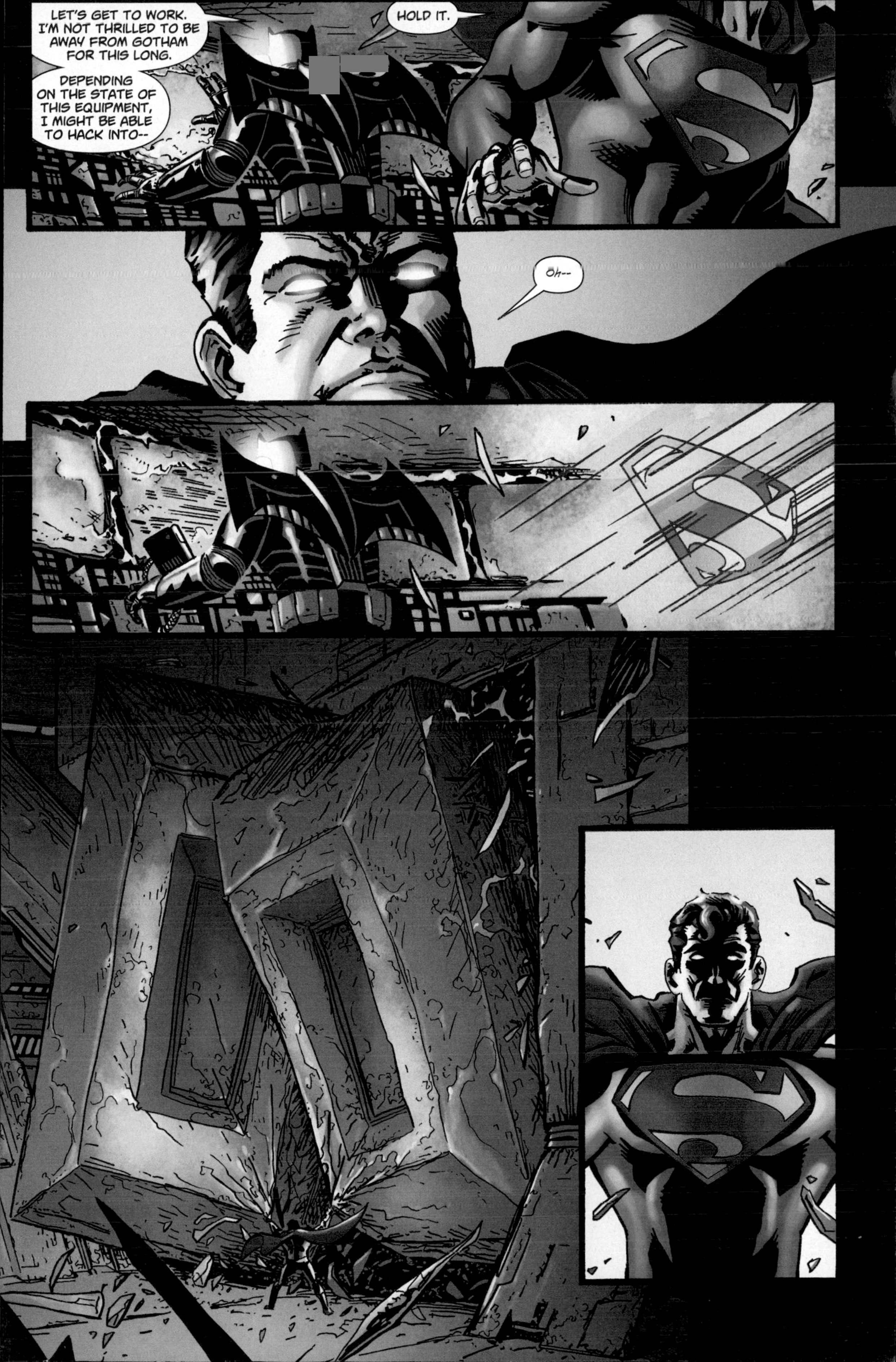
LET'S GET TO WORK. I'M NOT THRILLED TO BE AWAY FROM GOTHAM FOR THIS LONG.
HOLD IT.
DEPENDING ON THE STATE OF THIS EQUIPMENT, I MIGHT BE ABLE TO HACK INTO--
Oh--

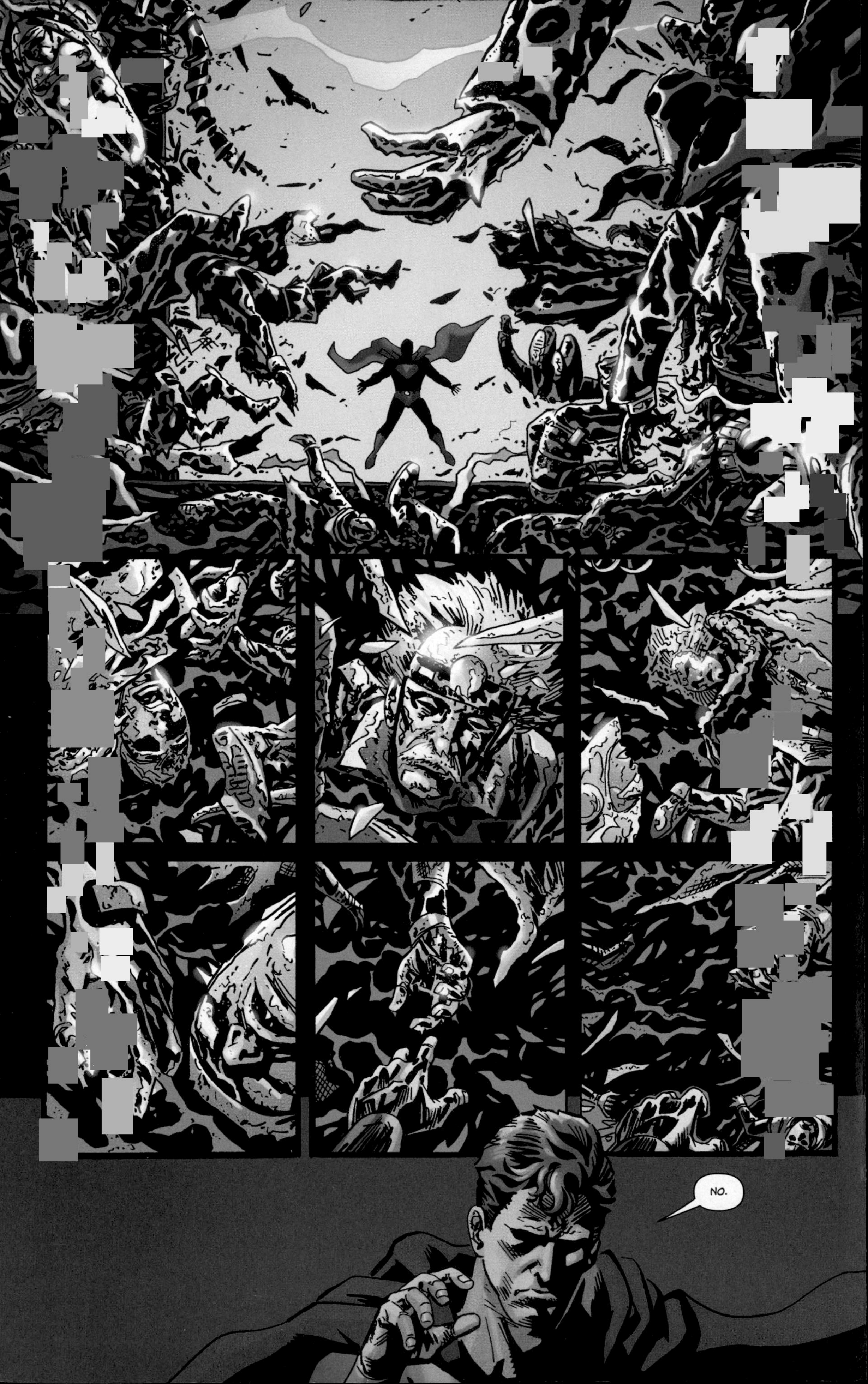
NO.

I COULD'VE TOLD YOU THAT YOU MIGHT FIND SOMETHING THAT HIT A LITTLE CLOSE TO HOME...

...NEVERTHELESS, I NEED YOUR HEAD IN THE GAME.

I'M HERE. IT WAS JUST...

...TO SEE SO MANY OF THEM...ALL AT ONCE...

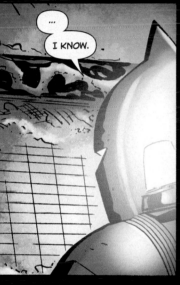

...

I KNOW.

A CRIPPLED SHIP. A BRIDGE FULL OF ALIEN INTRUDERS. A HOLD FULL OF MURDERED KRYPTONIANS.

ANY IDEAS...?

A FEW.

SEEMS LIKE I'VE BEEN ABLE TO BYPASS WHATEVER ENCRYPTION EXISTED WITHIN THIS SYSTEM. SO UNLESS I'M MISTAKEN--

--WHICH I DOUBT I AM--

--I'VE SUCCEEDED IN RECOVERING THE SHIP'S LOG.

YOU CAN TRANSLATE...?

SEEMS...A LITTLE MORE PRIMITIVE THAN THE KRYPTONIAN I'M USED TO...

...JUST GIVE ME A MOMENT.

OKAY, THERE'S SOME KIND OF DATE STAMP THAT I CAN'T DECIPHER...

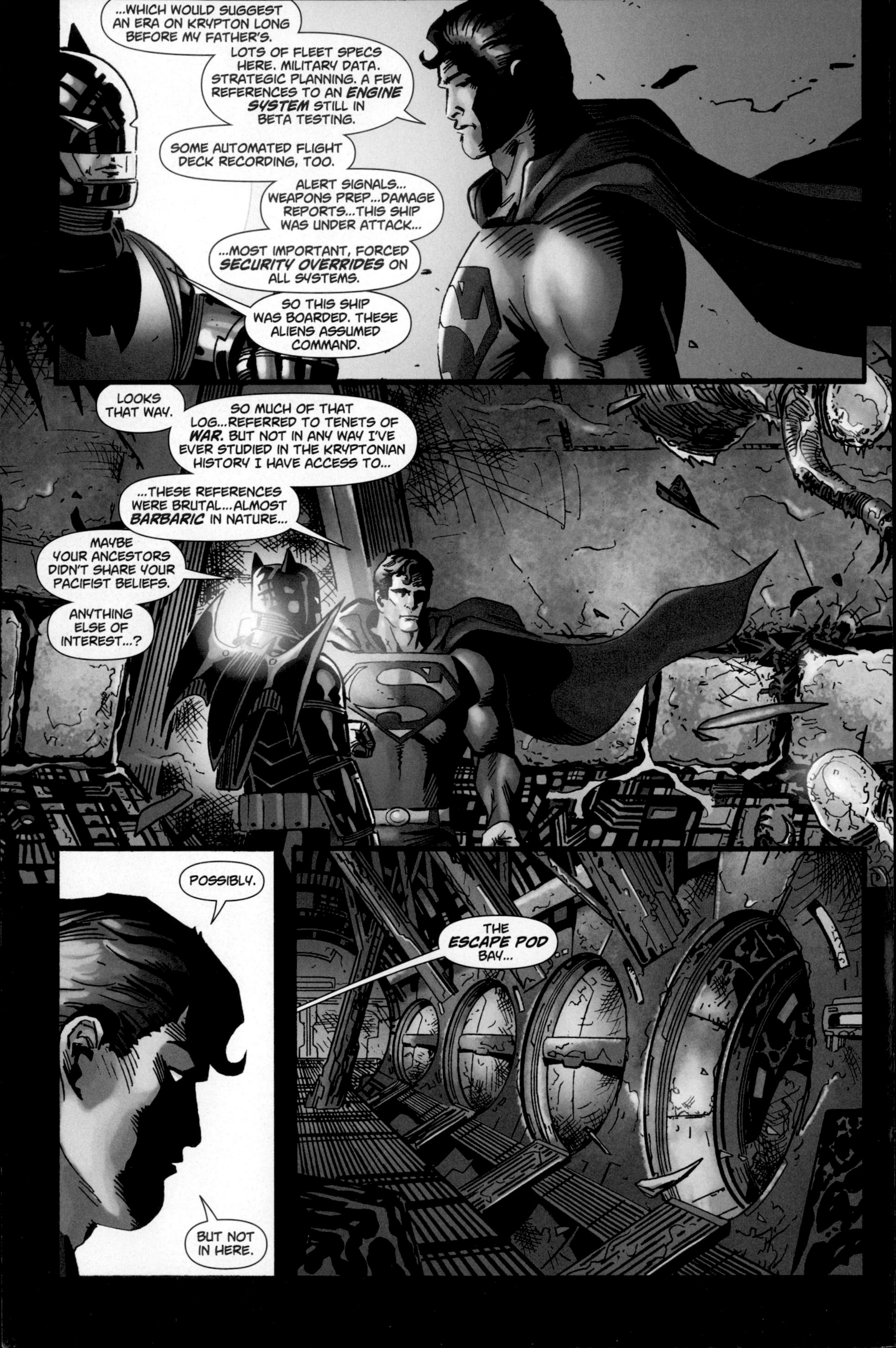
...WHICH WOULD SUGGEST AN ERA ON KRYPTON LONG BEFORE MY FATHER'S.
LOTS OF FLEET SPECS HERE. MILITARY DATA. STRATEGIC PLANNING. A FEW REFERENCES TO AN ENGINE SYSTEM STILL IN BETA TESTING.
SOME AUTOMATED FLIGHT DECK RECORDING, TOO.
ALERT SIGNALS... WEAPONS PREP...DAMAGE REPORTS...THIS SHIP WAS UNDER ATTACK...
...MOST IMPORTANT, FORCED SECURITY OVERRIDES ON ALL SYSTEMS.
SO THIS SHIP WAS BOARDED. THESE ALIENS ASSUMED COMMAND.
LOOKS THAT WAY.
SO MUCH OF THAT LOG...REFERRED TO TENETS OF WAR. BUT NOT IN ANY WAY I'VE EVER STUDIED IN THE KRYPTONIAN HISTORY I HAVE ACCESS TO...
...THESE REFERENCES WERE BRUTAL...ALMOST BARBARIC IN NATURE...
MAYBE YOUR ANCESTORS DIDN'T SHARE YOUR PACIFIST BELIEFS.
ANYTHING ELSE OF INTEREST...?
POSSIBLY.
BUT NOT IN HERE.
THE ESCAPE POD BAY...

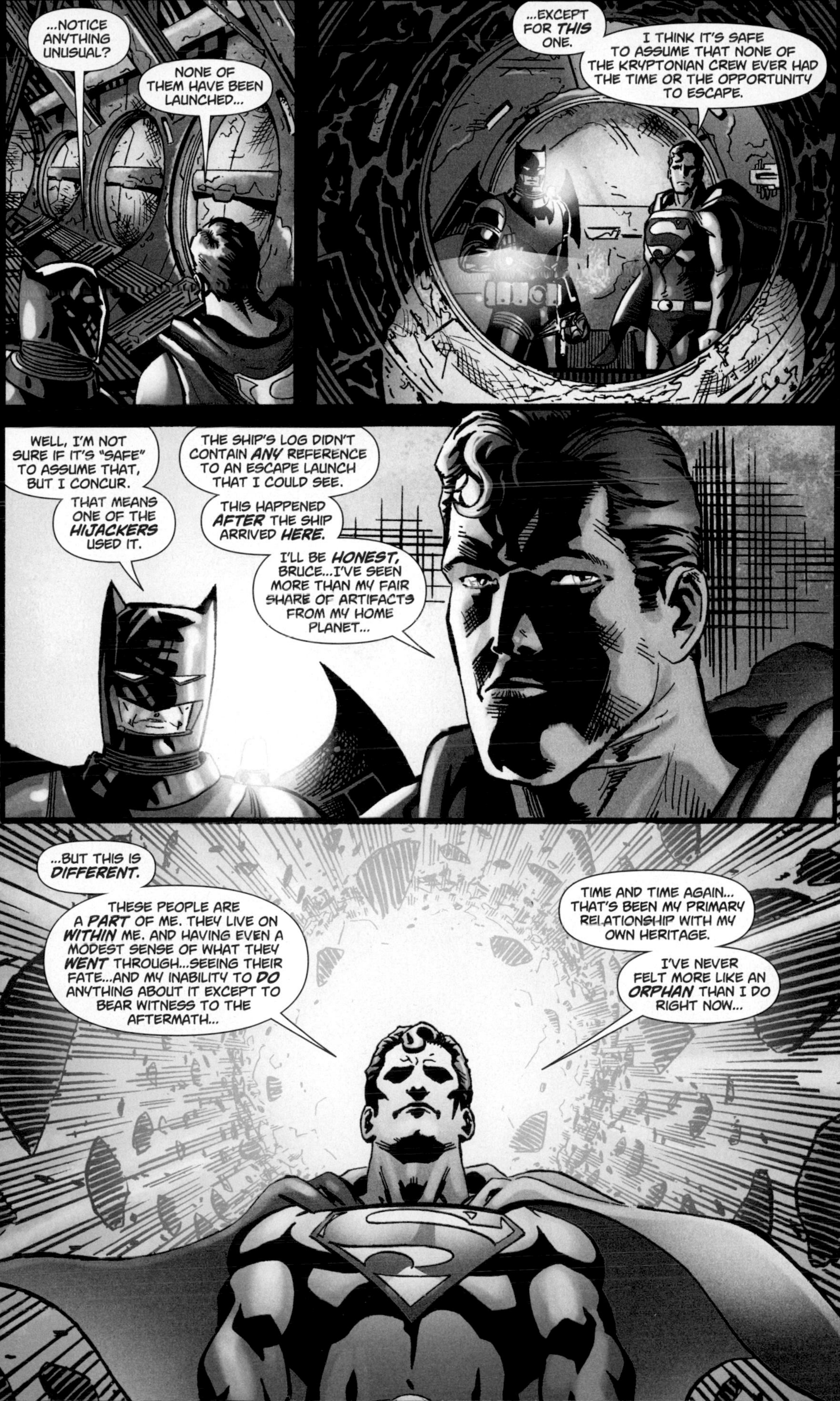
...NOTICE ANYTHING UNUSUAL?
NONE OF THEM HAVE BEEN LAUNCHED...
...EXCEPT FOR THIS ONE.
I THINK IT'S SAFE TO ASSUME THAT NONE OF THE KRYPTONIAN CREW EVER HAD THE TIME OR THE OPPORTUNITY TO ESCAPE.
WELL, I'M NOT SURE IF IT'S "SAFE" TO ASSUME THAT, BUT I CONCUR.
THAT MEANS ONE OF THE HIJACKERS USED IT.
THE SHIP'S LOG DIDN'T CONTAIN ANY REFERENCE TO AN ESCAPE LAUNCH THAT I COULD SEE.
THIS HAPPENED AFTER THE SHIP ARRIVED HERE.
I'LL BE HONEST, BRUCE...I'VE SEEN MORE THAN MY FAIR SHARE OF ARTIFACTS FROM MY HOME PLANET...
...BUT THIS IS DIFFERENT.
THESE PEOPLE ARE A PART OF ME. THEY LIVE ON WITHIN ME. AND HAVING EVEN A MODEST SENSE OF WHAT THEY WENT THROUGH...SEEING THEIR FATE...AND MY INABILITY TO DO ANYTHING ABOUT IT EXCEPT TO BEAR WITNESS TO THE AFTERMATH...
TIME AND TIME AGAIN... THAT'S BEEN MY PRIMARY RELATIONSHIP WITH MY OWN HERITAGE.
I'VE NEVER FELT MORE LIKE AN ORPHAN THAN I DO RIGHT NOW...

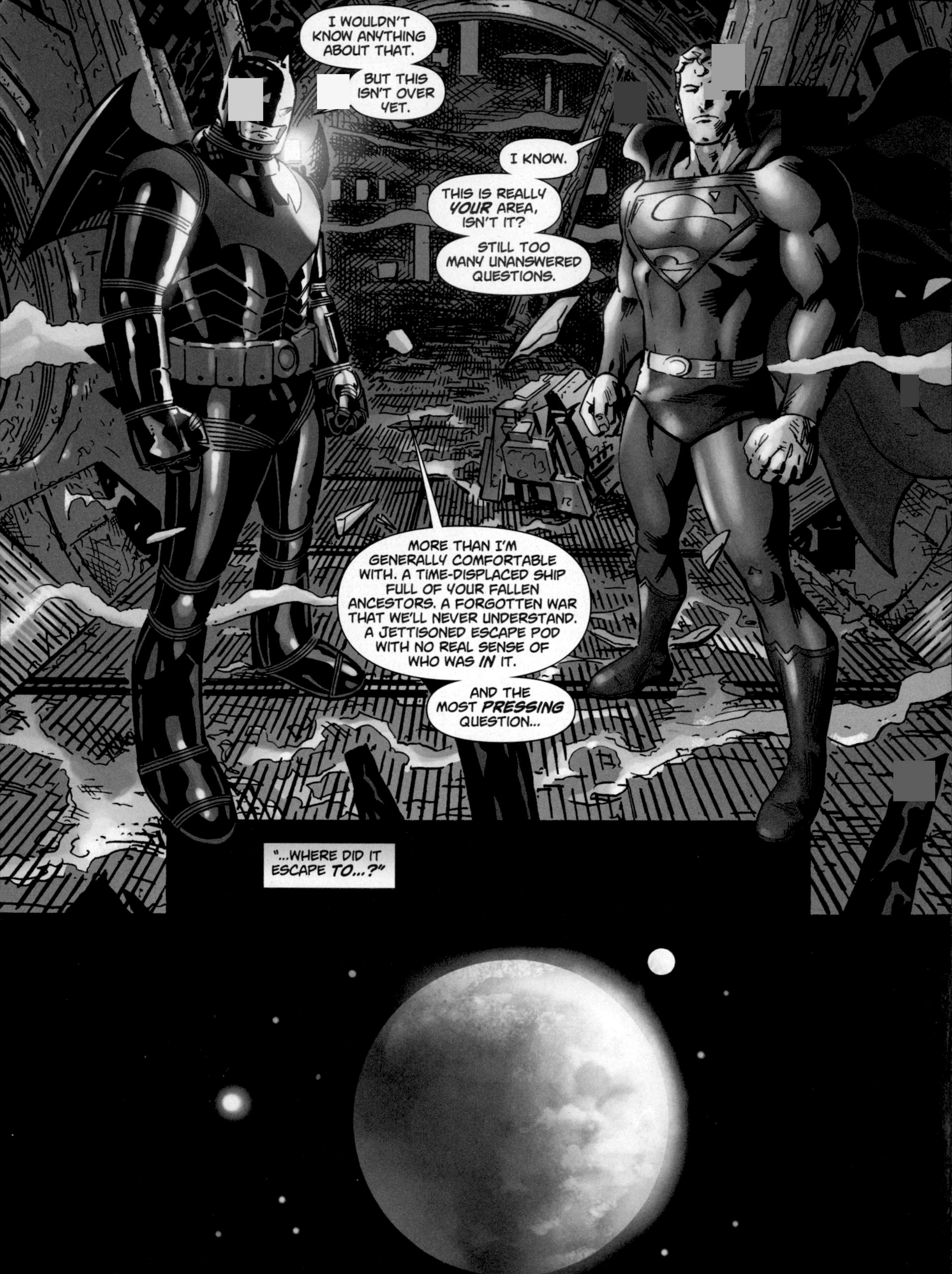
I WOULDN'T KNOW ANYTHING ABOUT THAT.
BUT THIS ISN'T OVER YET.
I KNOW.
THIS IS REALLY *YOUR* AREA, ISN'T IT?
STILL TOO MANY UNANSWERED QUESTIONS.
MORE THAN I'M GENERALLY COMFORTABLE WITH. A TIME-DISPLACED SHIP FULL OF YOUR FALLEN ANCESTORS. A FORGOTTEN WAR THAT WE'LL NEVER UNDERSTAND. A JETTISONED ESCAPE POD WITH NO REAL SENSE OF WHO WAS *IN* IT.
AND THE MOST *PRESSING* QUESTION...
"...WHERE DID IT ESCAPE *TO...?*"

SUPERMAN/BATMAN No. 68
Ardian Syaf, Vicente Cifuentes and Ulises Arreola

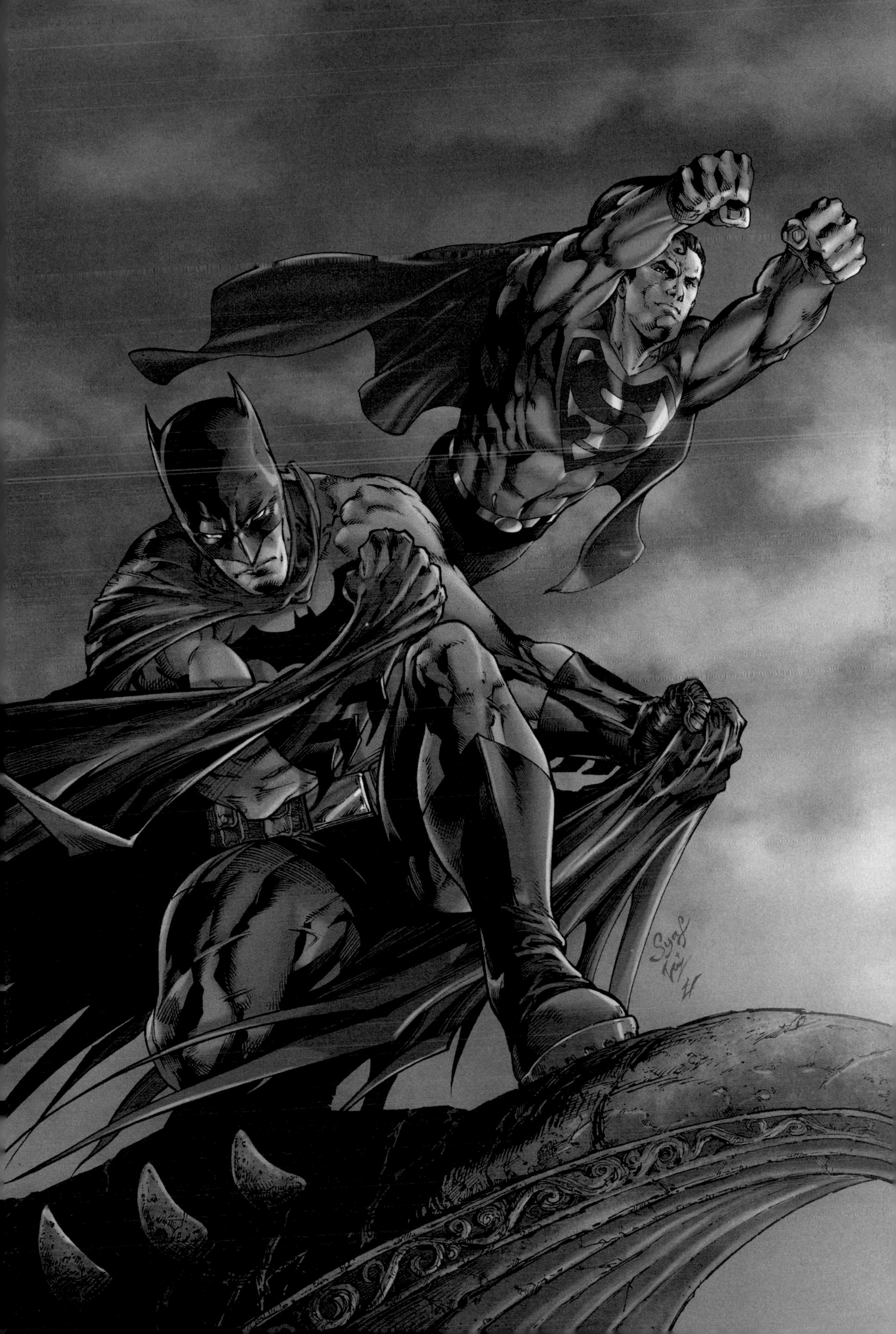

THE BIG NOISE PART 1: RUMBLE FACE

Penciller: Ardian Syaf

Inkers: Vicente Cifuentes and David Enebral

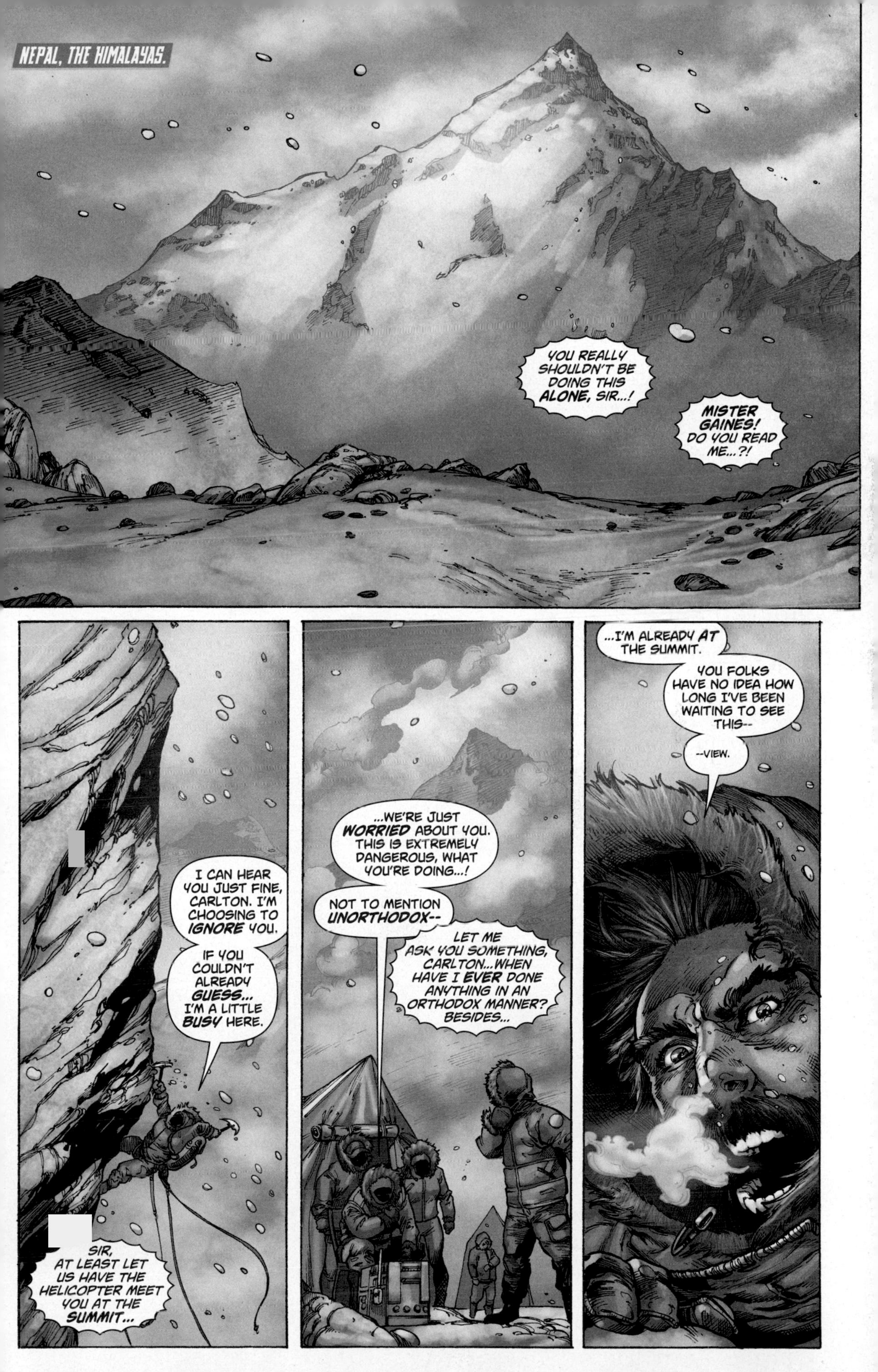
NEPAL, THE HIMALAYAS.
YOU REALLY SHOULDN'T BE DOING THIS ALONE, SIR...!
MISTER GAINES! DO YOU READ ME...?!
I CAN HEAR YOU JUST FINE, CARLTON. I'M CHOOSING TO IGNORE YOU.
IF YOU COULDN'T ALREADY GUESS... I'M A LITTLE BUSY HERE.
SIR, AT LEAST LET US HAVE THE HELICOPTER MEET YOU AT THE SUMMIT...
...WE'RE JUST WORRIED ABOUT YOU. THIS IS EXTREMELY DANGEROUS, WHAT YOU'RE DOING...!
NOT TO MENTION UNORTHODOX--
LET ME ASK YOU SOMETHING, CARLTON...WHEN HAVE I EVER DONE ANYTHING IN AN ORTHODOX MANNER? BESIDES...
...I'M ALREADY AT THE SUMMIT.
YOU FOLKS HAVE NO IDEA HOW LONG I'VE BEEN WAITING TO SEE THIS--
--VIEW.

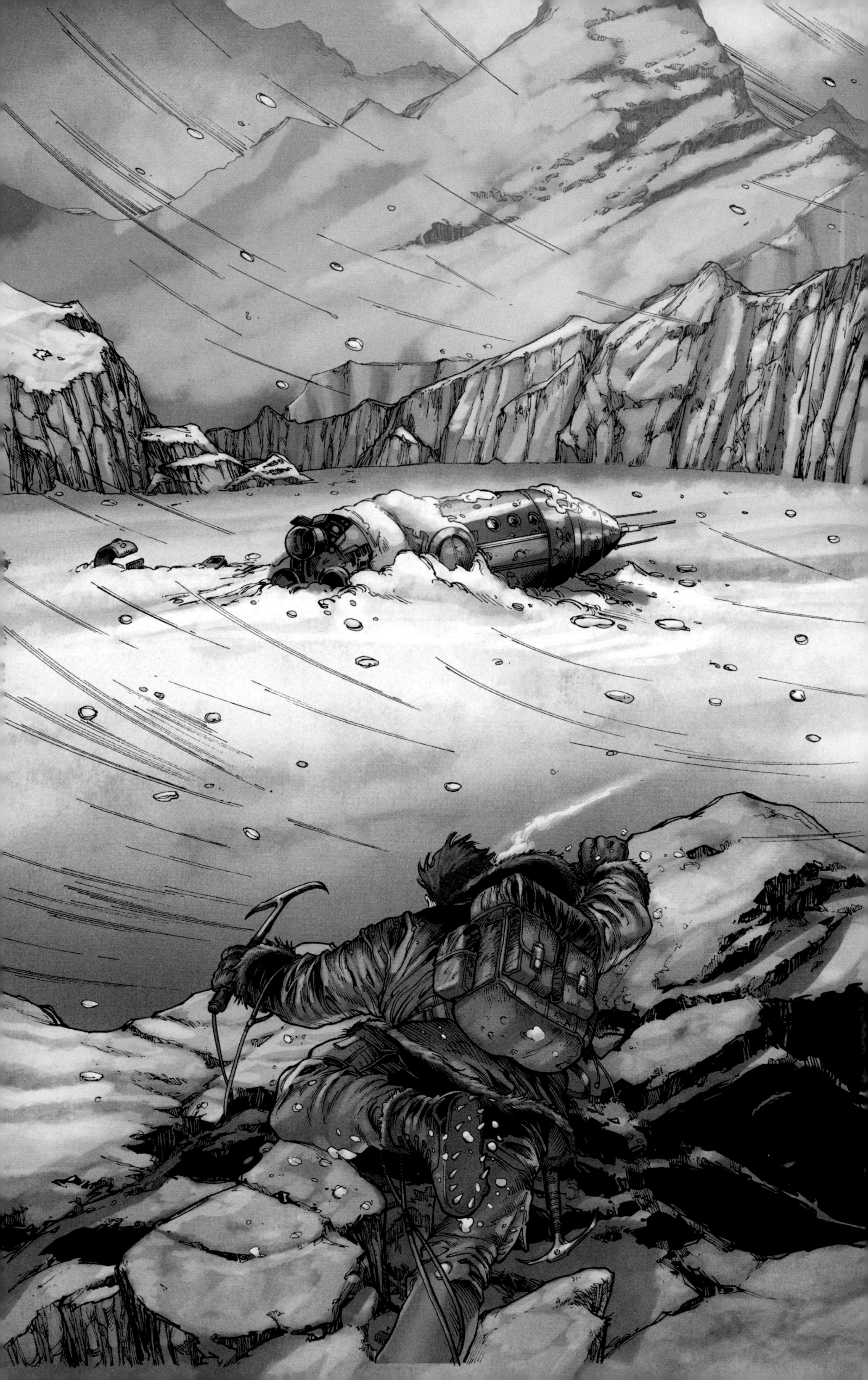

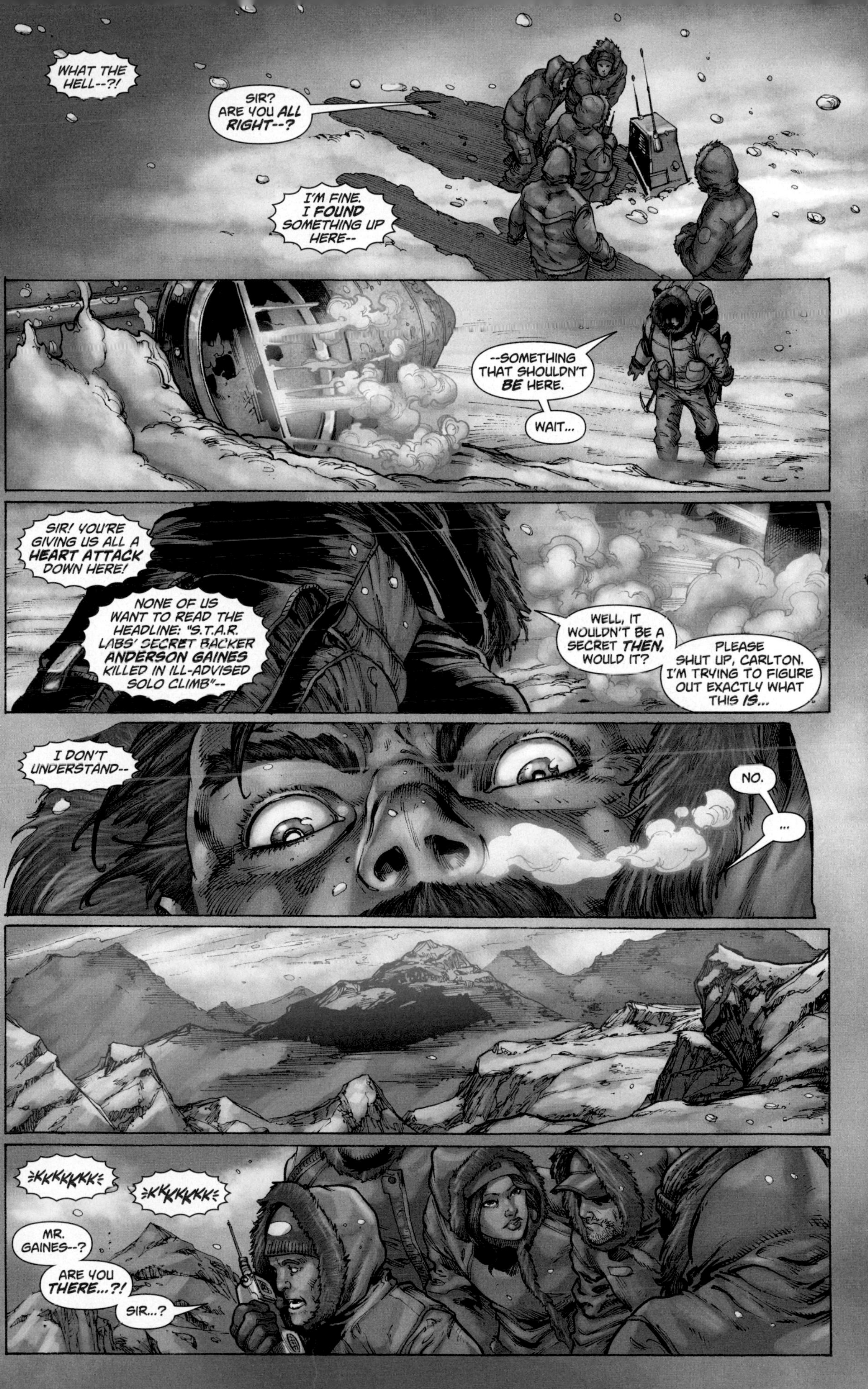

WHAT THE HELL--?!
SIR? ARE YOU ALL RIGHT--?
I'M FINE. I FOUND SOMETHING UP HERE--
--SOMETHING THAT SHOULDN'T BE HERE.
WAIT...
SIR! YOU'RE GIVING US ALL A HEART ATTACK DOWN HERE!
NONE OF US WANT TO READ THE HEADLINE: "S.T.A.R. LABS' SECRET BACKER ANDERSON GAINES KILLED IN ILL-ADVISED SOLO CLIMB"--
WELL, IT WOULDN'T BE A SECRET THEN, WOULD IT?
PLEASE SHUT UP, CARLTON. I'M TRYING TO FIGURE OUT EXACTLY WHAT THIS IS...
I DON'T UNDERSTAND--
NO.
...
KKKKKKK
KKKKKKK
MR. GAINES--?
ARE YOU THERE...?!
SIR...?

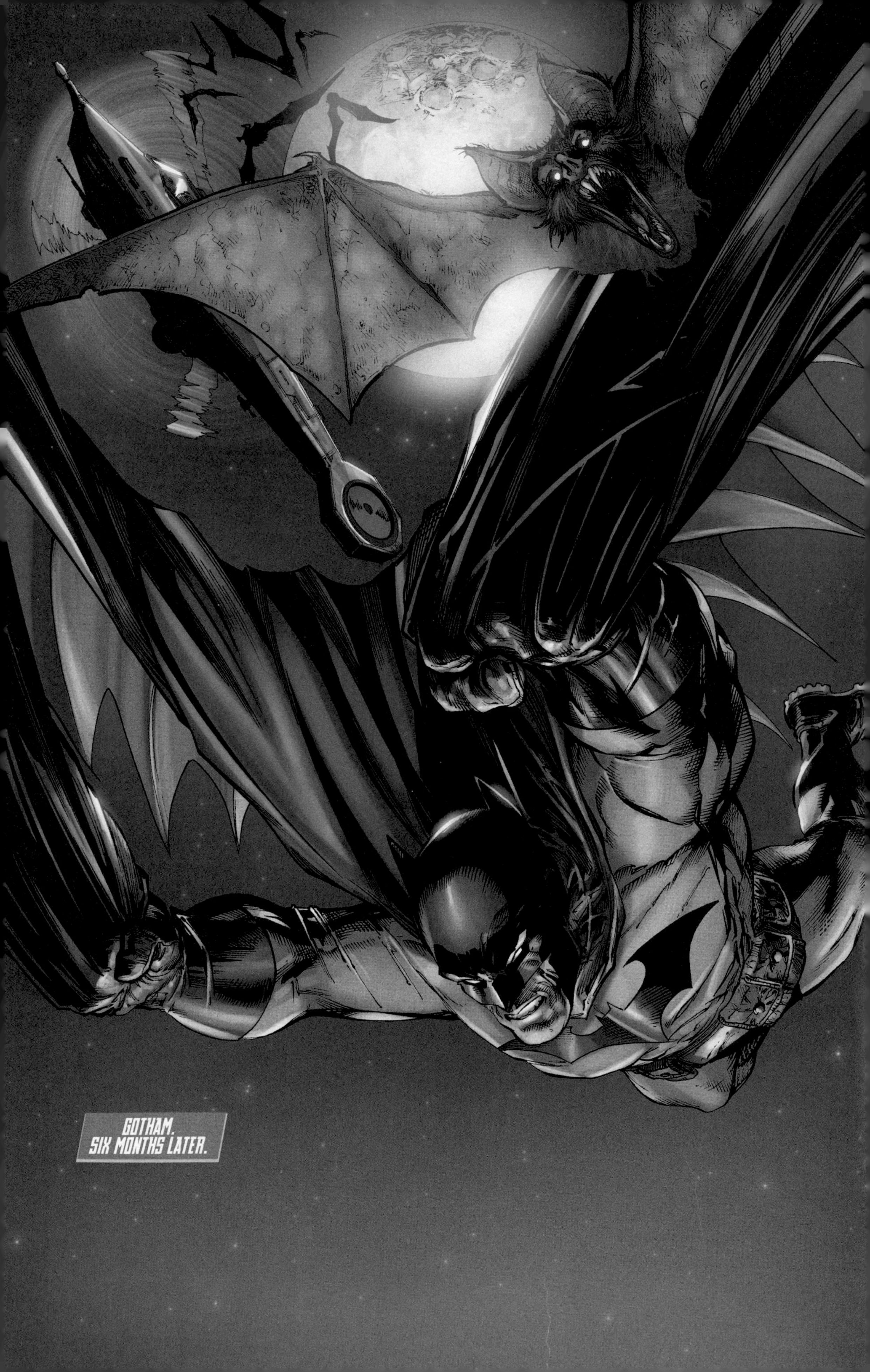
GOTHAM.
SIX MONTHS LATER.

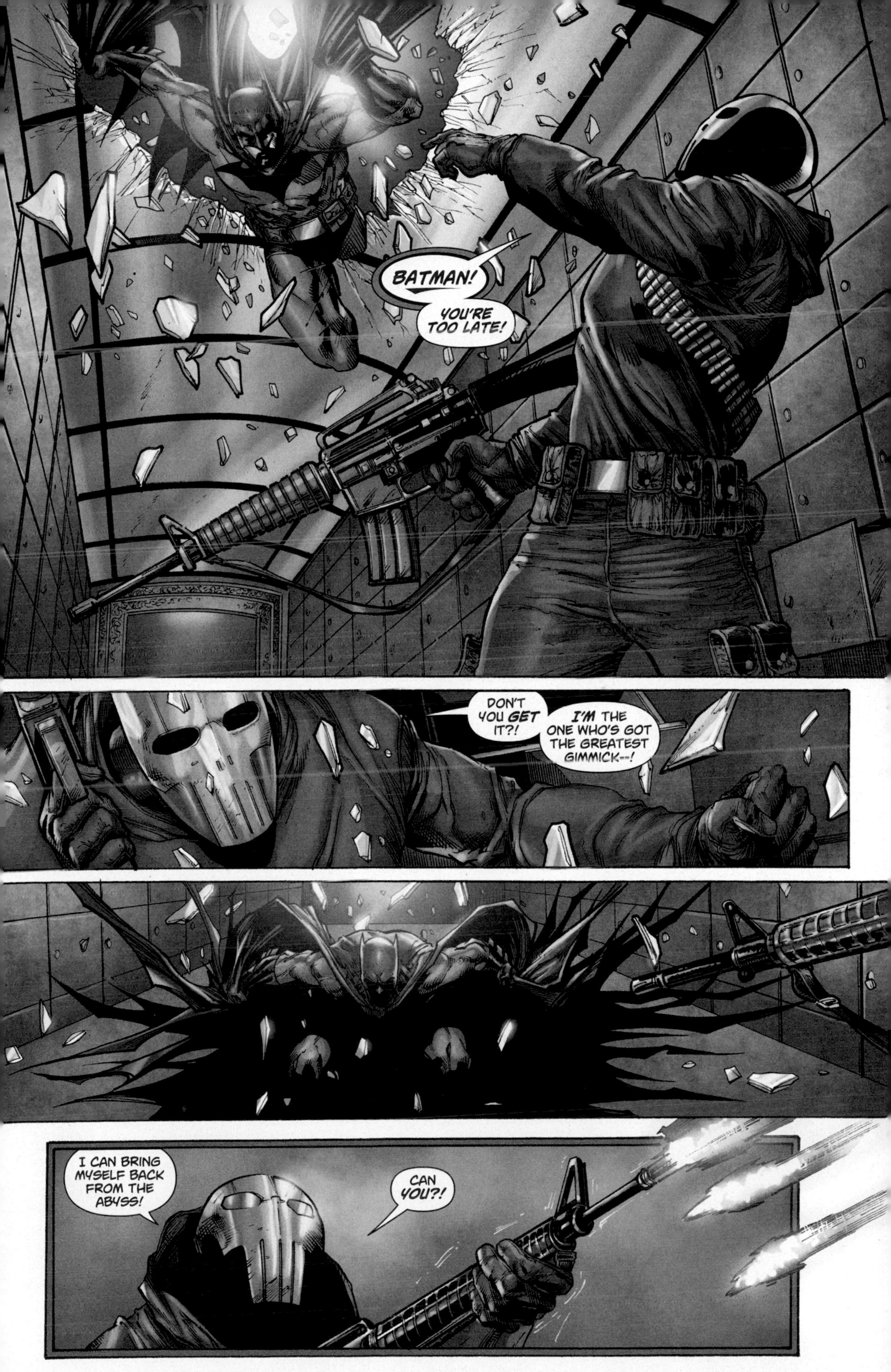
BATMAN!
YOU'RE TOO LATE!
DON'T YOU GET IT?!
I'M THE ONE WHO'S GOT THE GREATEST GIMMICK--!
I CAN BRING MYSELF BACK FROM THE ABYSS!
CAN YOU?!

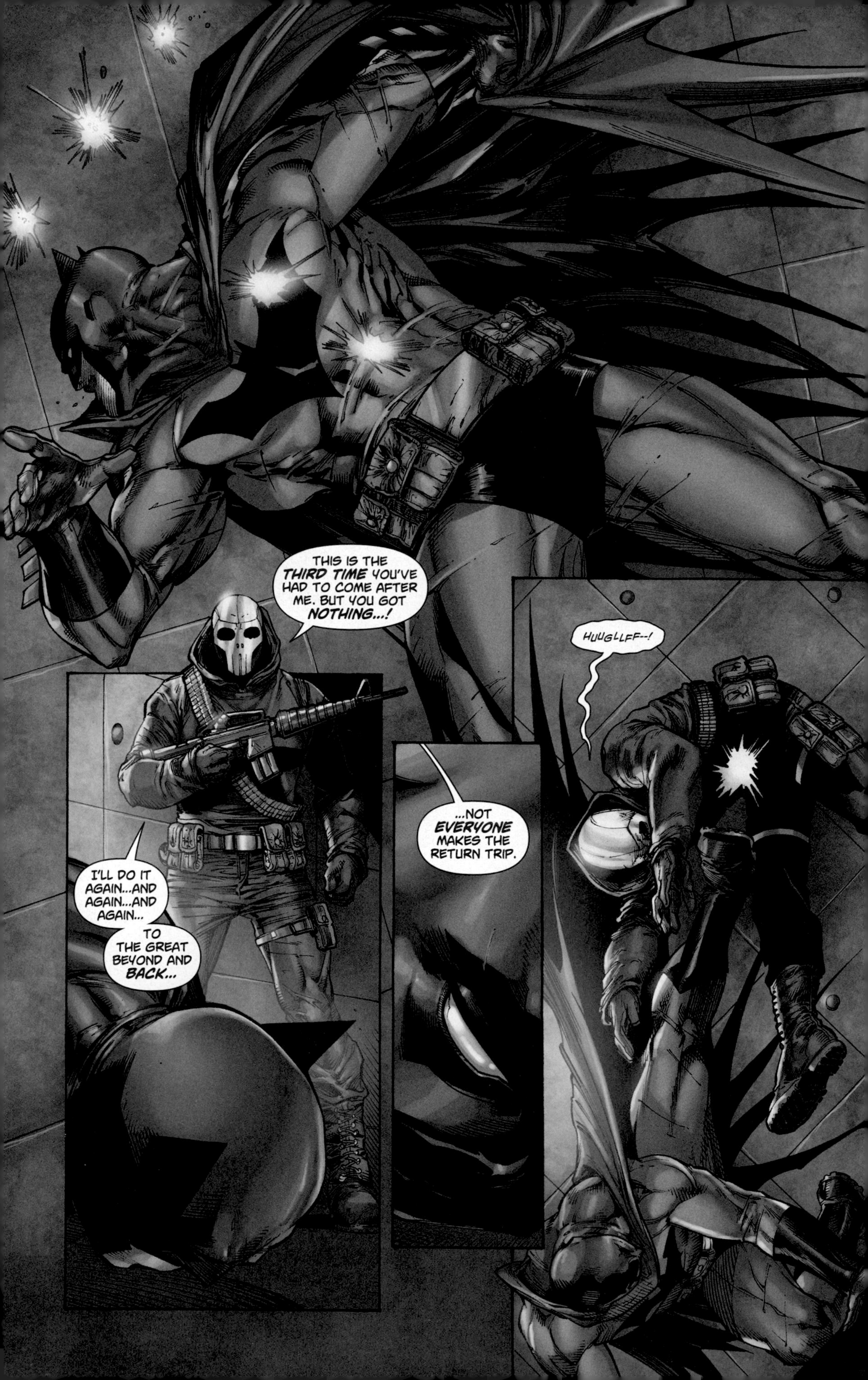
THIS IS THE THIRD TIME YOU'VE HAD TO COME AFTER ME. BUT YOU GOT NOTHING...!
I'LL DO IT AGAIN...AND AGAIN...AND AGAIN...
TO THE GREAT BEYOND AND BACK...
...NOT EVERYONE MAKES THE RETURN TRIP.
HUUGLLFF--!

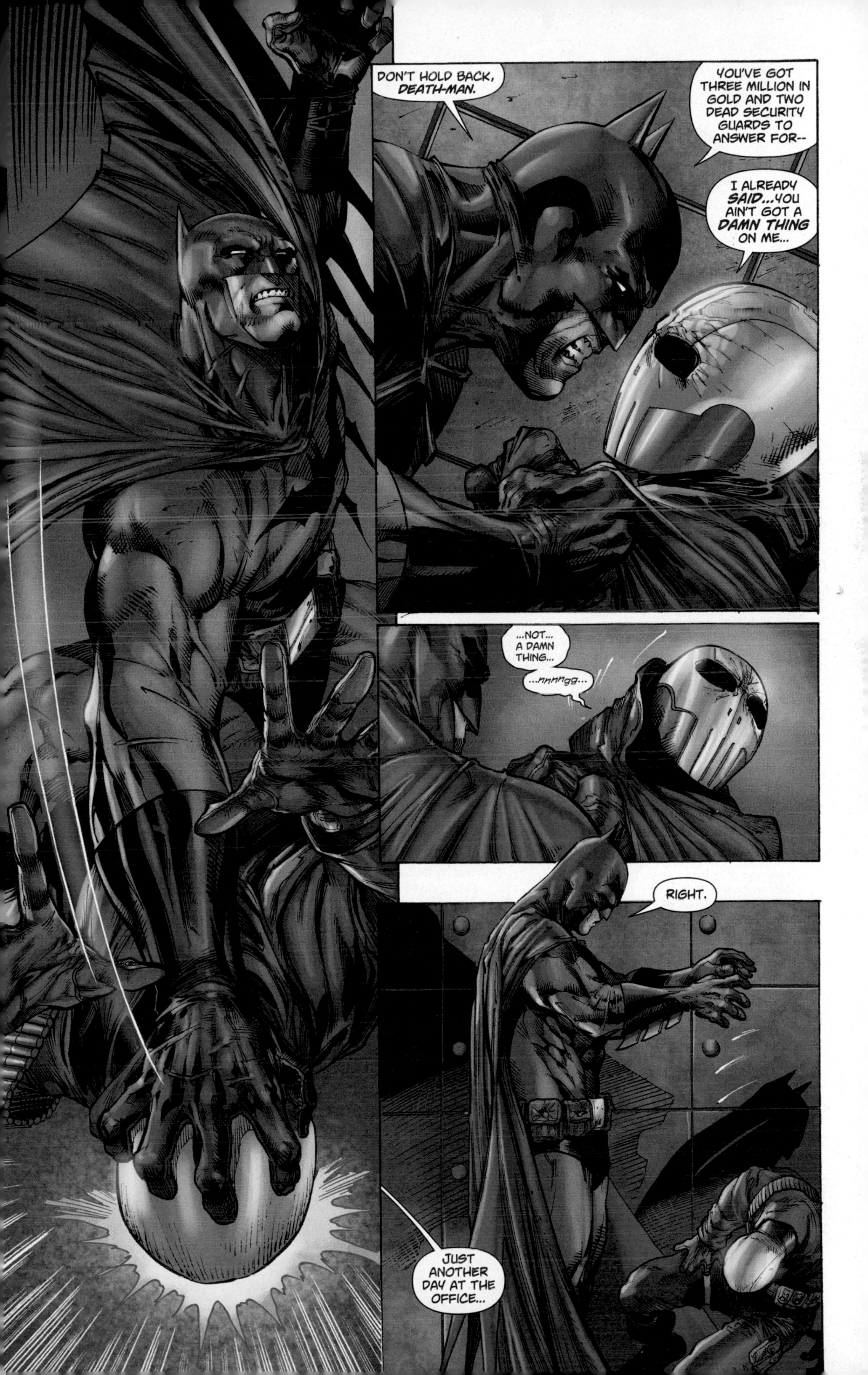
DON'T HOLD BACK, DEATH-MAN.
YOU'VE GOT THREE MILLION IN GOLD AND TWO DEAD SECURITY GUARDS TO ANSWER FOR--
I ALREADY SAID...YOU AIN'T GOT A DAMN THING ON ME...
...NOT... A DAMN THING...
...nnnngg...
RIGHT.
JUST ANOTHER DAY AT THE OFFICE...

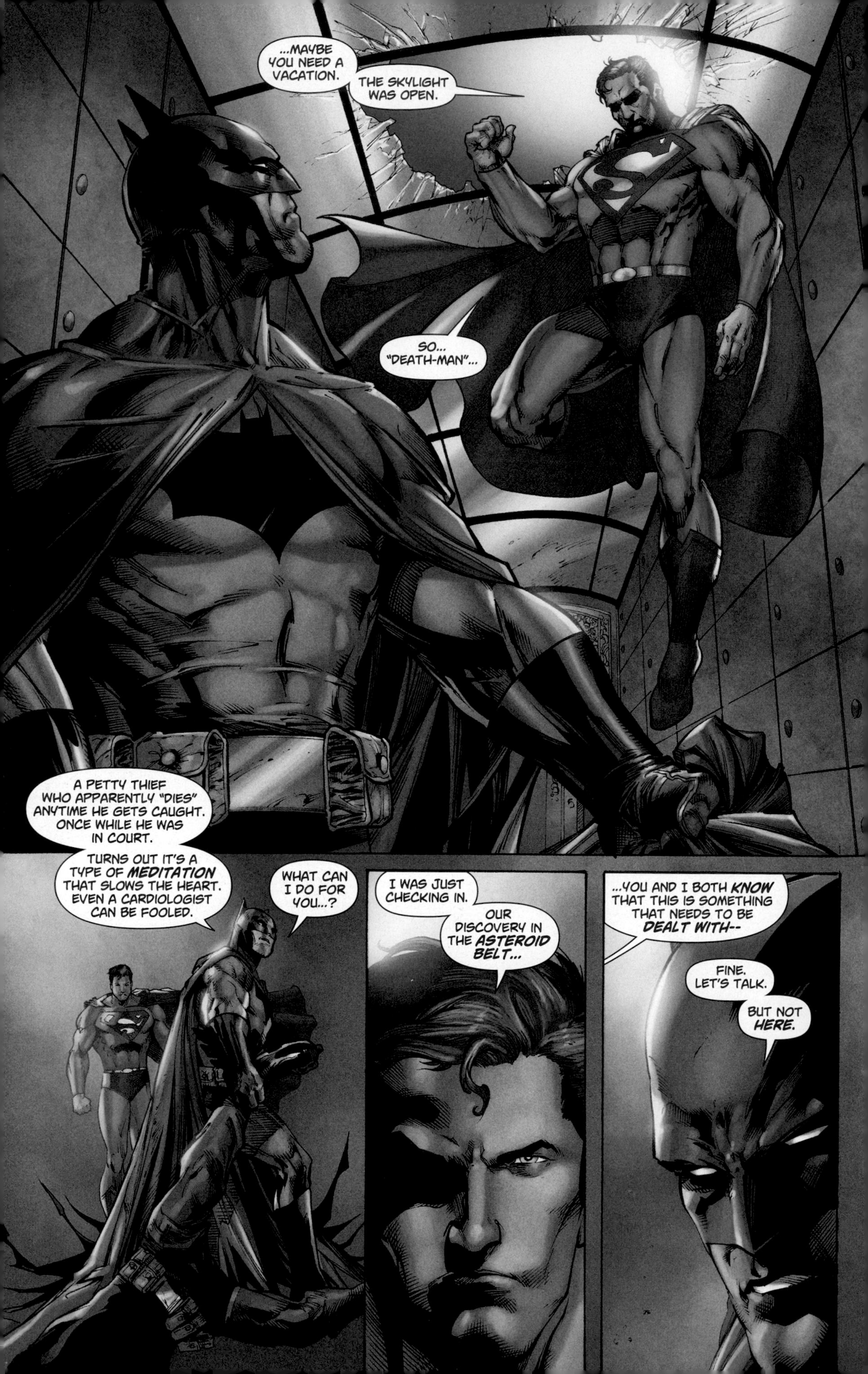
...MAYBE YOU NEED A VACATION.
THE SKYLIGHT WAS OPEN.
SO... "DEATH-MAN"...
A PETTY THIEF WHO APPARENTLY "DIES" ANYTIME HE GETS CAUGHT. ONCE WHILE HE WAS IN COURT.
TURNS OUT IT'S A TYPE OF MEDITATION THAT SLOWS THE HEART. EVEN A CARDIOLOGIST CAN BE FOOLED.
WHAT CAN I DO FOR YOU...?
I WAS JUST CHECKING IN.
OUR DISCOVERY IN THE ASTEROID BELT...
...YOU AND I BOTH KNOW THAT THIS IS SOMETHING THAT NEEDS TO BE DEALT WITH--
FINE. LET'S TALK.
BUT NOT HERE.

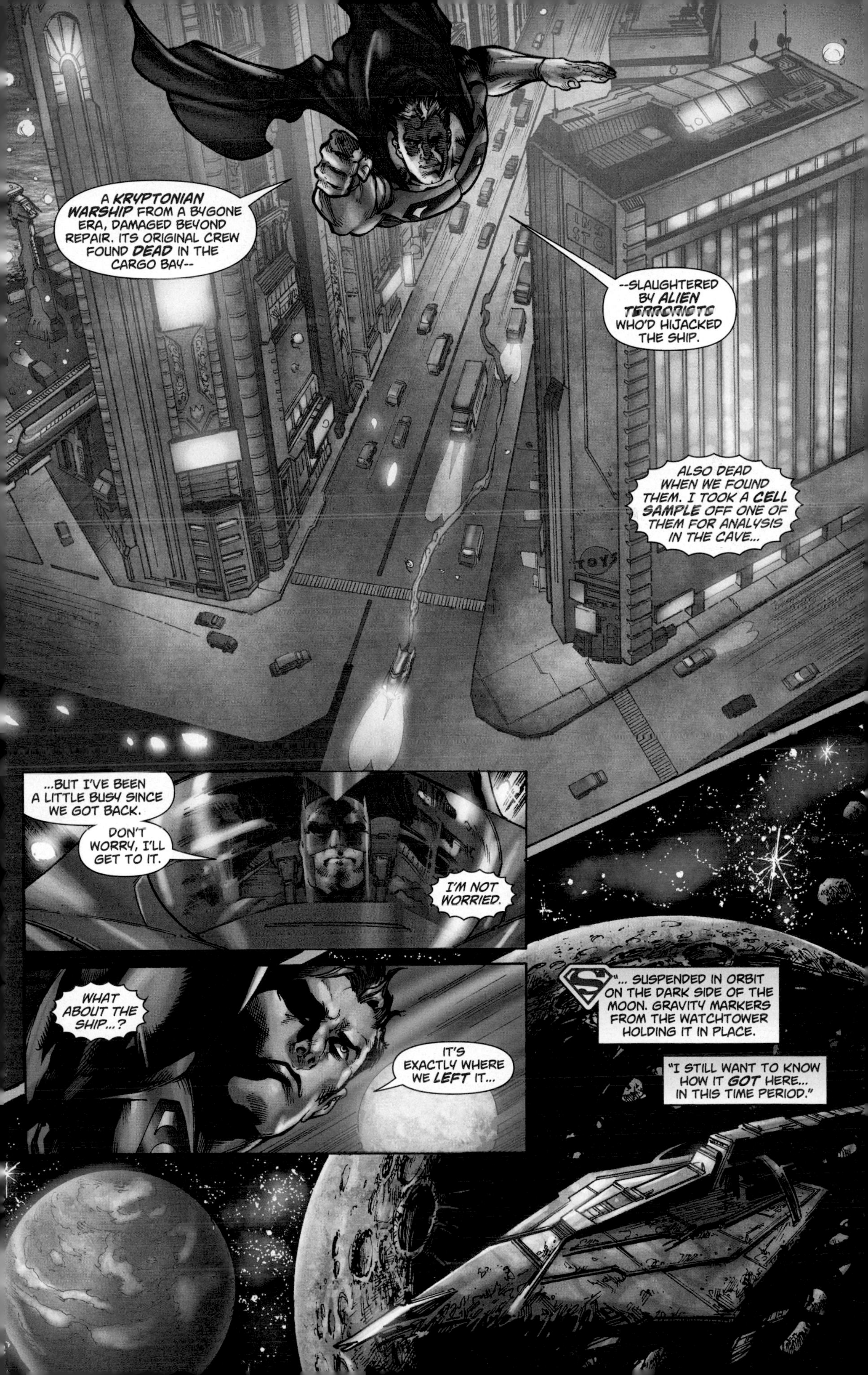
A KRYPTONIAN WARSHIP FROM A BYGONE ERA, DAMAGED BEYOND REPAIR. ITS ORIGINAL CREW FOUND DEAD IN THE CARGO BAY--
--SLAUGHTERED BY ALIEN TERRORISTS WHO'D HIJACKED THE SHIP.
ALSO DEAD WHEN WE FOUND THEM. I TOOK A CELL SAMPLE OFF ONE OF THEM FOR ANALYSIS IN THE CAVE...
...BUT I'VE BEEN A LITTLE BUSY SINCE WE GOT BACK.
DON'T WORRY, I'LL GET TO IT.
I'M NOT WORRIED.
WHAT ABOUT THE SHIP...?
IT'S EXACTLY WHERE WE LEFT IT...
"... SUSPENDED IN ORBIT ON THE DARK SIDE OF THE MOON. GRAVITY MARKERS FROM THE WATCHTOWER HOLDING IT IN PLACE.
"I STILL WANT TO KNOW HOW IT GOT HERE... IN THIS TIME PERIOD."

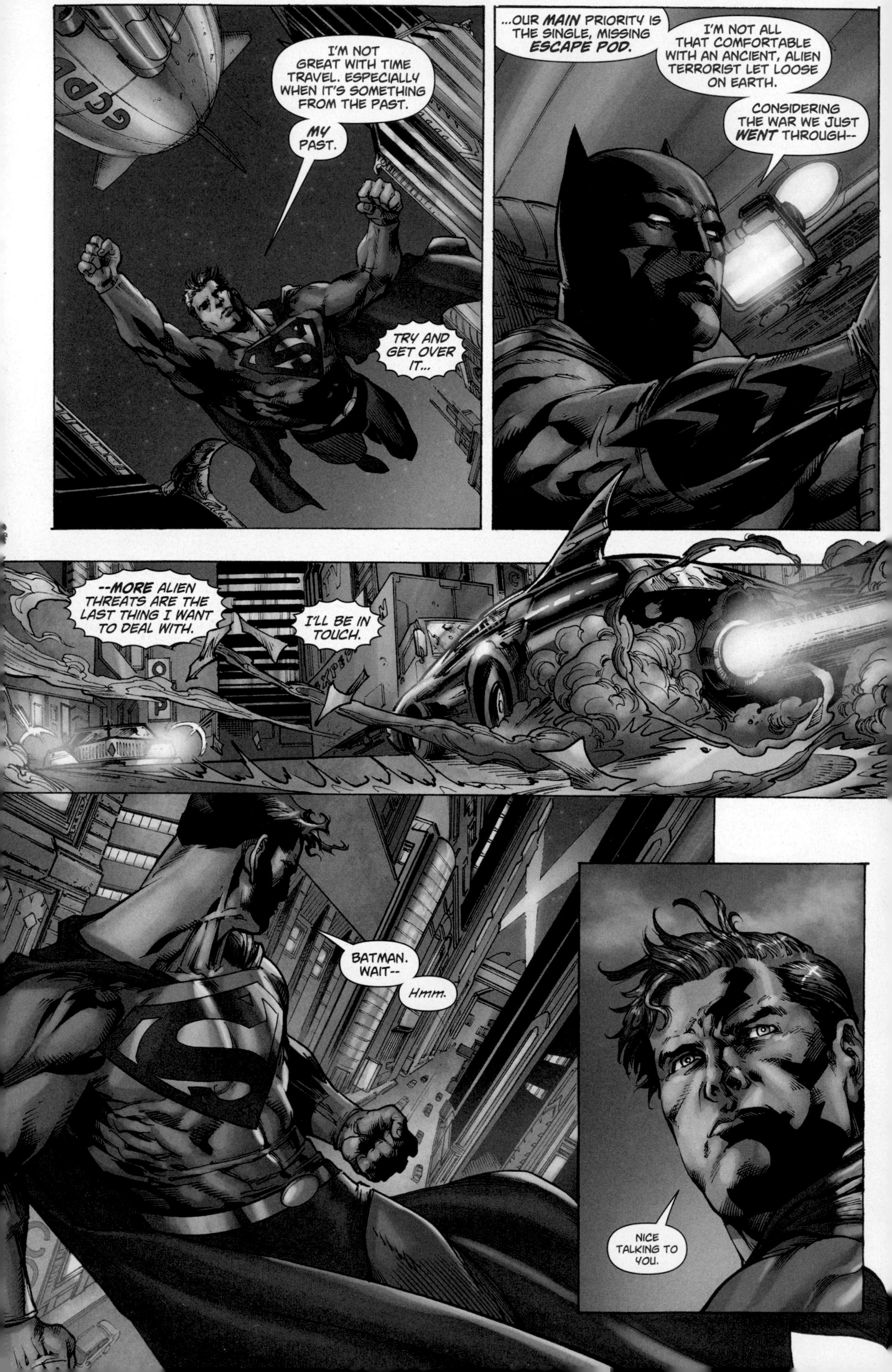
I'M NOT GREAT WITH TIME TRAVEL. ESPECIALLY WHEN IT'S SOMETHING FROM THE PAST.
MY PAST.
TRY AND GET OVER IT...
...OUR MAIN PRIORITY IS THE SINGLE, MISSING ESCAPE POD.
I'M NOT ALL THAT COMFORTABLE WITH AN ANCIENT, ALIEN TERRORIST LET LOOSE ON EARTH.
CONSIDERING THE WAR WE JUST WENT THROUGH--
--MORE ALIEN THREATS ARE THE LAST THING I WANT TO DEAL WITH.
I'LL BE IN TOUCH.
BATMAN. WAIT--
Hmm.
NICE TALKING TO YOU.

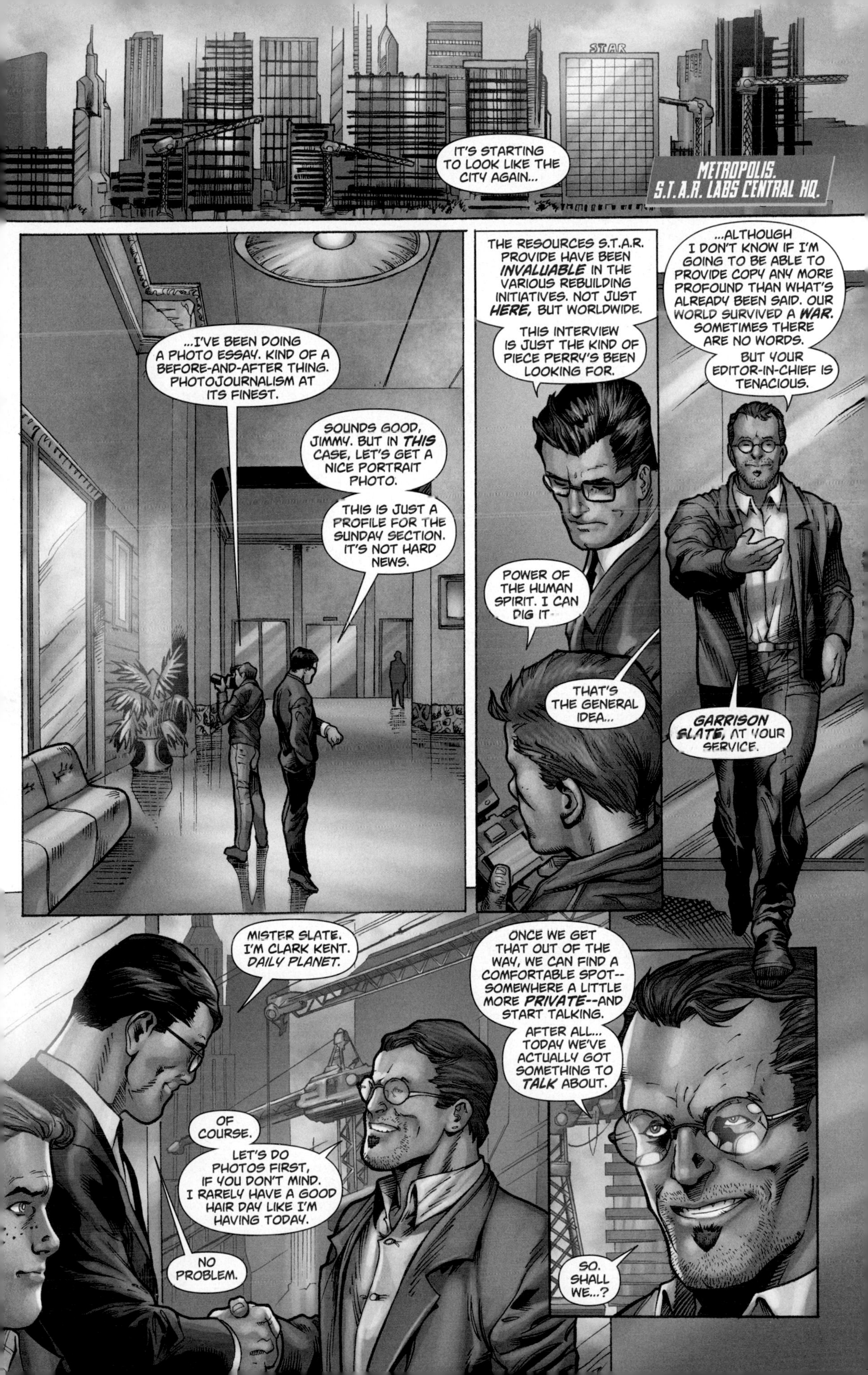
IT'S STARTING TO LOOK LIKE THE CITY AGAIN...
METROPOLIS. S.T.A.R. LABS CENTRAL HQ.
...I'VE BEEN DOING A PHOTO ESSAY. KIND OF A BEFORE-AND-AFTER THING. PHOTOJOURNALISM AT ITS FINEST.
SOUNDS GOOD, JIMMY. BUT IN THIS CASE, LET'S GET A NICE PORTRAIT PHOTO.
THIS IS JUST A PROFILE FOR THE SUNDAY SECTION. IT'S NOT HARD NEWS.
THE RESOURCES S.T.A.R. PROVIDE HAVE BEEN INVALUABLE IN THE VARIOUS REBUILDING INITIATIVES. NOT JUST HERE, BUT WORLDWIDE.
THIS INTERVIEW IS JUST THE KIND OF PIECE PERRY'S BEEN LOOKING FOR.
POWER OF THE HUMAN SPIRIT. I CAN DIG IT--
THAT'S THE GENERAL IDEA...
...ALTHOUGH I DON'T KNOW IF I'M GOING TO BE ABLE TO PROVIDE COPY ANY MORE PROFOUND THAN WHAT'S ALREADY BEEN SAID. OUR WORLD SURVIVED A WAR. SOMETIMES THERE ARE NO WORDS.
BUT YOUR EDITOR-IN-CHIEF IS TENACIOUS.
GARRISON SLATE, AT YOUR SERVICE.
MISTER SLATE. I'M CLARK KENT. DAILY PLANET.
OF COURSE.
LET'S DO PHOTOS FIRST, IF YOU DON'T MIND. I RARELY HAVE A GOOD HAIR DAY LIKE I'M HAVING TODAY.
NO PROBLEM.
ONCE WE GET THAT OUT OF THE WAY, WE CAN FIND A COMFORTABLE SPOT--SOMEWHERE A LITTLE MORE PRIVATE--AND START TALKING.
AFTER ALL... TODAY WE'VE ACTUALLY GOT SOMETHING TO TALK ABOUT.
SO. SHALL WE...?

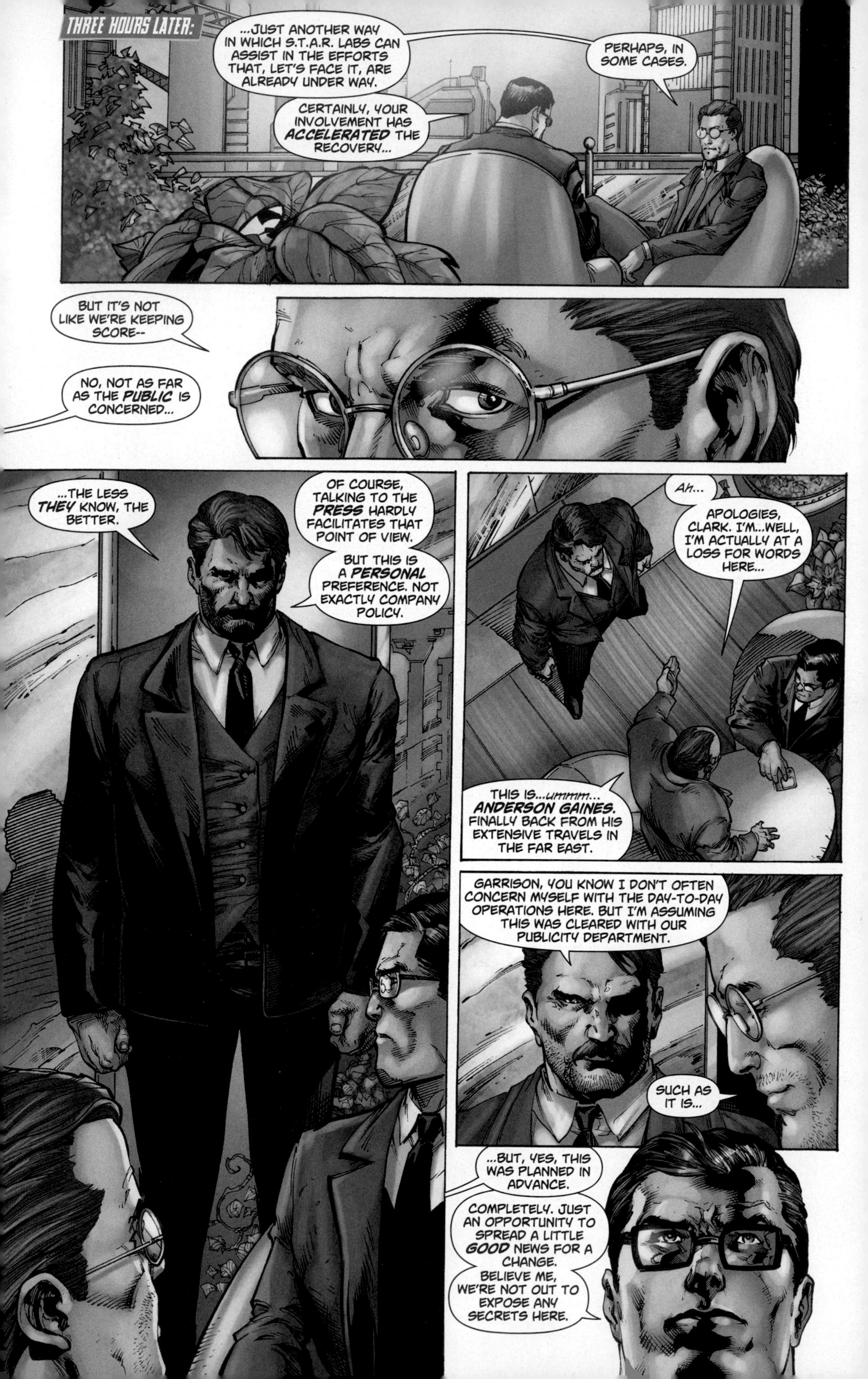
THREE HOURS LATER:
...JUST ANOTHER WAY IN WHICH S.T.A.R. LABS CAN ASSIST IN THE EFFORTS THAT, LET'S FACE IT, ARE ALREADY UNDER WAY.
PERHAPS, IN SOME CASES.
CERTAINLY, YOUR INVOLVEMENT HAS ACCELERATED THE RECOVERY...
BUT IT'S NOT LIKE WE'RE KEEPING SCORE--
NO, NOT AS FAR AS THE PUBLIC IS CONCERNED...
...THE LESS THEY KNOW, THE BETTER.
OF COURSE, TALKING TO THE PRESS HARDLY FACILITATES THAT POINT OF VIEW.
BUT THIS IS A PERSONAL PREFERENCE. NOT EXACTLY COMPANY POLICY.
Ah...
APOLOGIES, CLARK. I'M...WELL, I'M ACTUALLY AT A LOSS FOR WORDS HERE...
THIS IS...ummm... ANDERSON GAINES. FINALLY BACK FROM HIS EXTENSIVE TRAVELS IN THE FAR EAST.
GARRISON, YOU KNOW I DON'T OFTEN CONCERN MYSELF WITH THE DAY-TO-DAY OPERATIONS HERE. BUT I'M ASSUMING THIS WAS CLEARED WITH OUR PUBLICITY DEPARTMENT.
SUCH AS IT IS...
...BUT, YES, THIS WAS PLANNED IN ADVANCE.
COMPLETELY. JUST AN OPPORTUNITY TO SPREAD A LITTLE GOOD NEWS FOR A CHANGE.
BELIEVE ME, WE'RE NOT OUT TO EXPOSE ANY SECRETS HERE.

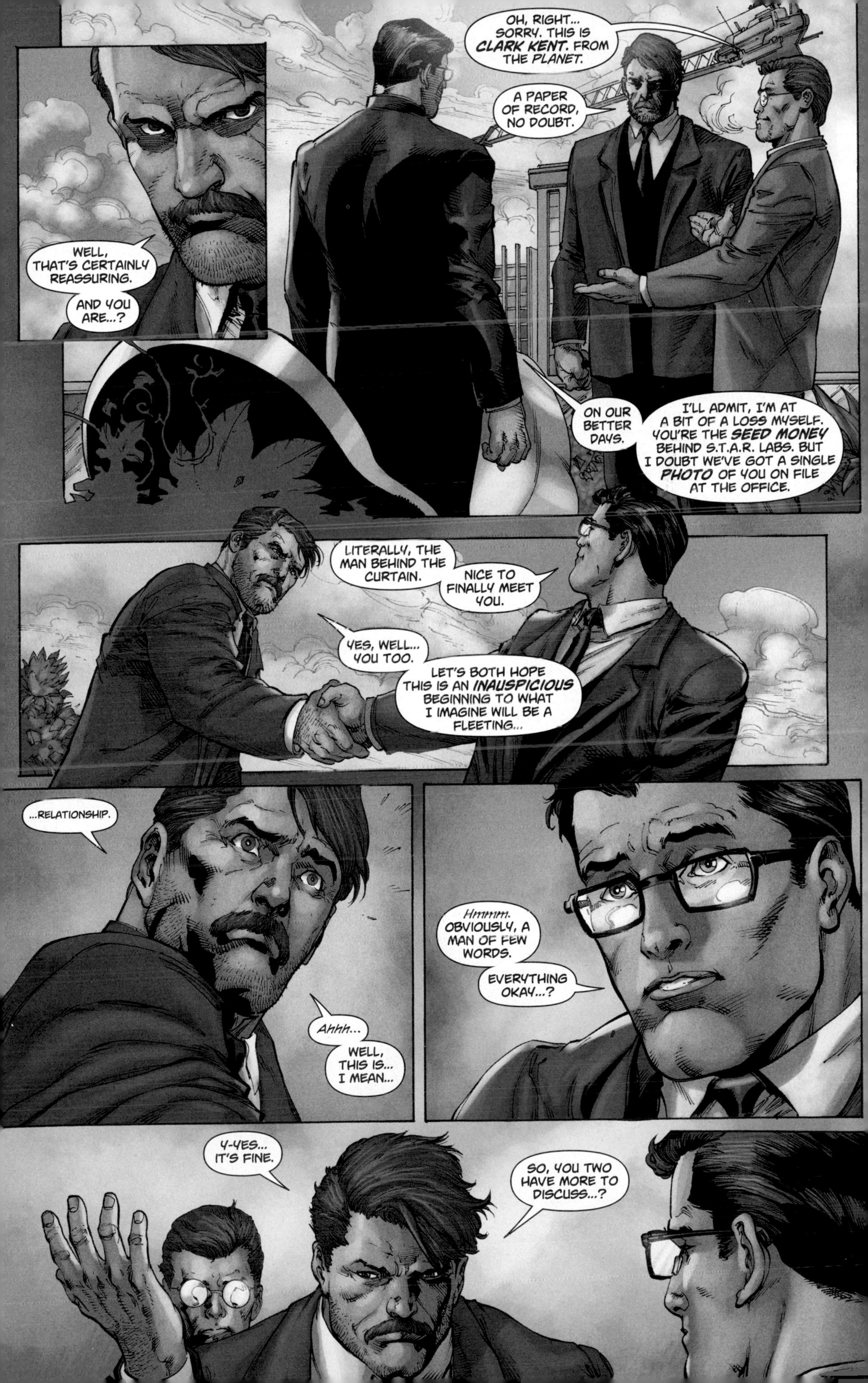
OH, RIGHT... SORRY. THIS IS CLARK KENT. FROM THE PLANET.
A PAPER OF RECORD, NO DOUBT.
WELL, THAT'S CERTAINLY REASSURING.
AND YOU ARE...?
ON OUR BETTER DAYS.
I'LL ADMIT, I'M AT A BIT OF A LOSS MYSELF. YOU'RE THE SEED MONEY BEHIND S.T.A.R. LABS. BUT I DOUBT WE'VE GOT A SINGLE PHOTO OF YOU ON FILE AT THE OFFICE.
LITERALLY, THE MAN BEHIND THE CURTAIN.
NICE TO FINALLY MEET YOU.
YES, WELL... YOU TOO.
LET'S BOTH HOPE THIS IS AN INAUSPICIOUS BEGINNING TO WHAT I IMAGINE WILL BE A FLEETING...
...RELATIONSHIP.
Hmmm. OBVIOUSLY, A MAN OF FEW WORDS.
EVERYTHING OKAY...?
Ahhh...
WELL, THIS IS... I MEAN...
Y-YES... IT'S FINE.
SO, YOU TWO HAVE MORE TO DISCUSS...?

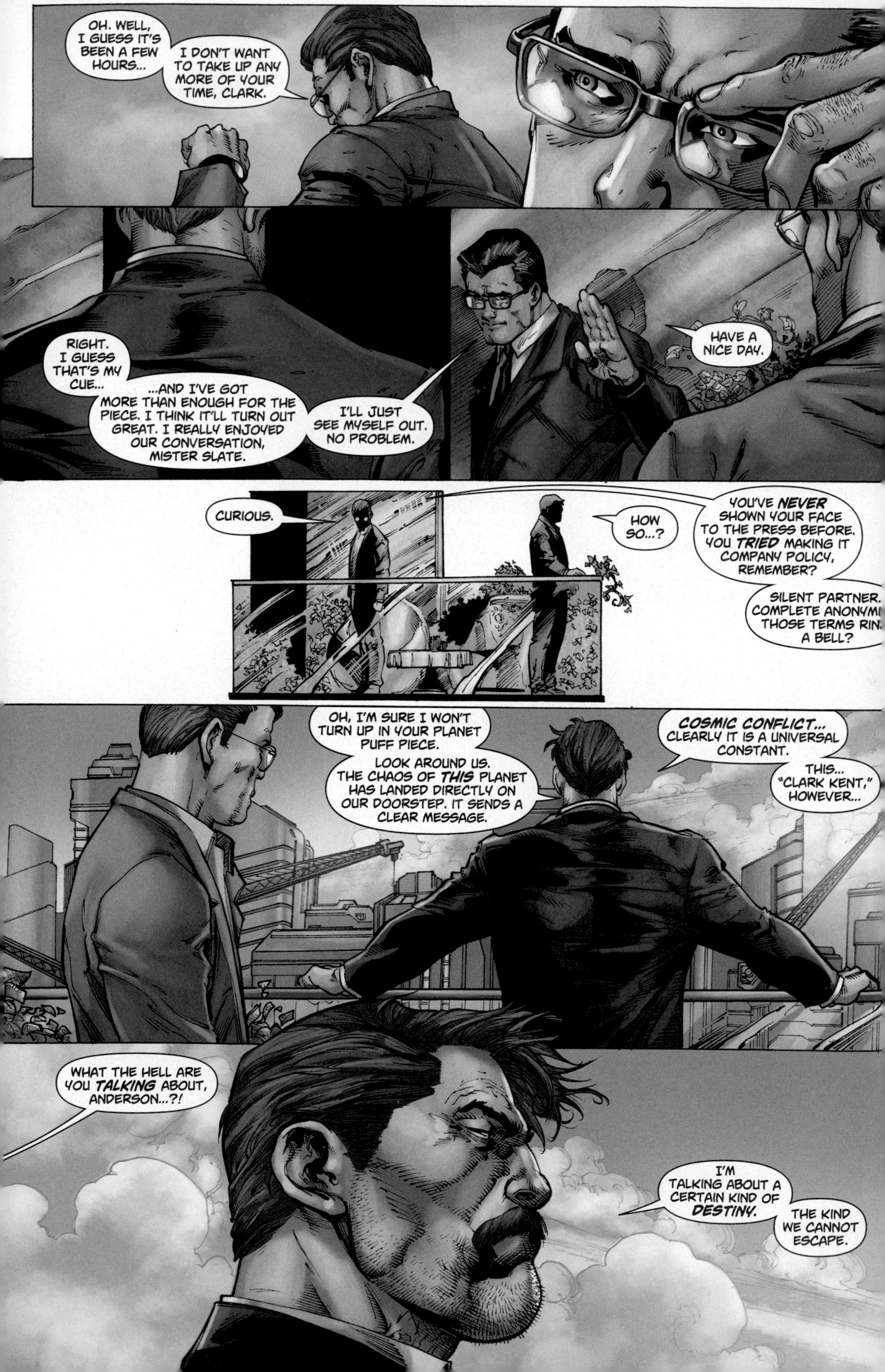
OH. WELL, I GUESS IT'S BEEN A FEW HOURS...
I DON'T WANT TO TAKE UP ANY MORE OF YOUR TIME, CLARK.
RIGHT. I GUESS THAT'S MY CUE...
...AND I'VE GOT MORE THAN ENOUGH FOR THE PIECE. I THINK IT'LL TURN OUT GREAT. I REALLY ENJOYED OUR CONVERSATION, MISTER SLATE.
I'LL JUST SEE MYSELF OUT. NO PROBLEM.
HAVE A NICE DAY.
CURIOUS.
HOW SO...?
YOU'VE NEVER SHOWN YOUR FACE TO THE PRESS BEFORE. YOU TRIED MAKING IT COMPANY POLICY, REMEMBER?
SILENT PARTNER. COMPLETE ANONYMI THOSE TERMS RIN A BELL?
OH, I'M SURE I WON'T TURN UP IN YOUR PLANET PUFF PIECE.
LOOK AROUND US. THE CHAOS OF THIS PLANET HAS LANDED DIRECTLY ON OUR DOORSTEP. IT SENDS A CLEAR MESSAGE.
COSMIC CONFLICT... CLEARLY IT IS A UNIVERSAL CONSTANT.
THIS... "CLARK KENT," HOWEVER...
WHAT THE HELL ARE YOU TALKING ABOUT, ANDERSON...?!
I'M TALKING ABOUT A CERTAIN KIND OF DESTINY.
THE KIND WE CANNOT ESCAPE.

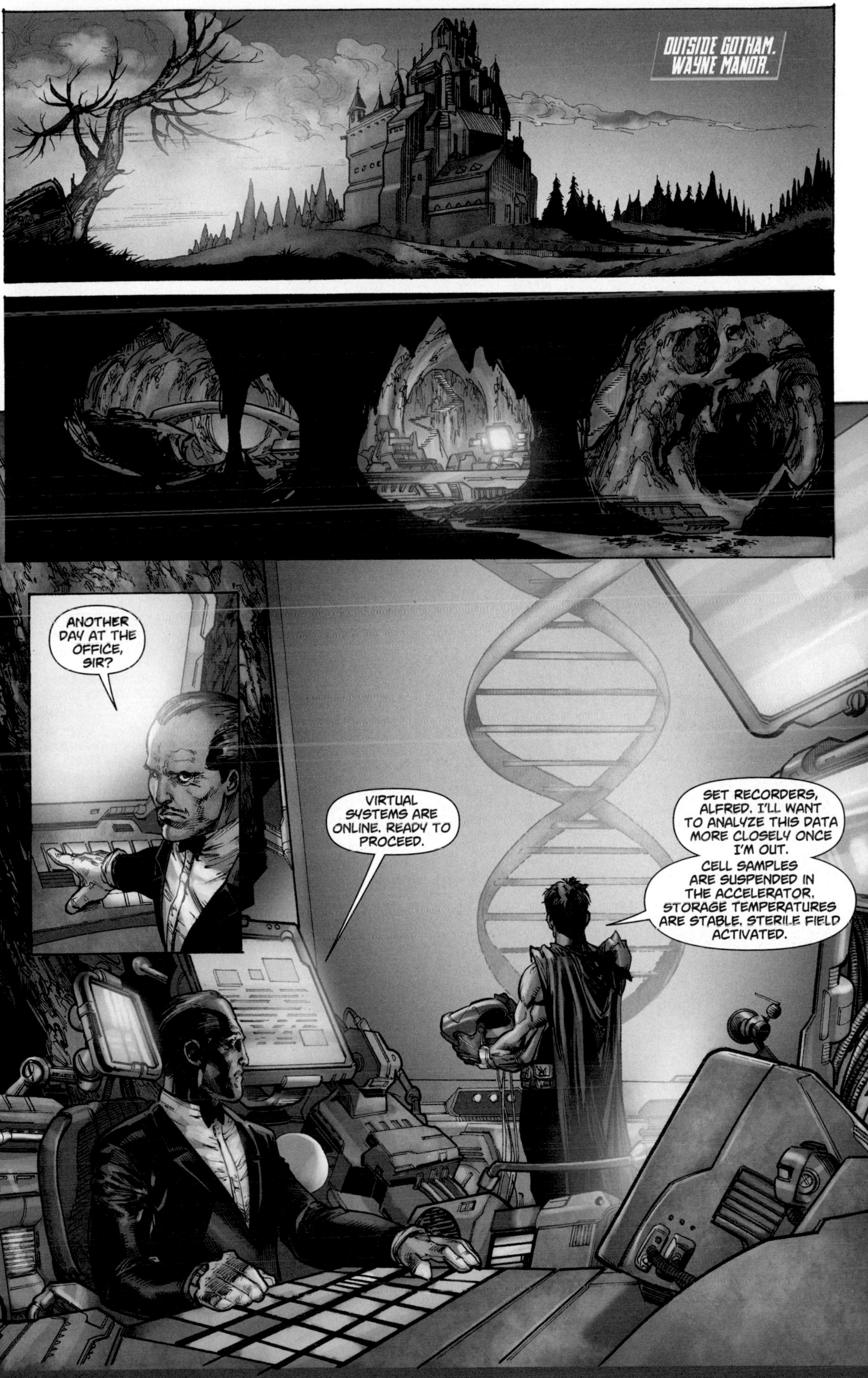
OUTSIDE GOTHAM. WAYNE MANOR.
ANOTHER DAY AT THE OFFICE, SIR?
VIRTUAL SYSTEMS ARE ONLINE. READY TO PROCEED.
SET RECORDERS, ALFRED. I'LL WANT TO ANALYZE THIS DATA MORE CLOSELY ONCE I'M OUT.
CELL SAMPLES ARE SUSPENDED IN THE ACCELERATOR, STORAGE TEMPERATURES ARE STABLE, STERILE FIELD ACTIVATED.

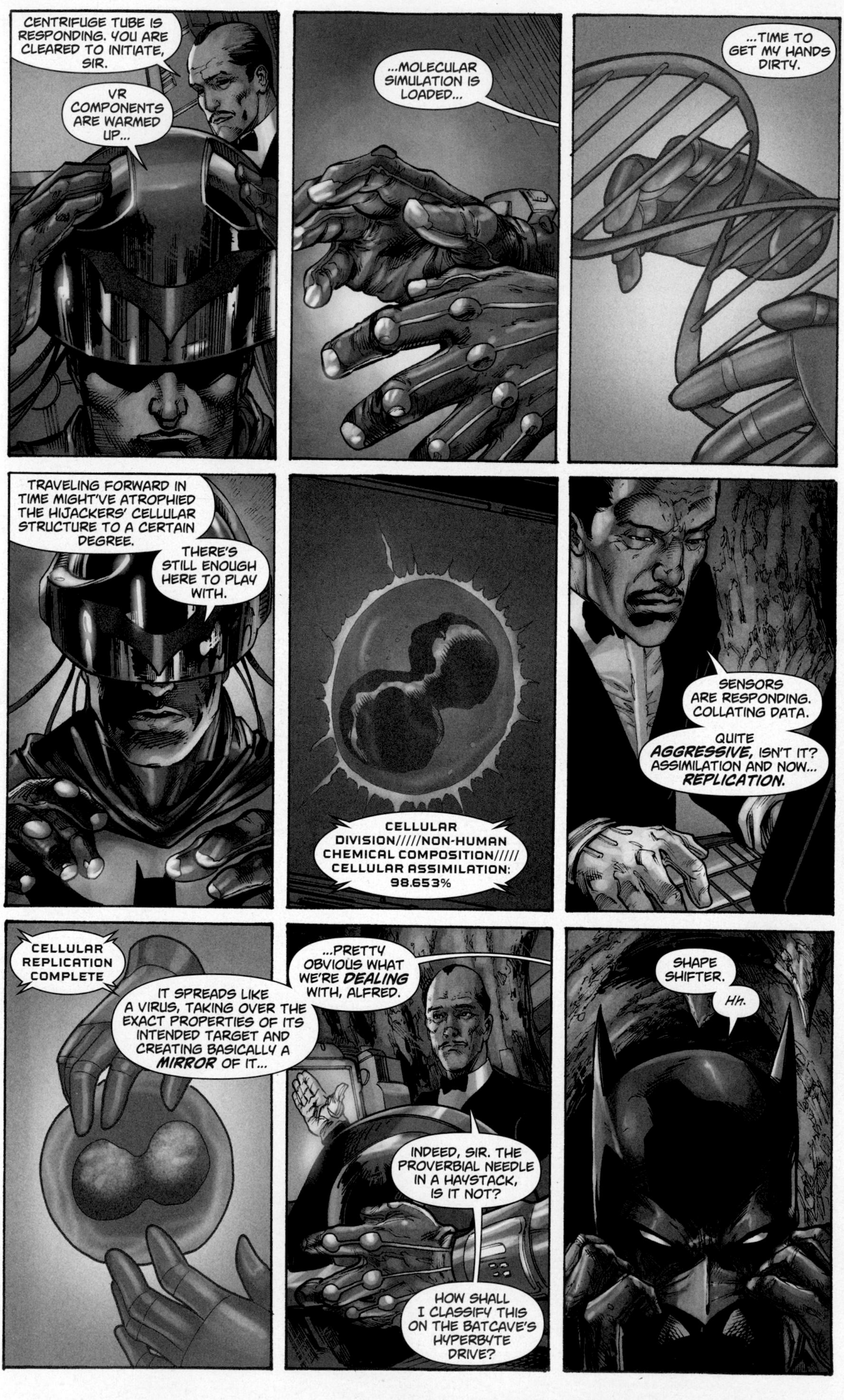

CENTRIFUGE TUBE IS RESPONDING. YOU ARE CLEARED TO INITIATE, SIR.
VR COMPONENTS ARE WARMED UP...
...MOLECULAR SIMULATION IS LOADED...
...TIME TO GET MY HANDS DIRTY.
TRAVELING FORWARD IN TIME MIGHT'VE ATROPHIED THE HIJACKERS' CELLULAR STRUCTURE TO A CERTAIN DEGREE.
THERE'S STILL ENOUGH HERE TO PLAY WITH.
CELLULAR DIVISION/////NON-HUMAN CHEMICAL COMPOSITION///// CELLULAR ASSIMILATION: 98.653%
SENSORS ARE RESPONDING. COLLATING DATA.
QUITE AGGRESSIVE, ISN'T IT? ASSIMILATION AND NOW... REPLICATION.
CELLULAR REPLICATION COMPLETE
IT SPREADS LIKE A VIRUS, TAKING OVER THE EXACT PROPERTIES OF ITS INTENDED TARGET AND CREATING BASICALLY A MIRROR OF IT...
...PRETTY OBVIOUS WHAT WE'RE DEALING WITH, ALFRED.
INDEED, SIR. THE PROVERBIAL NEEDLE IN A HAYSTACK, IS IT NOT?
HOW SHALL I CLASSIFY THIS ON THE BATCAVE'S HYPERBYTE DRIVE?
SHAPE SHIFTER.
Hh.

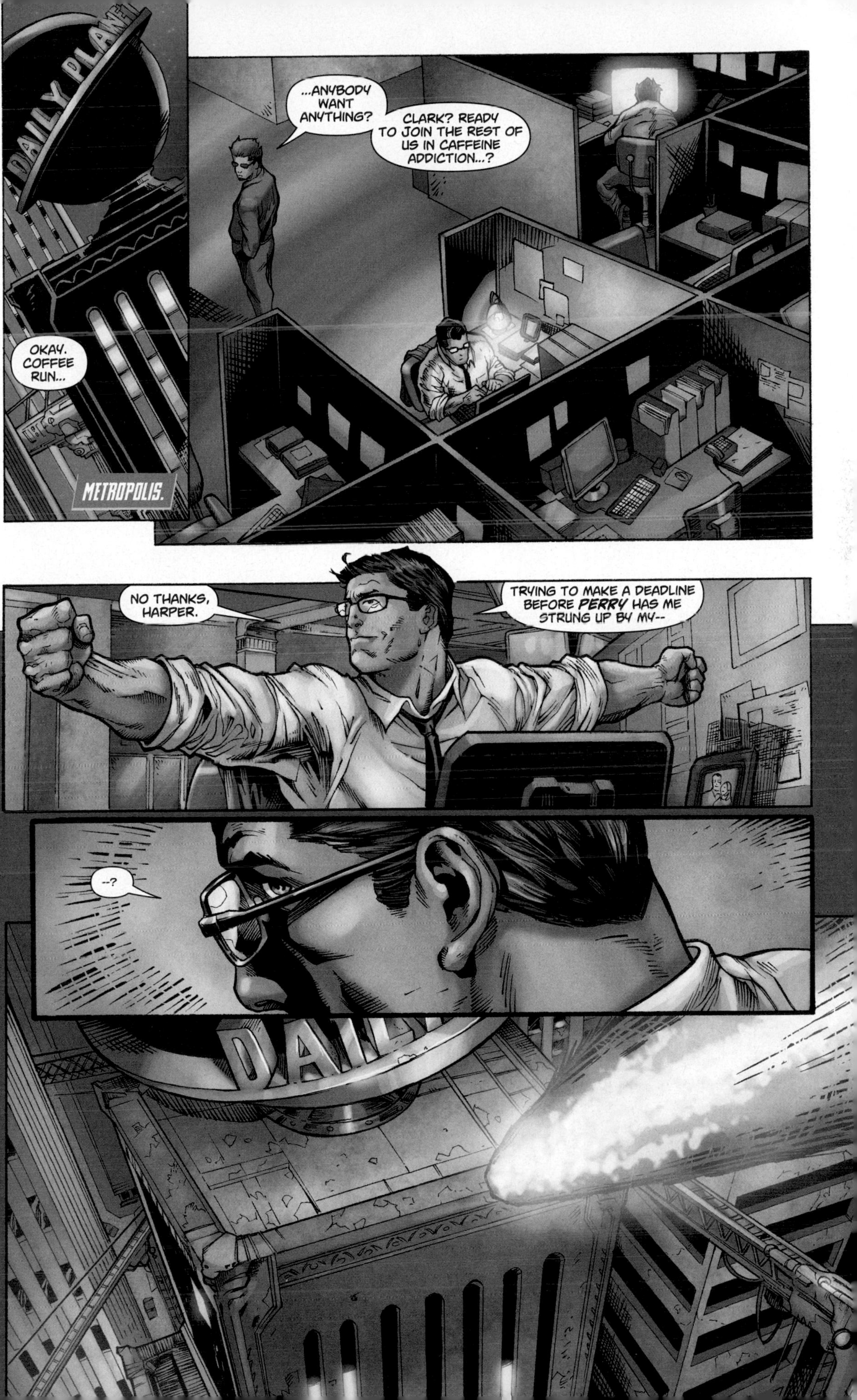
DAILY PLANET
METROPOLIS.
OKAY. COFFEE RUN...
...ANYBODY WANT ANYTHING?
CLARK? READY TO JOIN THE REST OF US IN CAFFEINE ADDICTION...?
NO THANKS, HARPER.
TRYING TO MAKE A DEADLINE BEFORE PERRY HAS ME STRUNG UP BY MY--
--?
DAIL

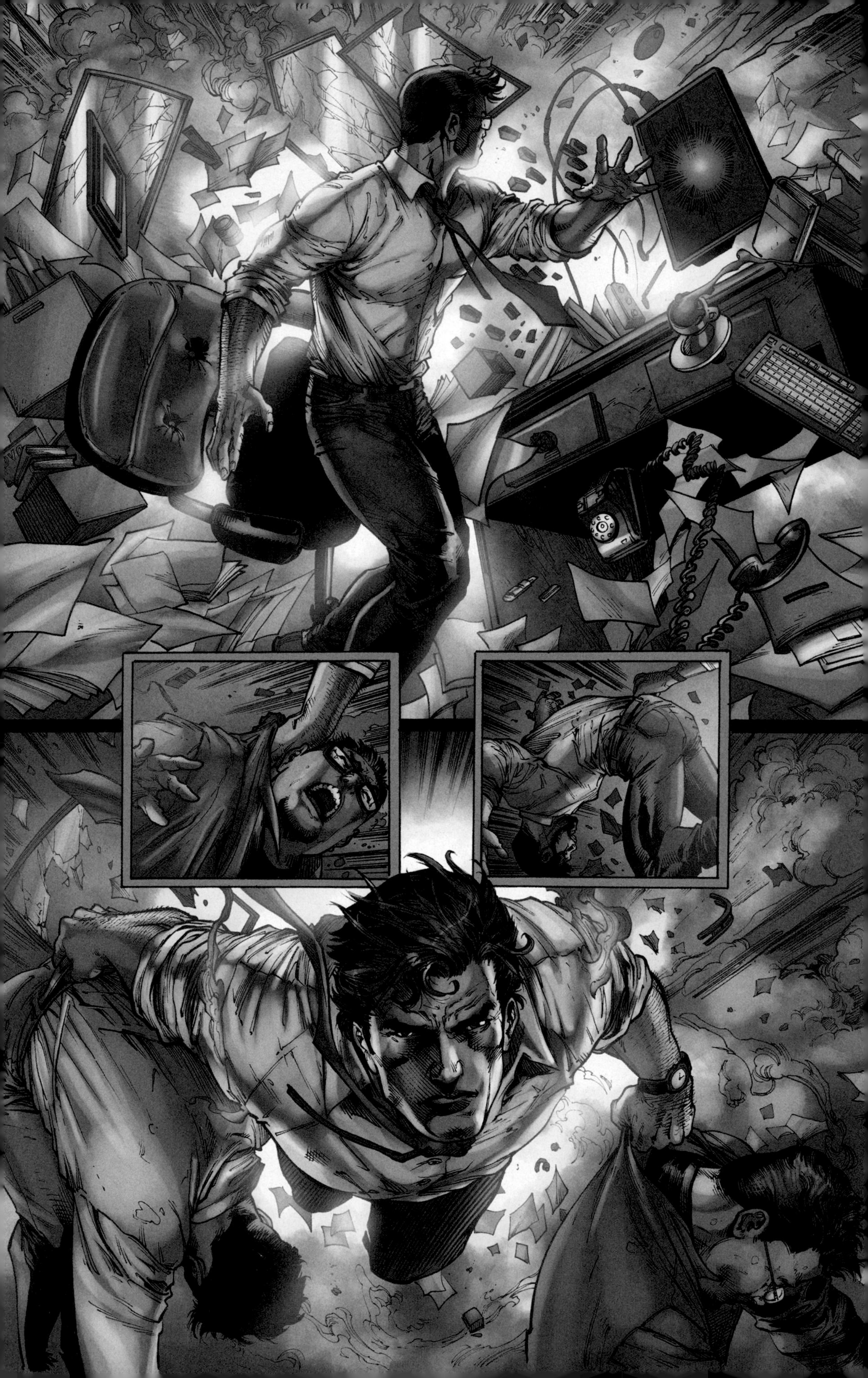

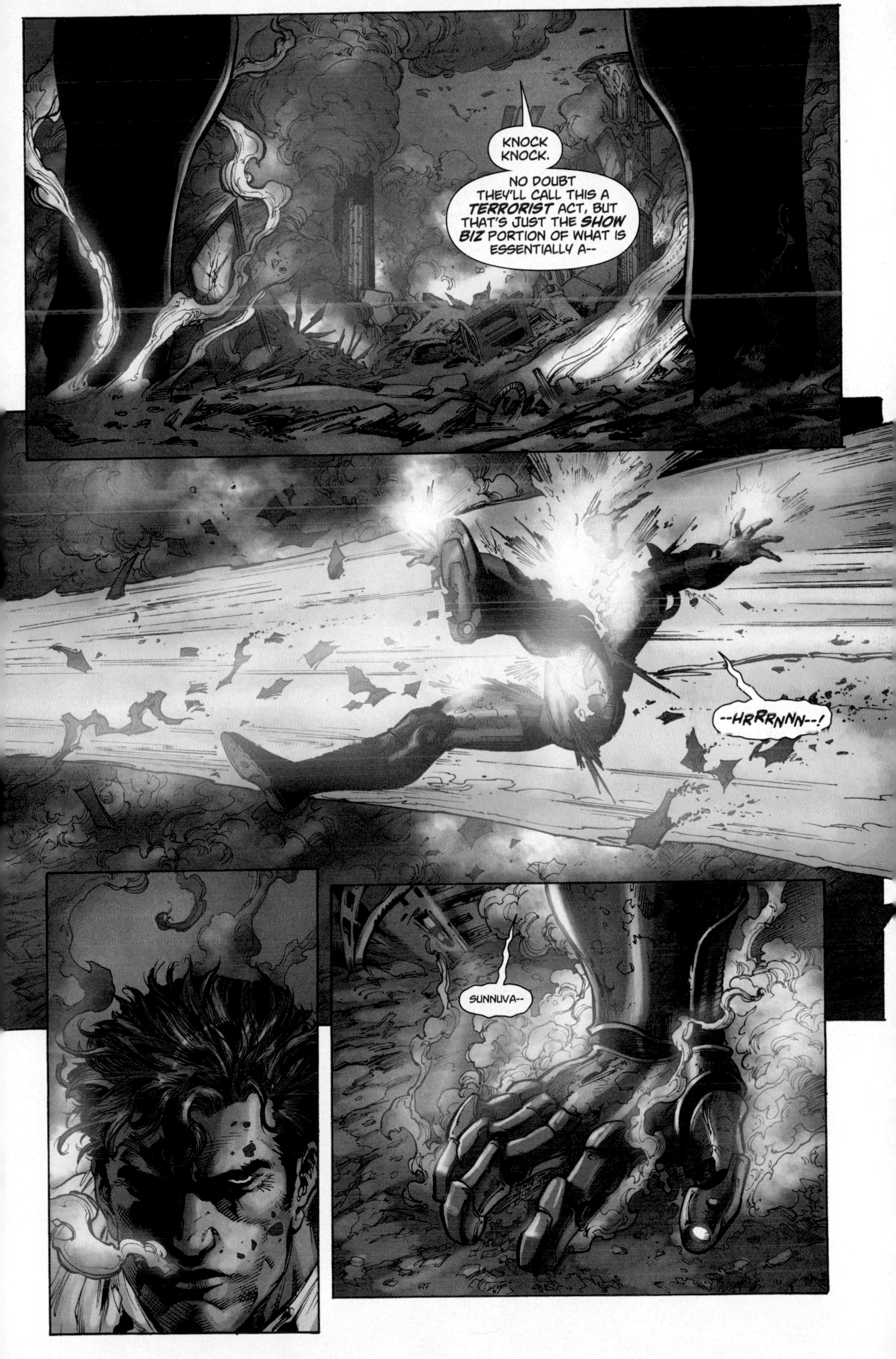
KNOCK KNOCK.
NO DOUBT THEY'LL CALL THIS A *TERRORIST* ACT, BUT THAT'S JUST THE *SHOW BIZ* PORTION OF WHAT IS ESSENTIALLY A--
--HRRRNNN--!
SUNNUVA--

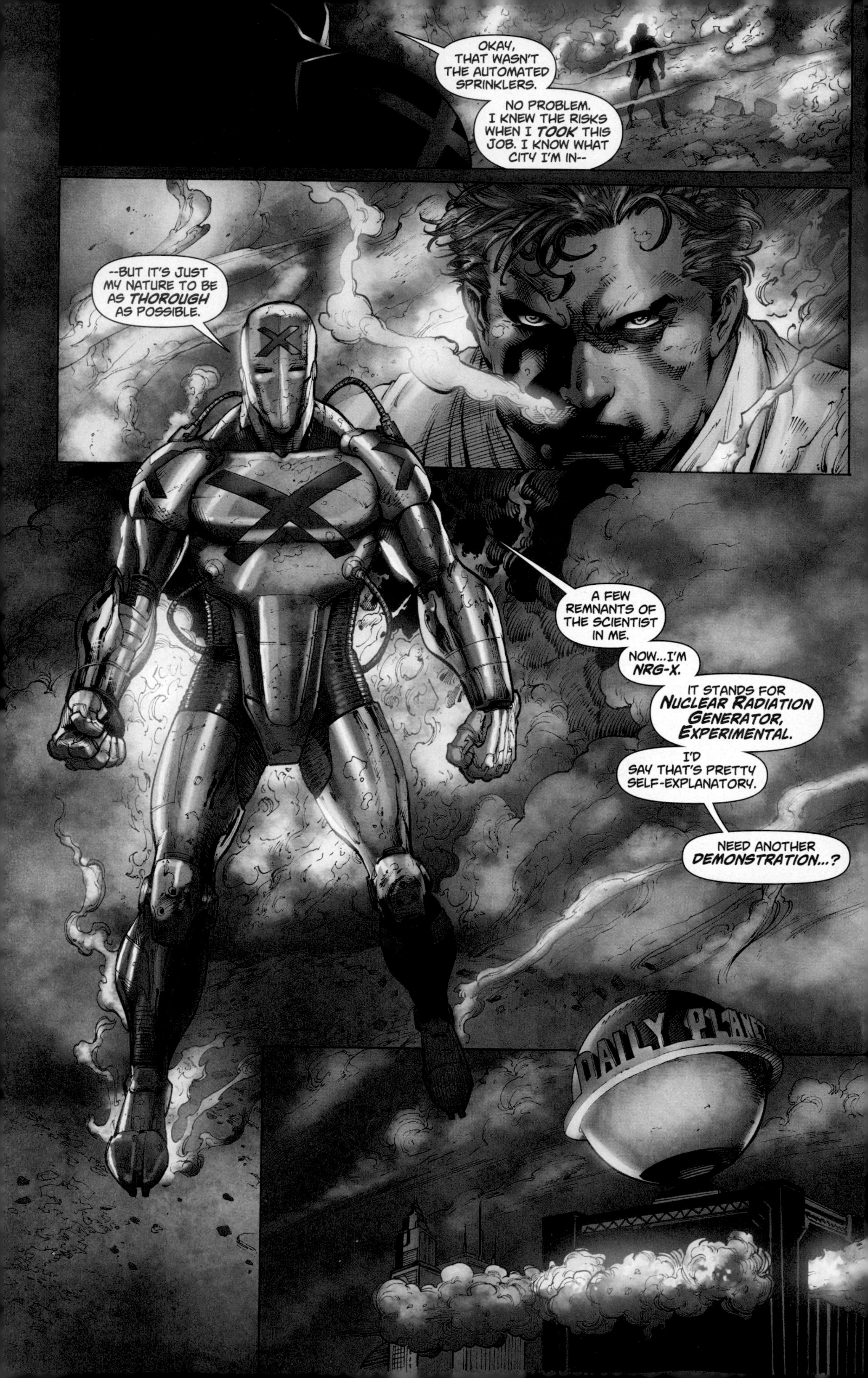

OKAY, THAT WASN'T THE AUTOMATED SPRINKLERS.
NO PROBLEM. I KNEW THE RISKS WHEN I *TOOK* THIS JOB. I KNOW WHAT CITY I'M IN--
--BUT IT'S JUST MY NATURE TO BE AS *THOROUGH* AS POSSIBLE.
A FEW REMNANTS OF THE SCIENTIST IN ME.
NOW...I'M *NRG-X.*
IT STANDS FOR *NUCLEAR RADIATION GENERATOR, EXPERIMENTAL.*
I'D SAY THAT'S PRETTY SELF-EXPLANATORY.
NEED ANOTHER *DEMONSTRATION...?*
DAILY PLANET

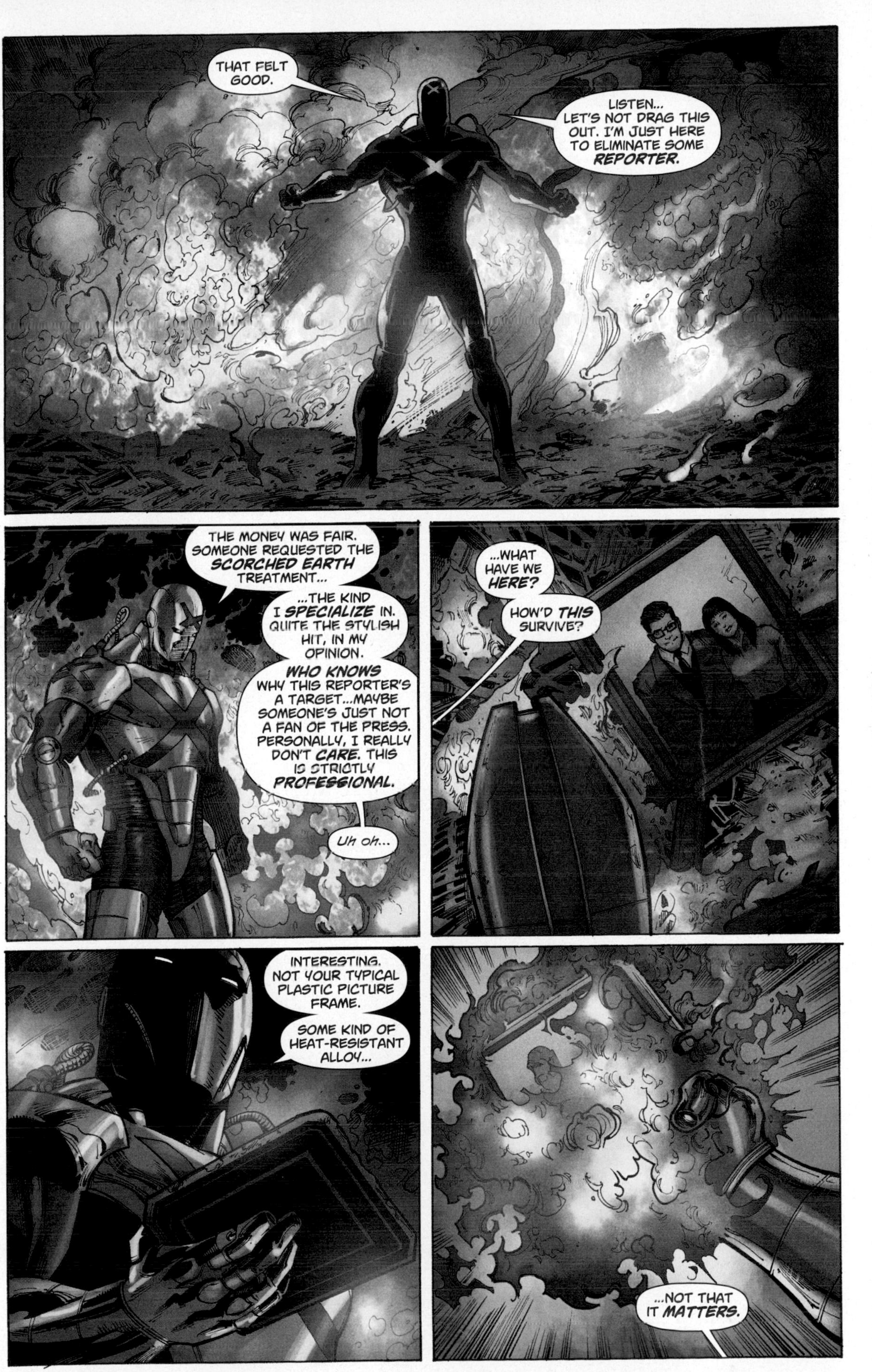
THAT FELT GOOD.
LISTEN... LET'S NOT DRAG THIS OUT. I'M JUST HERE TO ELIMINATE SOME REPORTER.
THE MONEY WAS FAIR. SOMEONE REQUESTED THE SCORCHED EARTH TREATMENT...
...THE KIND I SPECIALIZE IN. QUITE THE STYLISH HIT, IN MY OPINION.
WHO KNOWS WHY THIS REPORTER'S A TARGET...MAYBE SOMEONE'S JUST NOT A FAN OF THE PRESS. PERSONALLY, I REALLY DON'T CARE. THIS IS STRICTLY PROFESSIONAL.
Uh oh...
...WHAT HAVE WE HERE?
HOW'D THIS SURVIVE?
INTERESTING. NOT YOUR TYPICAL PLASTIC PICTURE FRAME.
SOME KIND OF HEAT-RESISTANT ALLOY...
...NOT THAT IT MATTERS.

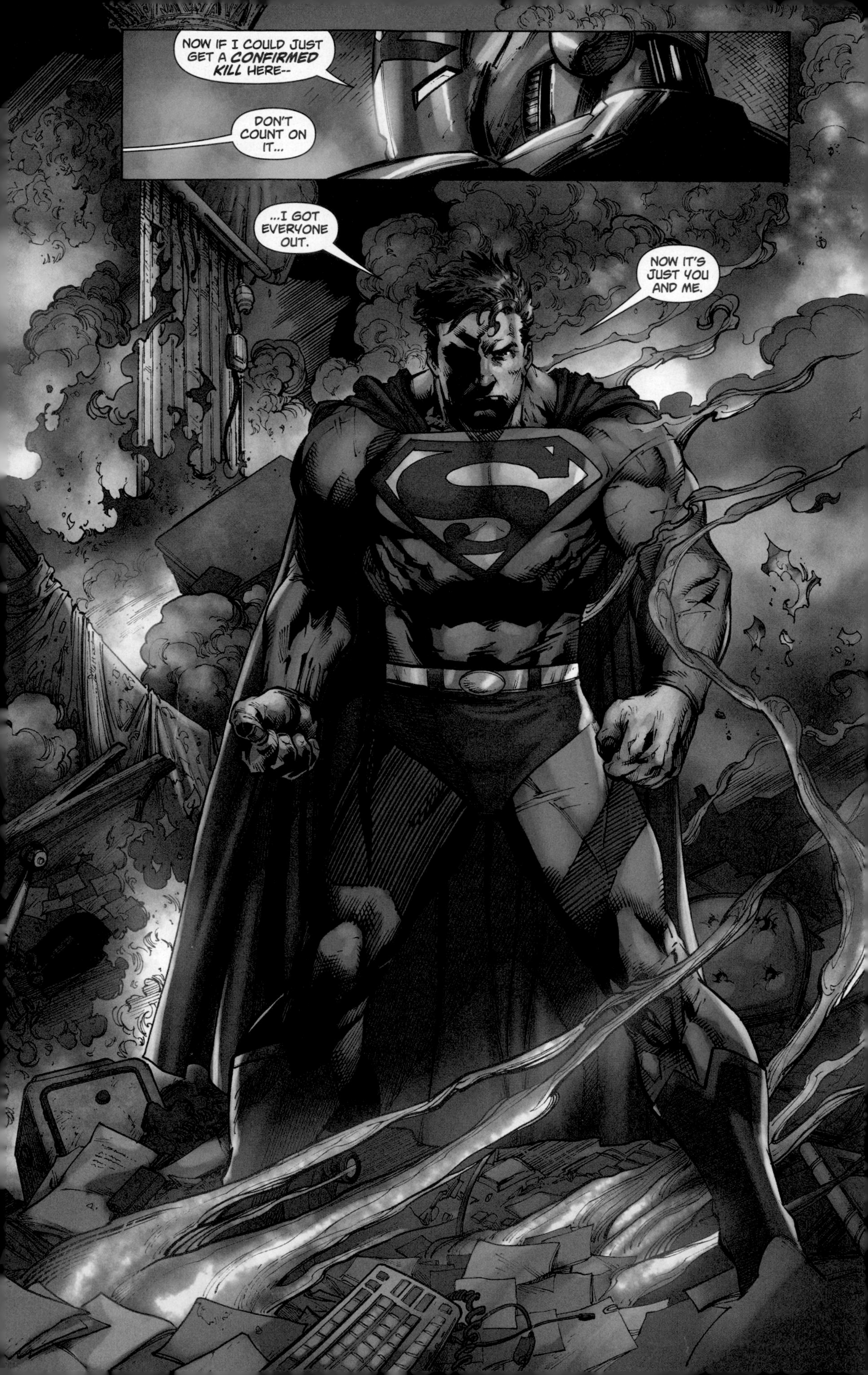
NOW IF I COULD JUST GET A CONFIRMED KILL HERE--
DON'T COUNT ON IT...
...I GOT EVERYONE OUT.
NOW IT'S JUST YOU AND ME.

SUPERMAN/BATMAN No. 69
Ardian Syaf, Vicente Cifuentes and Ulises Arreola

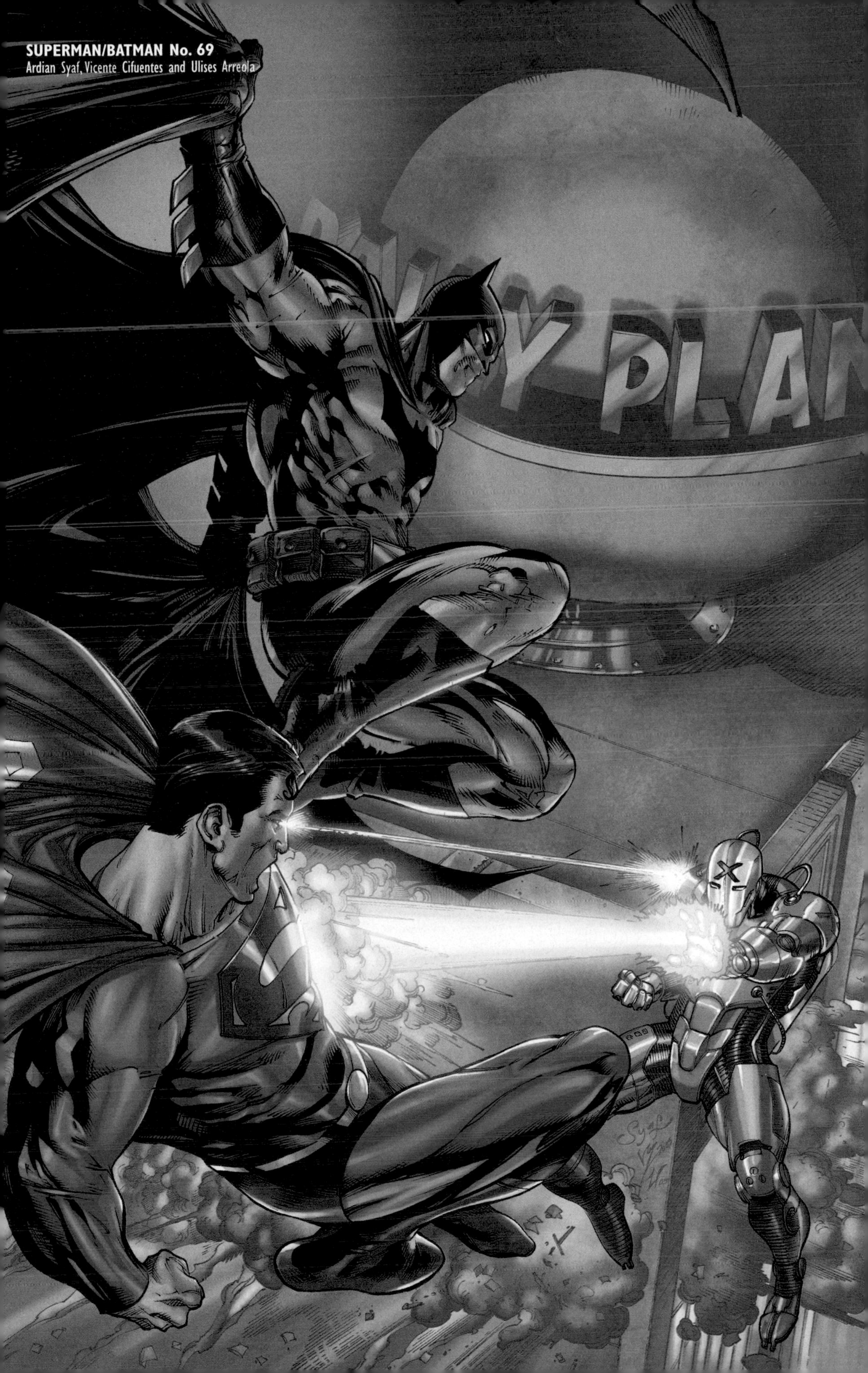

THE BIG NOISE PART 2: BENEDICTION REDUX

Penciller: Ardian Syaf
Inker: Vicente Cifuentes

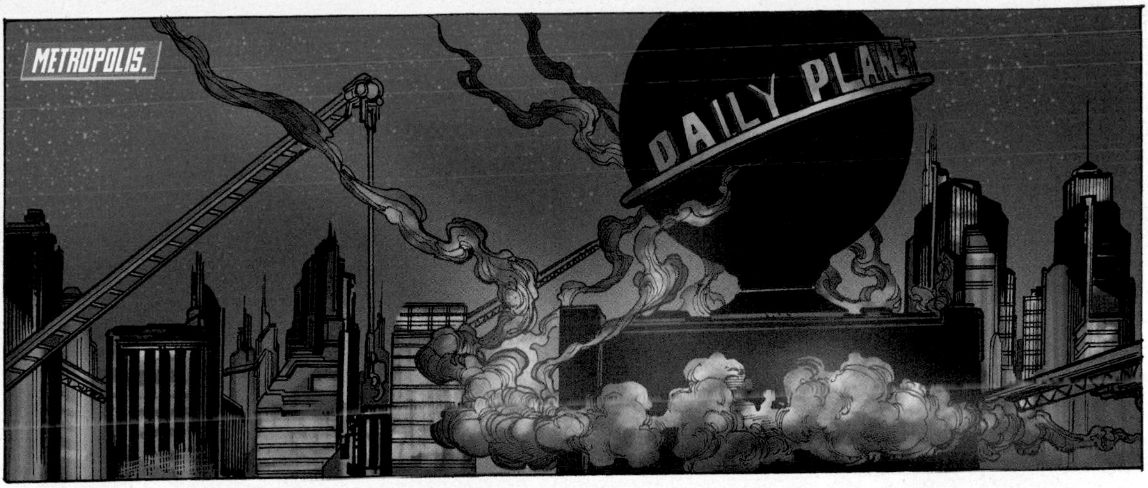
METROPOLIS.
DAILY PLANET

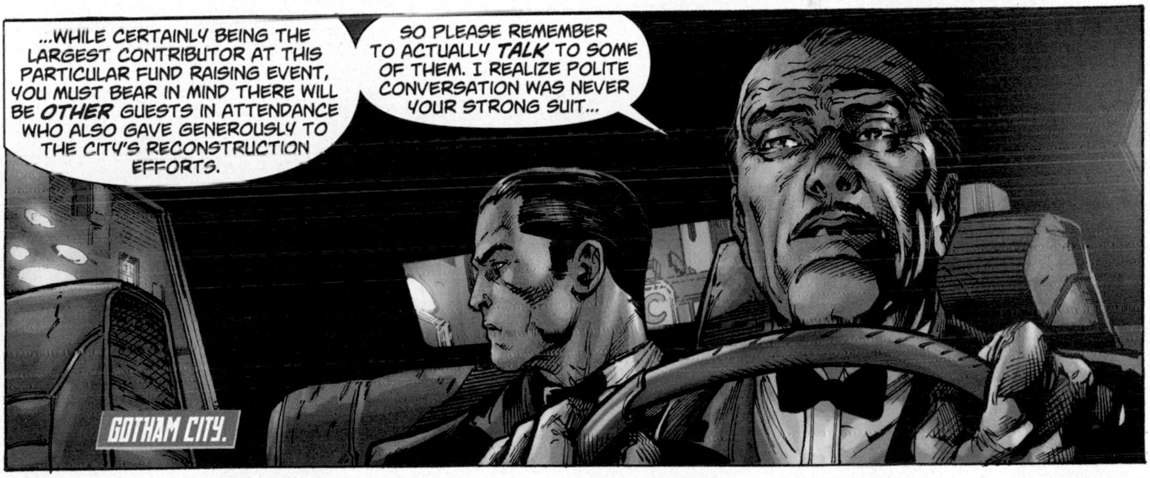
...WHILE CERTAINLY BEING THE LARGEST CONTRIBUTOR AT THIS PARTICULAR FUND RAISING EVENT, YOU MUST BEAR IN MIND THERE WILL BE OTHER GUESTS IN ATTENDANCE WHO ALSO GAVE GENEROUSLY TO THE CITY'S RECONSTRUCTION EFFORTS.
SO PLEASE REMEMBER TO ACTUALLY TALK TO SOME OF THEM. I REALIZE POLITE CONVERSATION WAS NEVER YOUR STRONG SUIT...
GOTHAM CITY.

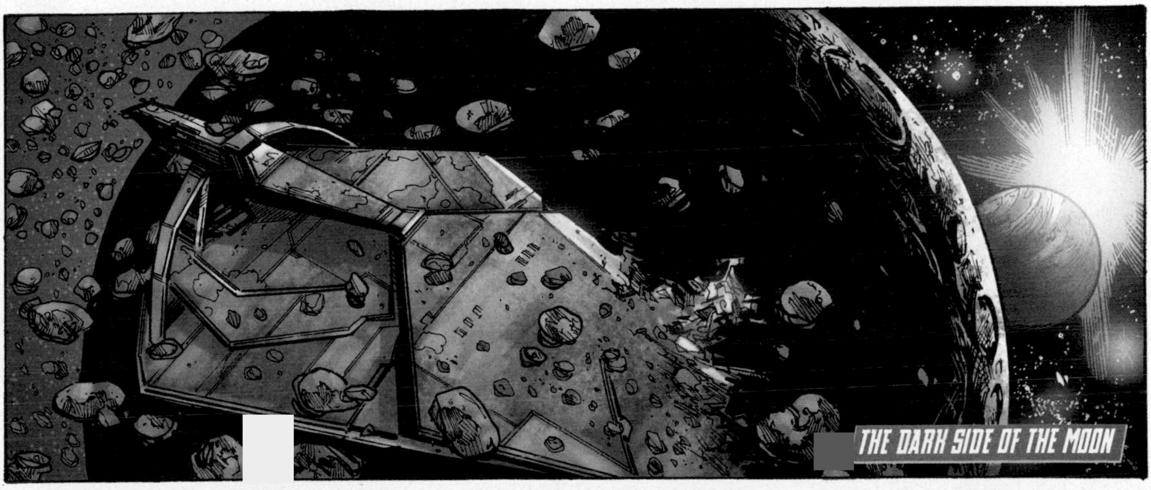
THE DARK SIDE OF THE MOON

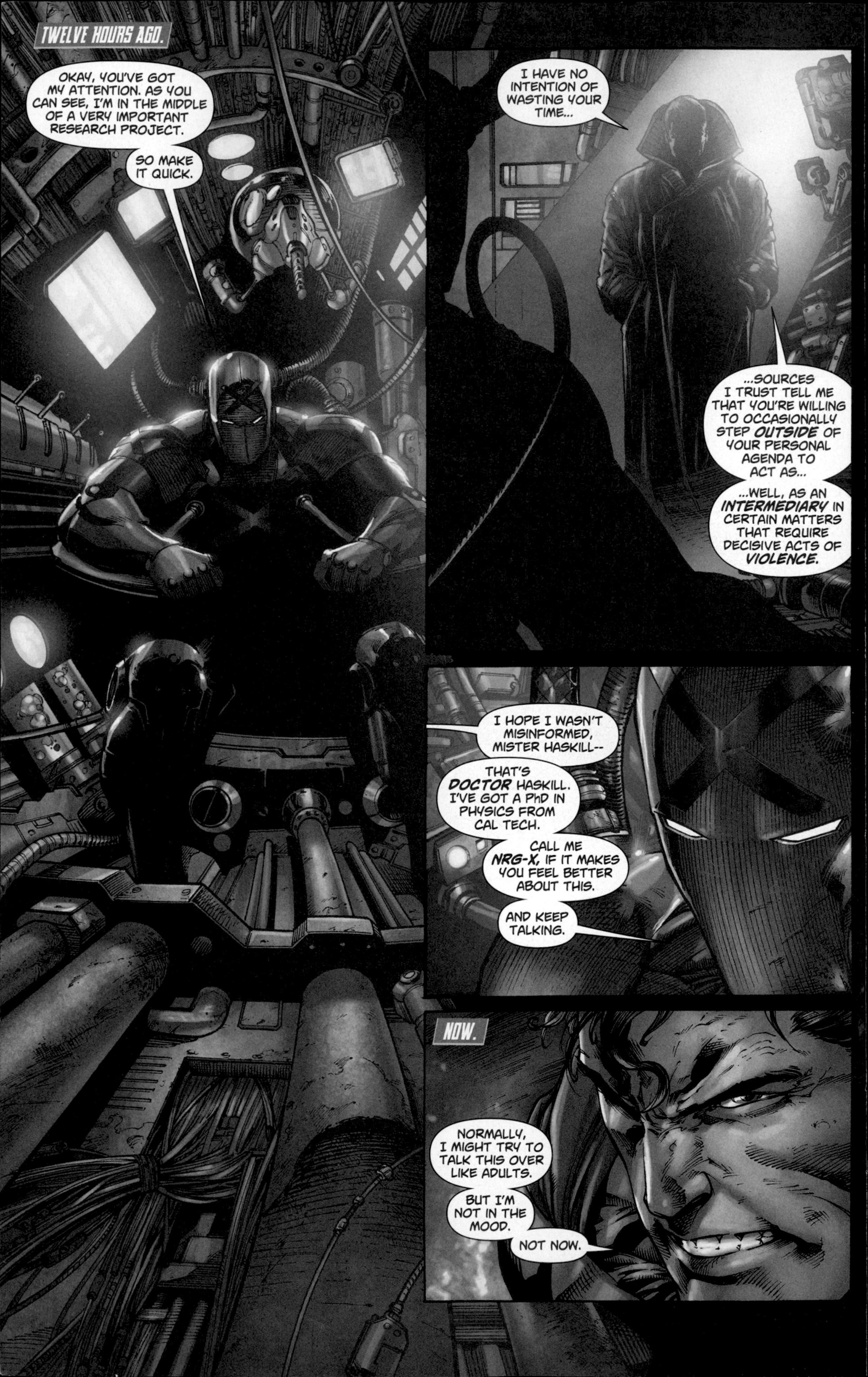
TWELVE HOURS AGO.
OKAY, YOU'VE GOT MY ATTENTION. AS YOU CAN SEE, I'M IN THE MIDDLE OF A VERY IMPORTANT RESEARCH PROJECT.
SO MAKE IT QUICK.
I HAVE NO INTENTION OF WASTING YOUR TIME...
...SOURCES I TRUST TELL ME THAT YOU'RE WILLING TO OCCASIONALLY STEP OUTSIDE OF YOUR PERSONAL AGENDA TO ACT AS...
...WELL, AS AN INTERMEDIARY IN CERTAIN MATTERS THAT REQUIRE DECISIVE ACTS OF VIOLENCE.
I HOPE I WASN'T MISINFORMED, MISTER HASKILL--
THAT'S DOCTOR HASKILL. I'VE GOT A PhD IN PHYSICS FROM CAL TECH.
CALL ME NRG-X, IF IT MAKES YOU FEEL BETTER ABOUT THIS.
AND KEEP TALKING.
NOW.
NORMALLY, I MIGHT TRY TO TALK THIS OVER LIKE ADULTS.
BUT I'M NOT IN THE MOOD.
NOT NOW.

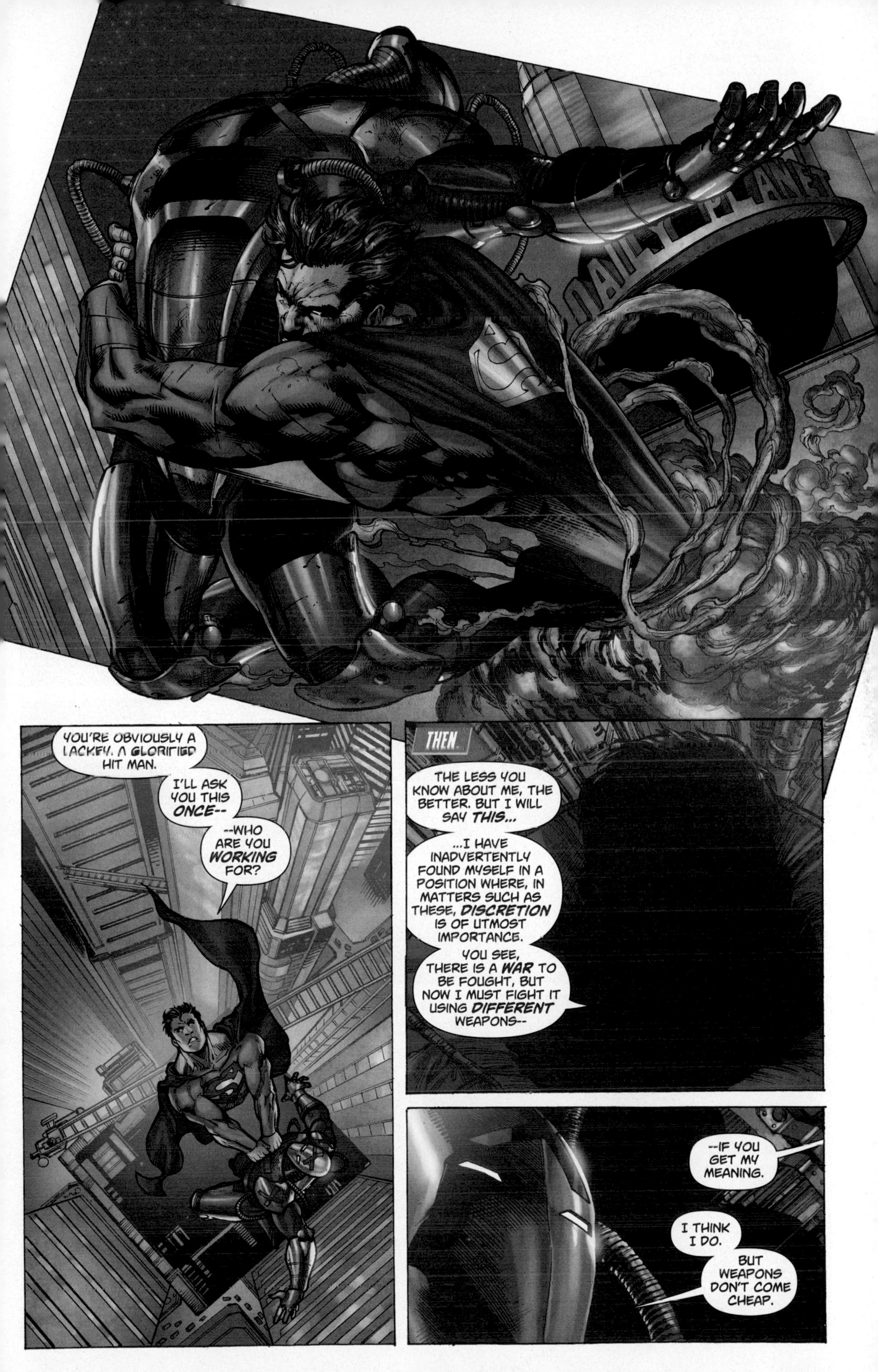
YOU'RE OBVIOUSLY A LACKEY. A GLORIFIED HIT MAN.
I'LL ASK YOU THIS ONCE--
--WHO ARE YOU WORKING FOR?
THEN.
THE LESS YOU KNOW ABOUT ME, THE BETTER. BUT I WILL SAY THIS...
...I HAVE INADVERTENTLY FOUND MYSELF IN A POSITION WHERE, IN MATTERS SUCH AS THESE, DISCRETION IS OF UTMOST IMPORTANCE.
YOU SEE, THERE IS A WAR TO BE FOUGHT, BUT NOW I MUST FIGHT IT USING DIFFERENT WEAPONS--
--IF YOU GET MY MEANING.
I THINK I DO.
BUT WEAPONS DON'T COME CHEAP.

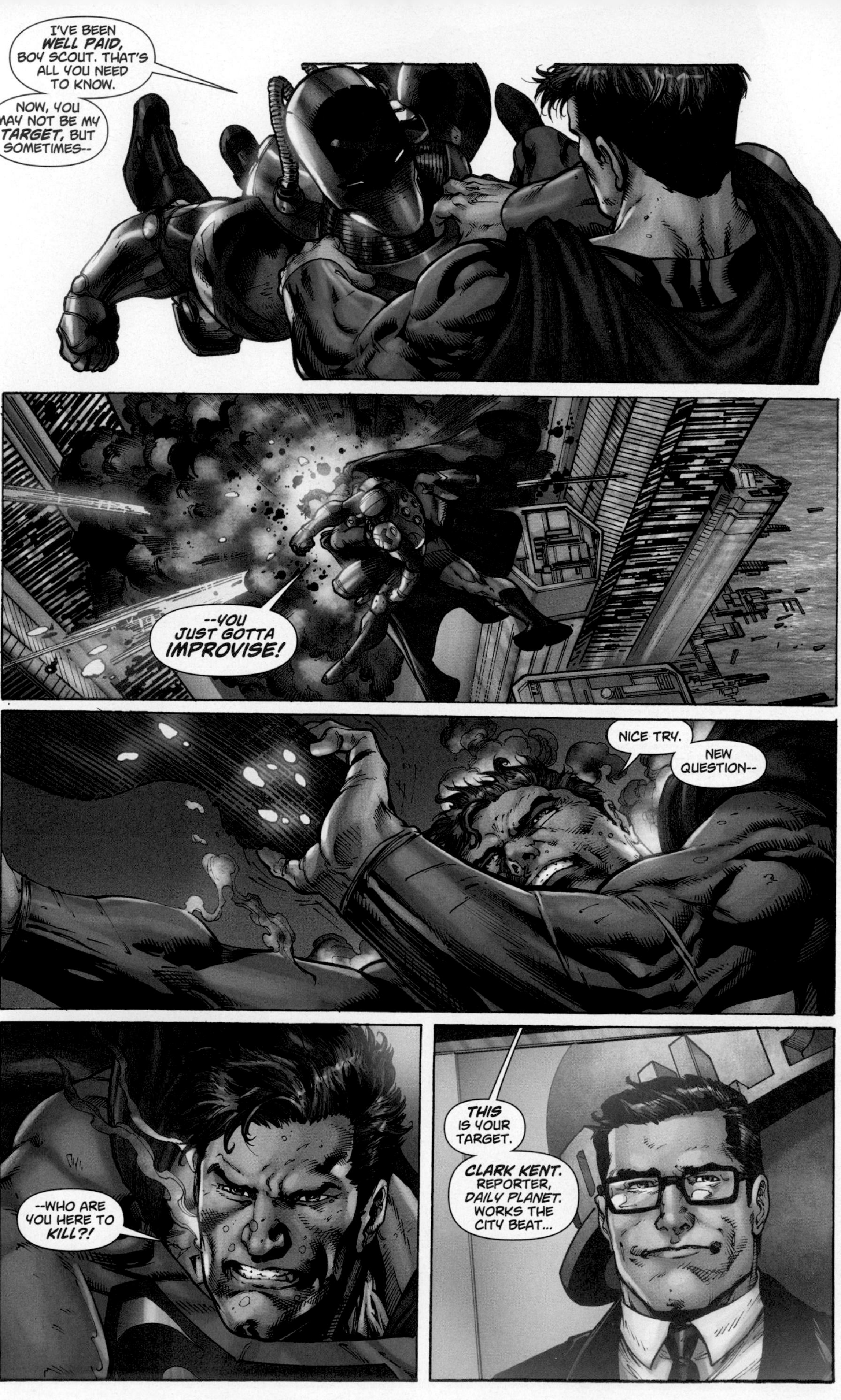
I'VE BEEN WELL PAID, BOY SCOUT. THAT'S ALL YOU NEED TO KNOW.
NOW, YOU MAY NOT BE MY TARGET, BUT SOMETIMES--
--YOU JUST GOTTA IMPROVISE!
NICE TRY.
NEW QUESTION--
--WHO ARE YOU HERE TO KILL?!
THIS IS YOUR TARGET.
CLARK KENT. REPORTER, DAILY PLANET. WORKS THE CITY BEAT...

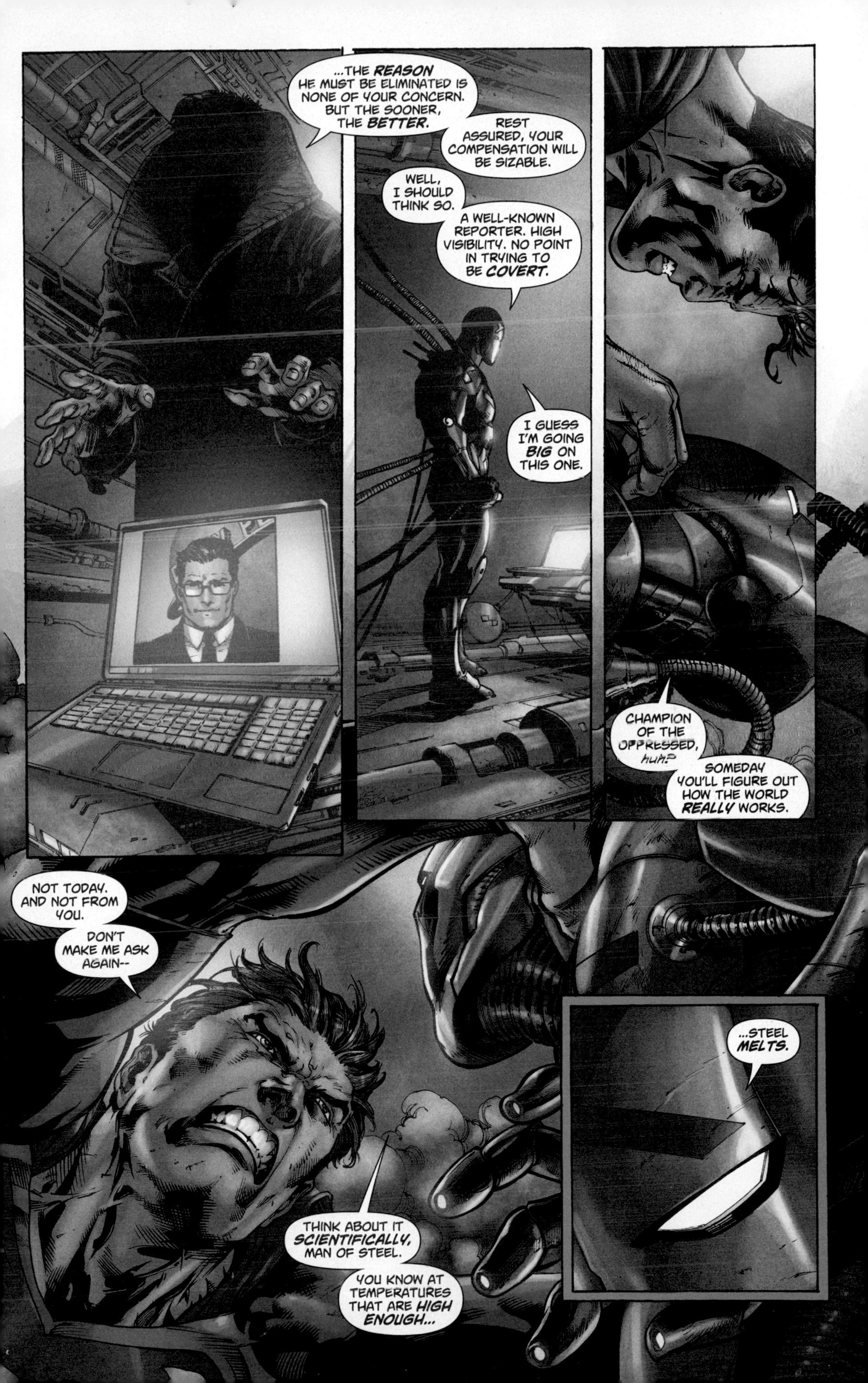
...THE REASON HE MUST BE ELIMINATED IS NONE OF YOUR CONCERN. BUT THE SOONER, THE BETTER.
REST ASSURED, YOUR COMPENSATION WILL BE SIZABLE.
WELL, I SHOULD THINK SO.
A WELL-KNOWN REPORTER. HIGH VISIBILITY. NO POINT IN TRYING TO BE COVERT.
I GUESS I'M GOING BIG ON THIS ONE.
CHAMPION OF THE OPPRESSED, huh?
SOMEDAY YOU'LL FIGURE OUT HOW THE WORLD REALLY WORKS.
NOT TODAY. AND NOT FROM YOU.
DON'T MAKE ME ASK AGAIN--
THINK ABOUT IT SCIENTIFICALLY, MAN OF STEEL.
YOU KNOW AT TEMPERATURES THAT ARE HIGH ENOUGH...
...STEEL MELTS.

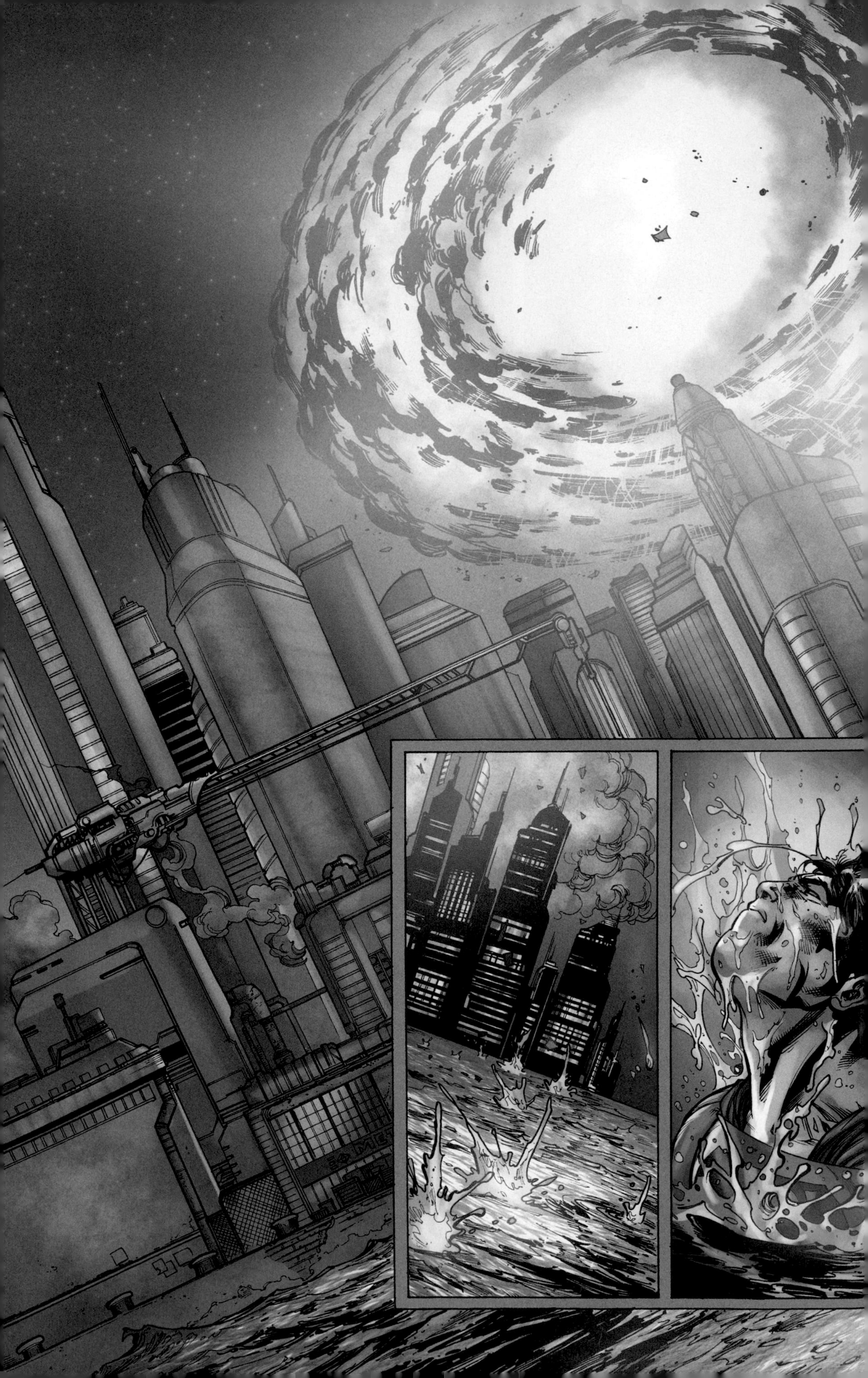

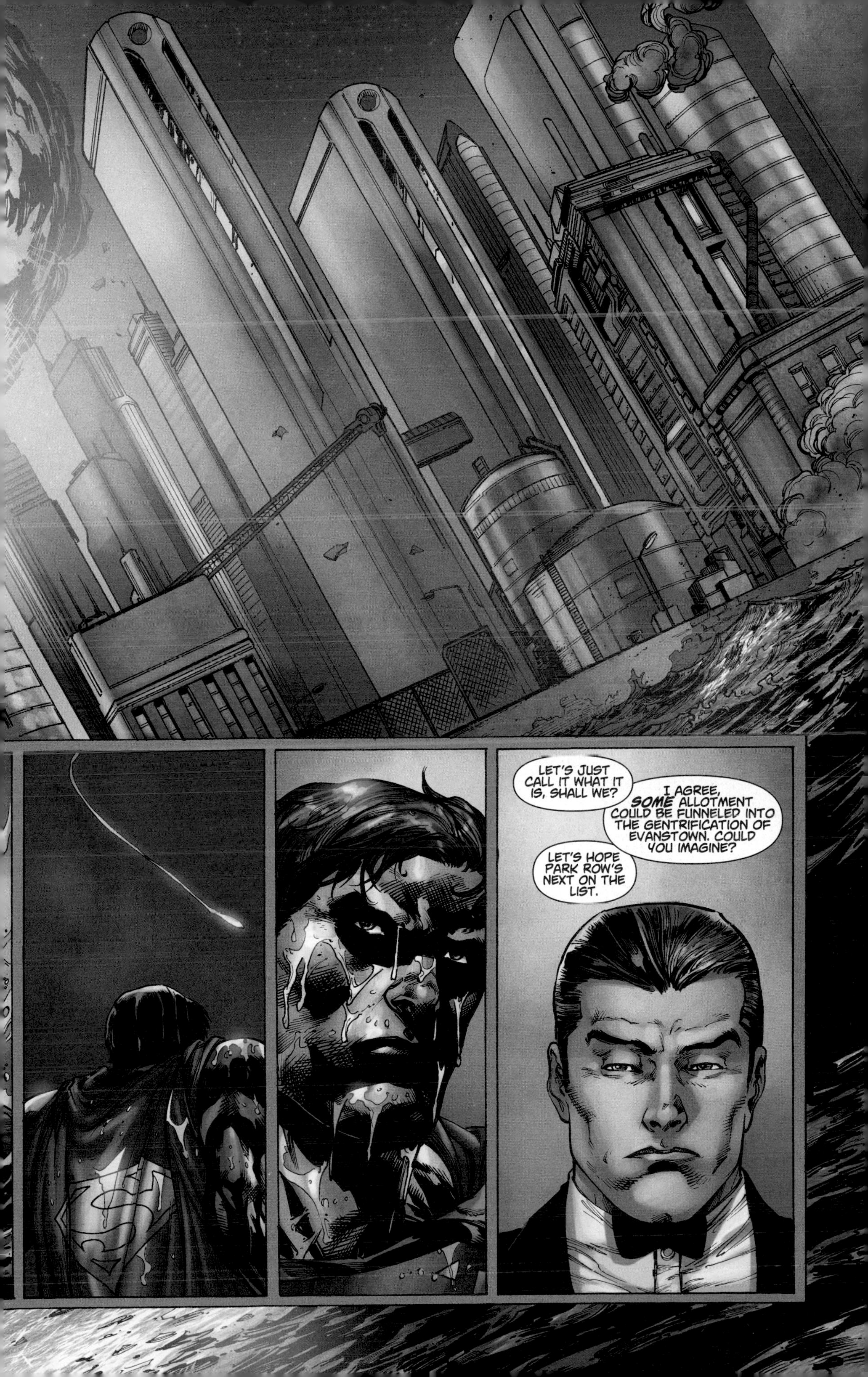
LET'S JUST CALL IT WHAT IT IS, SHALL WE?
I AGREE, SOME ALLOTMENT COULD BE FUNNELED INTO THE GENTRIFICATION OF EVANSTOWN. COULD YOU IMAGINE?
LET'S HOPE PARK ROW'S NEXT ON THE LIST.

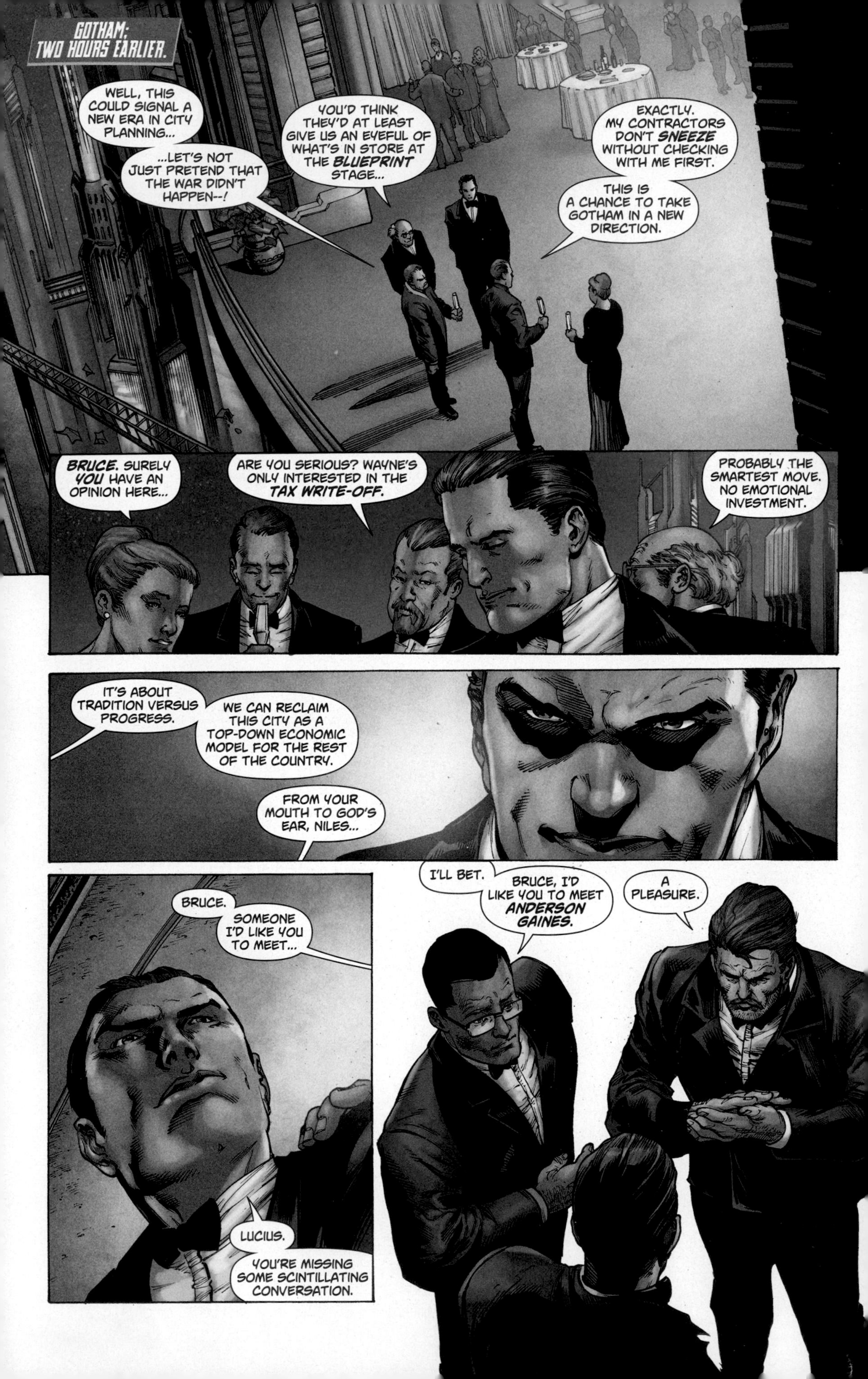
GOTHAM; TWO HOURS EARLIER.
WELL, THIS COULD SIGNAL A NEW ERA IN CITY PLANNING...
...LET'S NOT JUST PRETEND THAT THE WAR DIDN'T HAPPEN--!
YOU'D THINK THEY'D AT LEAST GIVE US AN EYEFUL OF WHAT'S IN STORE AT THE BLUEPRINT STAGE...
EXACTLY. MY CONTRACTORS DON'T SNEEZE WITHOUT CHECKING WITH ME FIRST.
THIS IS A CHANCE TO TAKE GOTHAM IN A NEW DIRECTION.
BRUCE. SURELY YOU HAVE AN OPINION HERE...
ARE YOU SERIOUS? WAYNE'S ONLY INTERESTED IN THE TAX WRITE-OFF.
PROBABLY THE SMARTEST MOVE. NO EMOTIONAL INVESTMENT.
IT'S ABOUT TRADITION VERSUS PROGRESS.
WE CAN RECLAIM THIS CITY AS A TOP-DOWN ECONOMIC MODEL FOR THE REST OF THE COUNTRY.
FROM YOUR MOUTH TO GOD'S EAR, NILES...
BRUCE.
SOMEONE I'D LIKE YOU TO MEET...
LUCIUS.
YOU'RE MISSING SOME SCINTILLATING CONVERSATION.
I'LL BET.
BRUCE, I'D LIKE YOU TO MEET ANDERSON GAINES.
A PLEASURE.

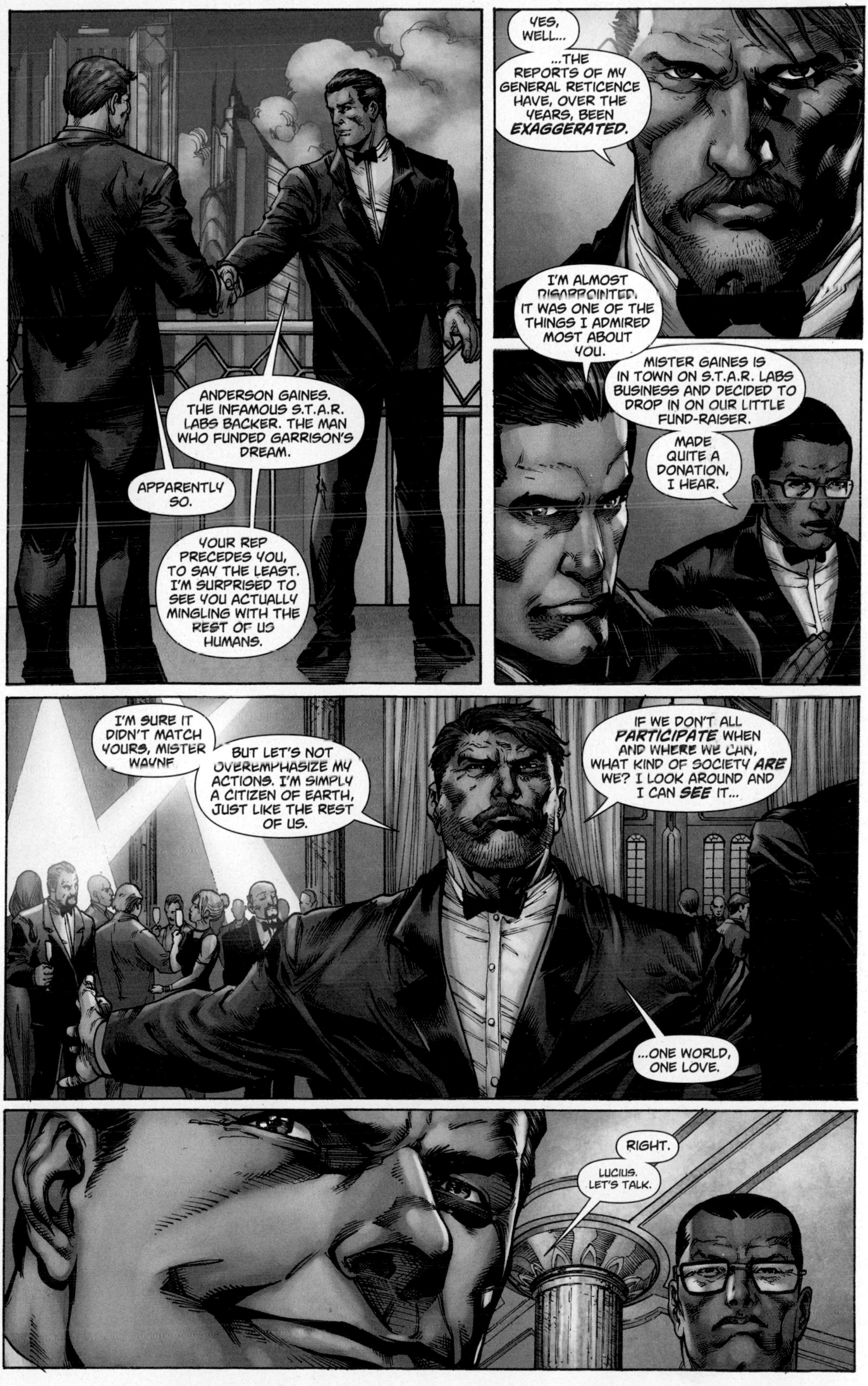
ANDERSON GAINES. THE INFAMOUS S.T.A.R. LABS BACKER. THE MAN WHO FUNDED GARRISON'S DREAM.
APPARENTLY SO.
YOUR REP PRECEDES YOU, TO SAY THE LEAST. I'M SURPRISED TO SEE YOU ACTUALLY MINGLING WITH THE REST OF US HUMANS.
YES, WELL...
...THE REPORTS OF MY GENERAL RETICENCE HAVE, OVER THE YEARS, BEEN EXAGGERATED.
I'M ALMOST DISAPPOINTED. IT WAS ONE OF THE THINGS I ADMIRED MOST ABOUT YOU.
MISTER GAINES IS IN TOWN ON S.T.A.R. LABS BUSINESS AND DECIDED TO DROP IN ON OUR LITTLE FUND-RAISER.
MADE QUITE A DONATION, I HEAR.
I'M SURE IT DIDN'T MATCH YOURS, MISTER WAYNE.
BUT LET'S NOT OVEREMPHASIZE MY ACTIONS. I'M SIMPLY A CITIZEN OF EARTH, JUST LIKE THE REST OF US.
IF WE DON'T ALL PARTICIPATE WHEN AND WHERE WE CAN, WHAT KIND OF SOCIETY ARE WE? I LOOK AROUND AND I CAN SEE IT...
...ONE WORLD, ONE LOVE.
RIGHT.
LUCIUS. LET'S TALK.

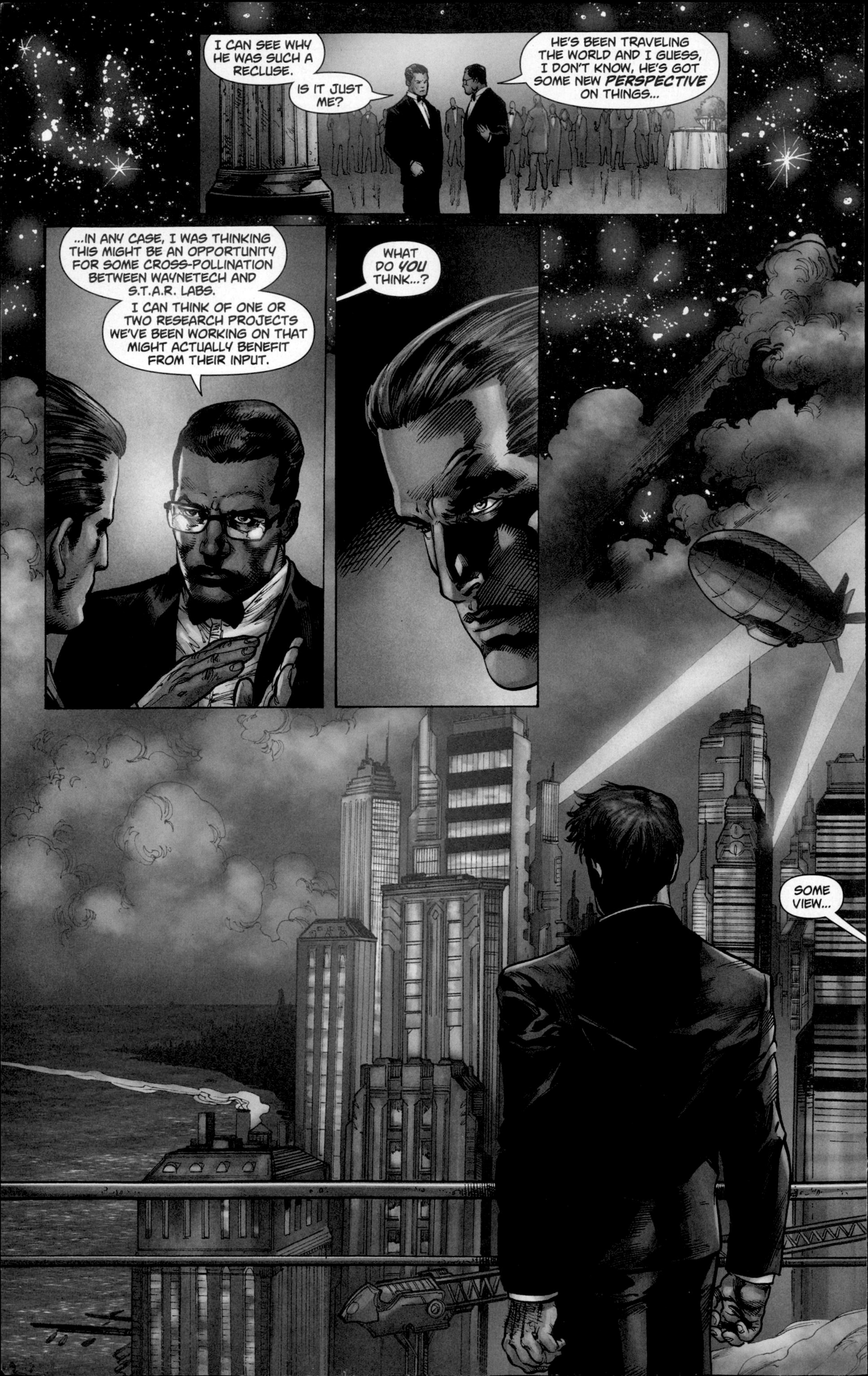
I CAN SEE WHY HE WAS SUCH A RECLUSE.
IS IT JUST ME?
HE'S BEEN TRAVELING THE WORLD AND I GUESS, I DON'T KNOW, HE'S GOT SOME NEW PERSPECTIVE ON THINGS...
...IN ANY CASE, I WAS THINKING THIS MIGHT BE AN OPPORTUNITY FOR SOME CROSS-POLLINATION BETWEEN WAYNETECH AND S.T.A.R. LABS.
I CAN THINK OF ONE OR TWO RESEARCH PROJECTS WE'VE BEEN WORKING ON THAT MIGHT ACTUALLY BENEFIT FROM THEIR INPUT.
WHAT DO YOU THINK...?
SOME VIEW...

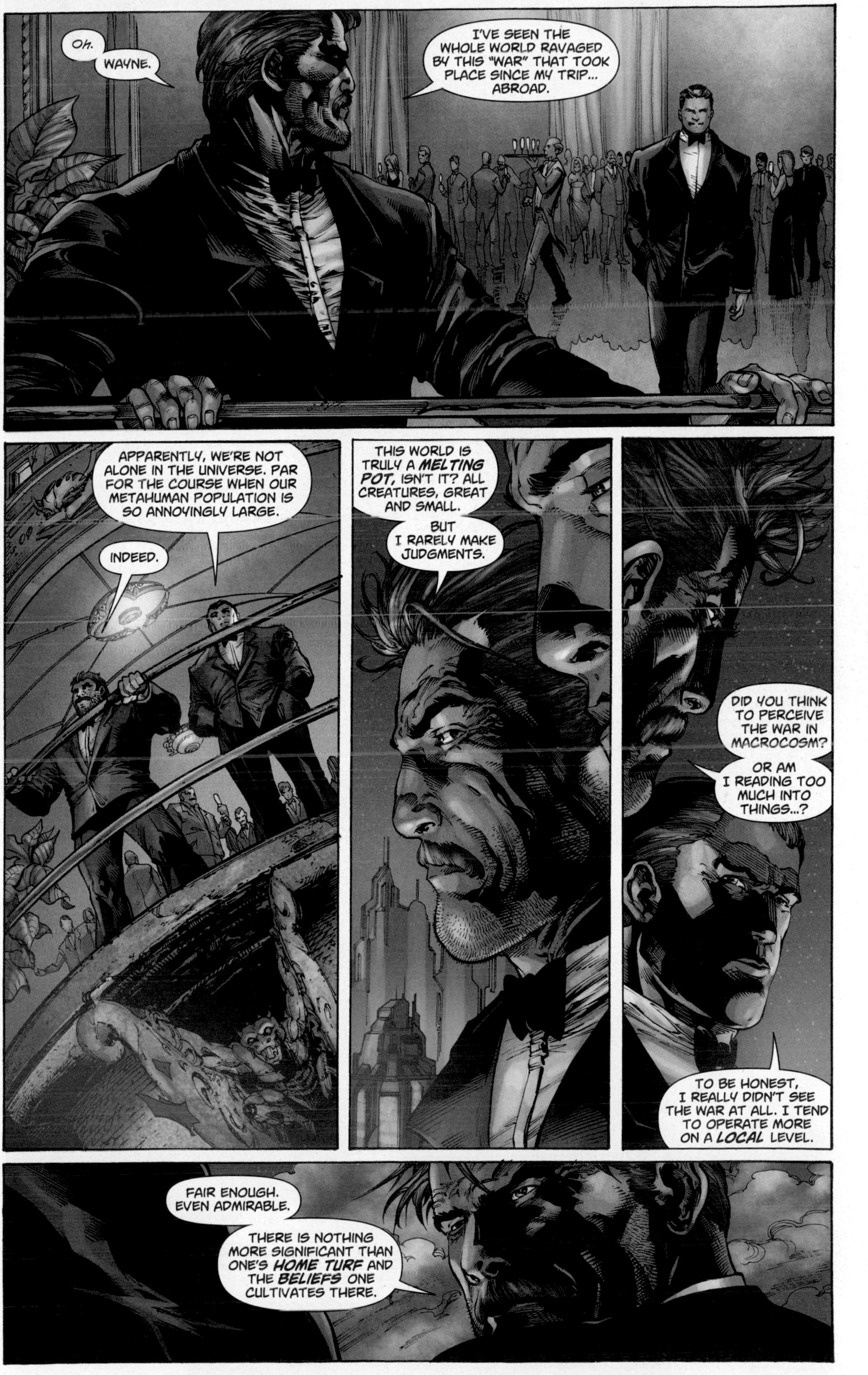

OH. WAYNE.
I'VE SEEN THE WHOLE WORLD RAVAGED BY THIS "WAR" THAT TOOK PLACE SINCE MY TRIP... ABROAD.
APPARENTLY, WE'RE NOT ALONE IN THE UNIVERSE. PAR FOR THE COURSE WHEN OUR METAHUMAN POPULATION IS SO ANNOYINGLY LARGE.
INDEED.
THIS WORLD IS TRULY A MELTING POT, ISN'T IT? ALL CREATURES, GREAT AND SMALL.
BUT I RARELY MAKE JUDGMENTS.
DID YOU THINK TO PERCEIVE THE WAR IN MACROCOSM?
OR AM I READING TOO MUCH INTO THINGS...?
TO BE HONEST, I REALLY DIDN'T SEE THE WAR AT ALL. I TEND TO OPERATE MORE ON A LOCAL LEVEL.
FAIR ENOUGH. EVEN ADMIRABLE.
THERE IS NOTHING MORE SIGNIFICANT THAN ONE'S HOME TURF AND THE BELIEFS ONE CULTIVATES THERE.

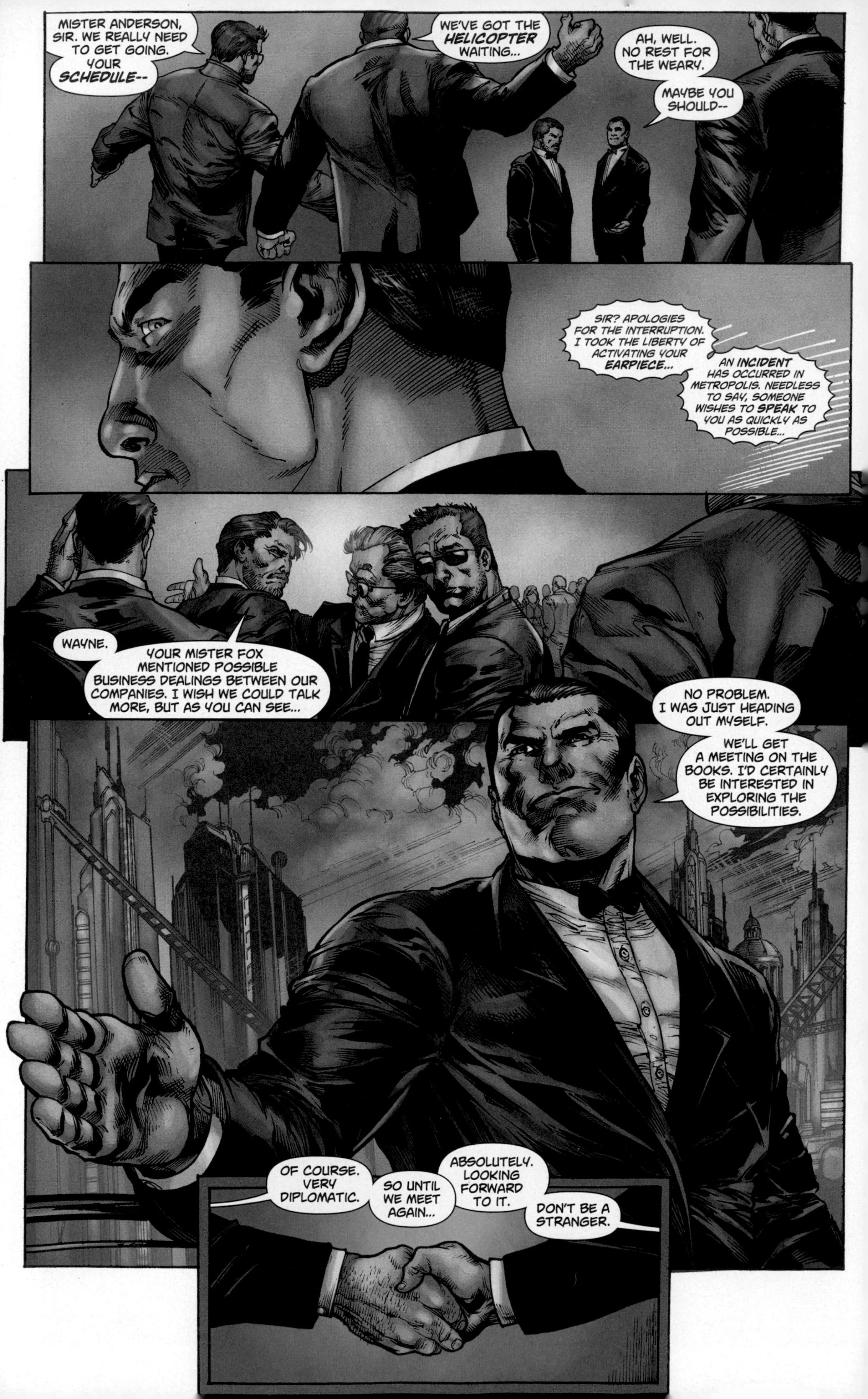
MISTER ANDERSON, SIR. WE REALLY NEED TO GET GOING. YOUR SCHEDULE--
WE'VE GOT THE HELICOPTER WAITING...
AH, WELL. NO REST FOR THE WEARY.
MAYBE YOU SHOULD--
SIR? APOLOGIES FOR THE INTERRUPTION. I TOOK THE LIBERTY OF ACTIVATING YOUR EARPIECE...
AN INCIDENT HAS OCCURRED IN METROPOLIS. NEEDLESS TO SAY, SOMEONE WISHES TO SPEAK TO YOU AS QUICKLY AS POSSIBLE...
WAYNE.
YOUR MISTER FOX MENTIONED POSSIBLE BUSINESS DEALINGS BETWEEN OUR COMPANIES. I WISH WE COULD TALK MORE, BUT AS YOU CAN SEE...
NO PROBLEM. I WAS JUST HEADING OUT MYSELF.
WE'LL GET A MEETING ON THE BOOKS. I'D CERTAINLY BE INTERESTED IN EXPLORING THE POSSIBILITIES.
OF COURSE. VERY DIPLOMATIC.
SO UNTIL WE MEET AGAIN...
ABSOLUTELY. LOOKING FORWARD TO IT.
DON'T BE A STRANGER.

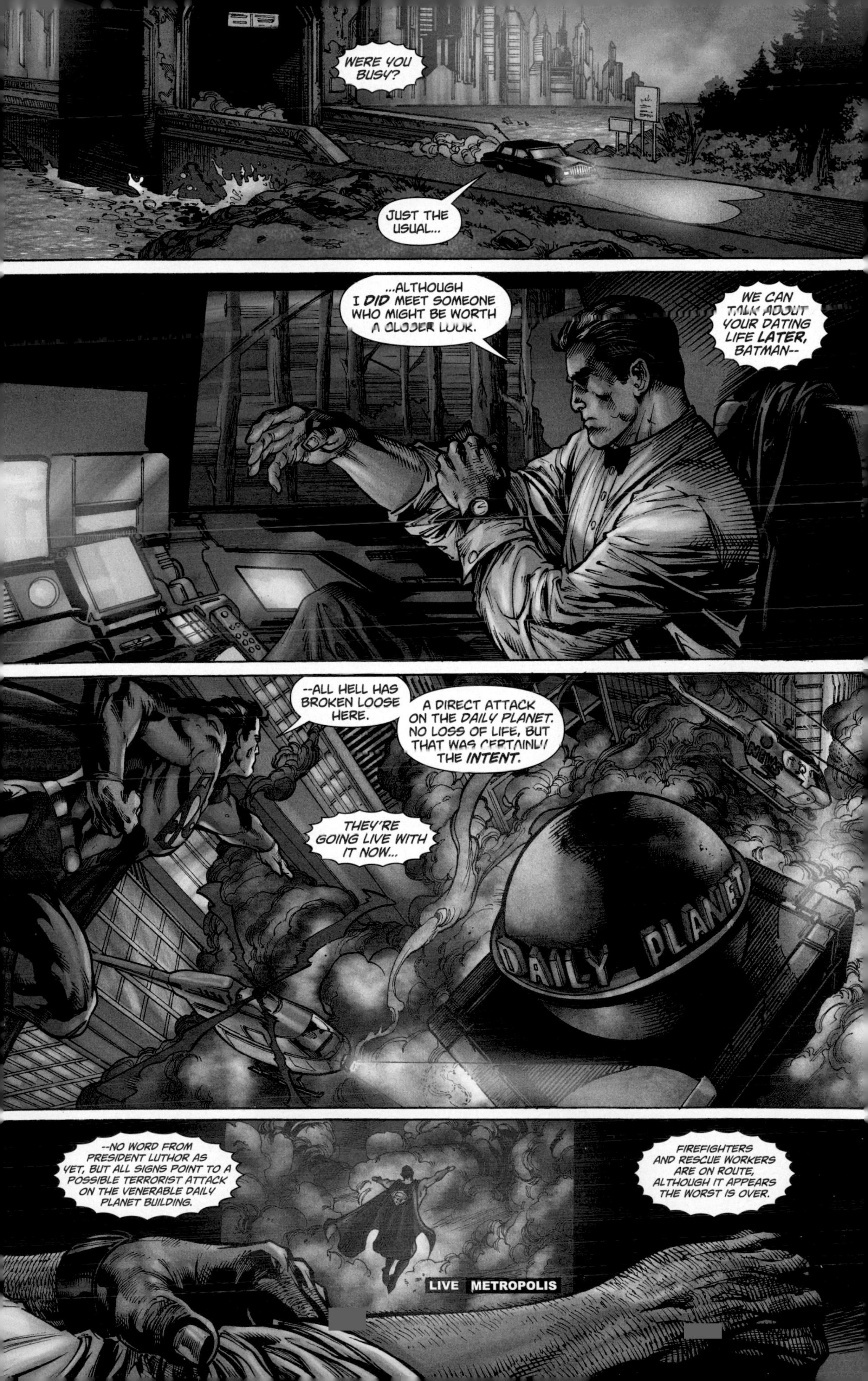
WERE YOU BUSY?
JUST THE USUAL...
...ALTHOUGH I DID MEET SOMEONE WHO MIGHT BE WORTH A CLOSER LOOK.
WE CAN TALK ABOUT YOUR DATING LIFE LATER, BATMAN--
--ALL HELL HAS BROKEN LOOSE HERE.
A DIRECT ATTACK ON THE DAILY PLANET. NO LOSS OF LIFE, BUT THAT WAS CERTAINLY THE INTENT.
THEY'RE GOING LIVE WITH IT NOW...
DAILY PLANET
--NO WORD FROM PRESIDENT LUTHOR AS YET, BUT ALL SIGNS POINT TO A POSSIBLE TERRORIST ATTACK ON THE VENERABLE DAILY PLANET BUILDING.
FIREFIGHTERS AND RESCUE WORKERS ARE ON ROUTE, ALTHOUGH IT APPEARS THE WORST IS OVER.
LIVE METROPOLIS

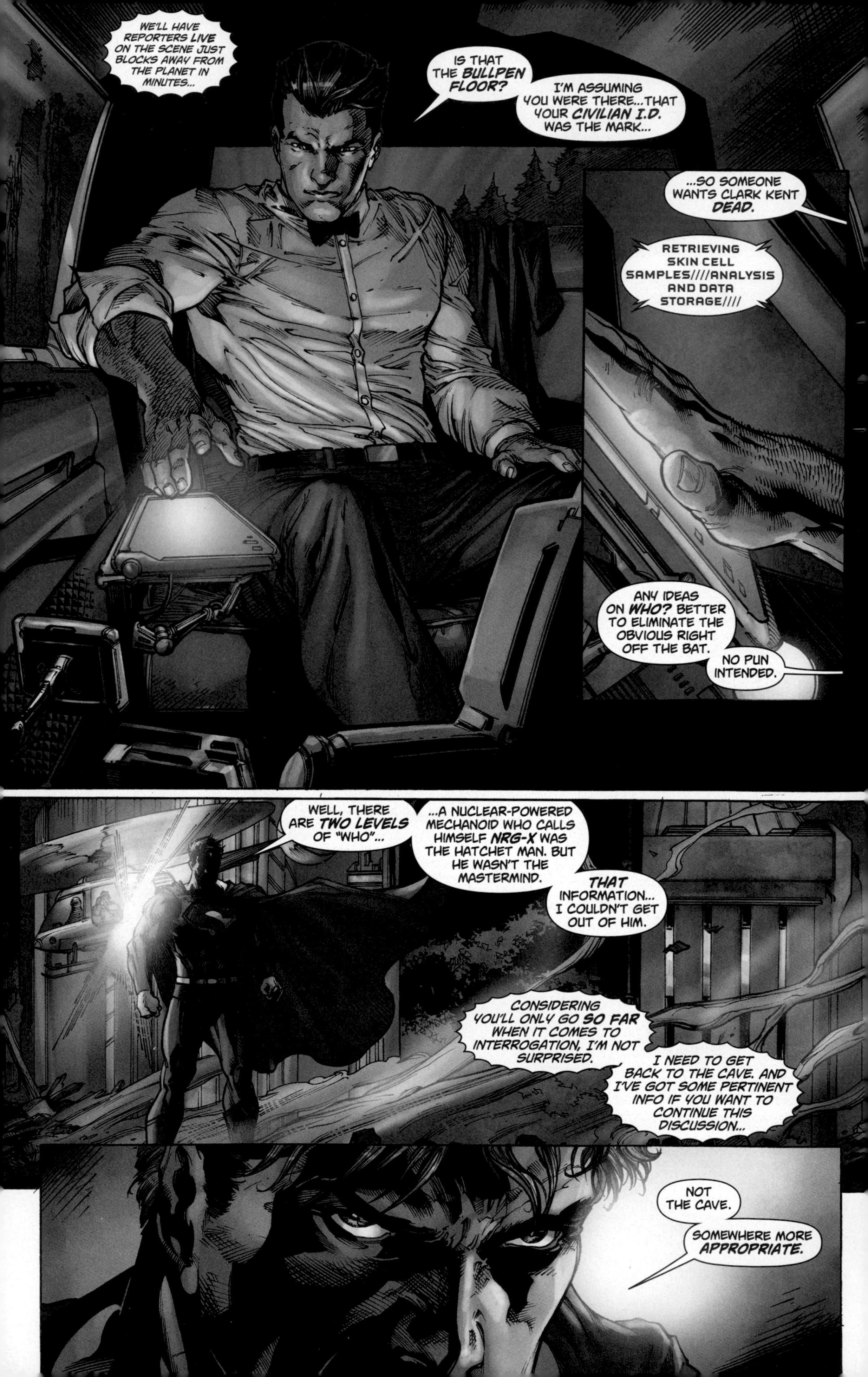
WE'LL HAVE REPORTERS LIVE ON THE SCENE JUST BLOCKS AWAY FROM THE PLANET IN MINUTES...
IS THAT THE BULLPEN FLOOR?
I'M ASSUMING YOU WERE THERE...THAT YOUR CIVILIAN I.D. WAS THE MARK...
...SO SOMEONE WANTS CLARK KENT DEAD.
RETRIEVING SKIN CELL SAMPLES////ANALYSIS AND DATA STORAGE////
ANY IDEAS ON WHO? BETTER TO ELIMINATE THE OBVIOUS RIGHT OFF THE BAT.
NO PUN INTENDED.
WELL, THERE ARE TWO LEVELS OF "WHO"...
...A NUCLEAR-POWERED MECHANOID WHO CALLS HIMSELF NRG-X WAS THE HATCHET MAN. BUT HE WASN'T THE MASTERMIND.
THAT INFORMATION... I COULDN'T GET OUT OF HIM.
CONSIDERING YOU'LL ONLY GO SO FAR WHEN IT COMES TO INTERROGATION, I'M NOT SURPRISED.
I NEED TO GET BACK TO THE CAVE. AND I'VE GOT SOME PERTINENT INFO IF YOU WANT TO CONTINUE THIS DISCUSSION...
NOT THE CAVE.
SOMEWHERE MORE APPROPRIATE.

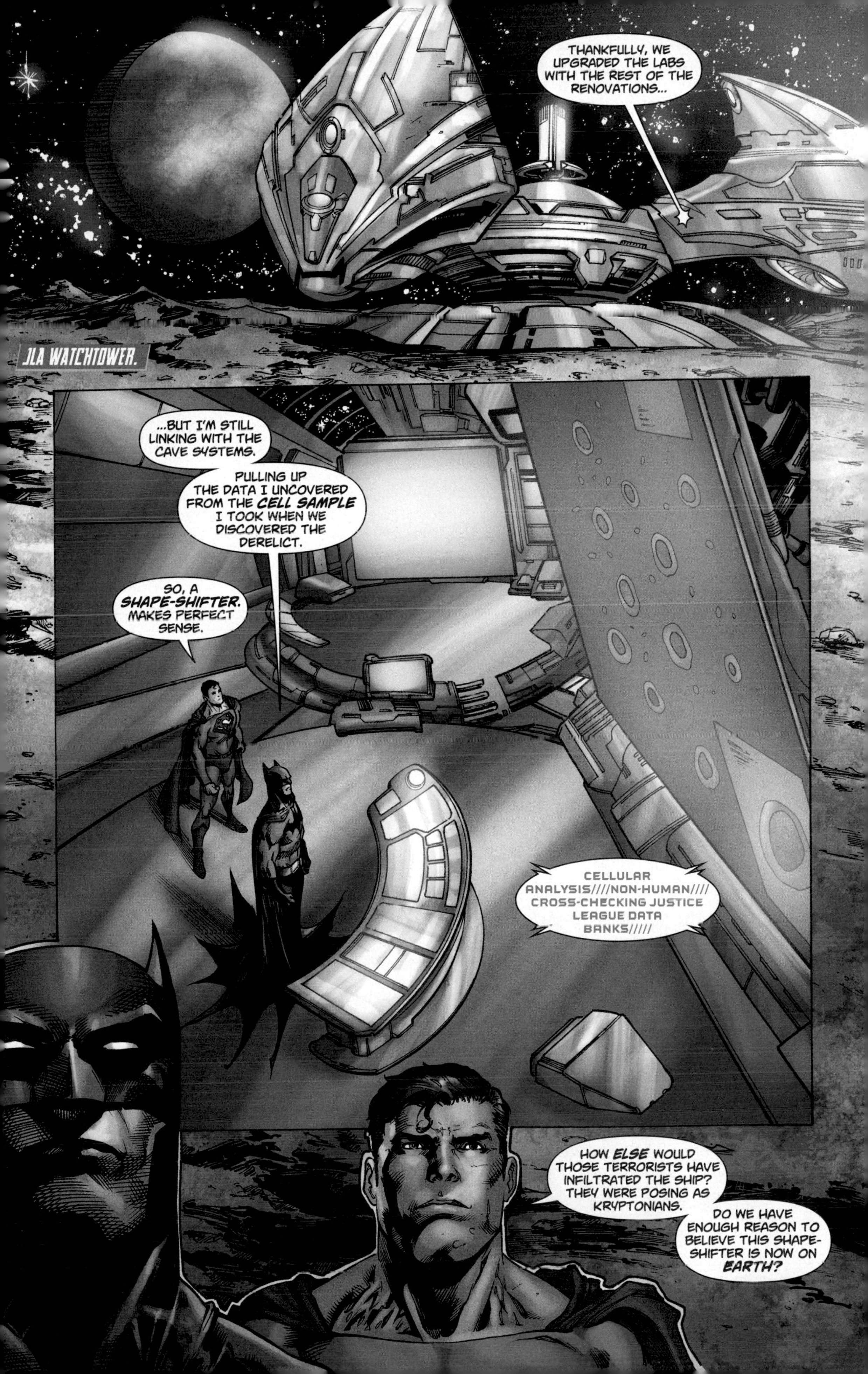
THANKFULLY, WE UPGRADED THE LABS WITH THE REST OF THE RENOVATIONS...
JLA WATCHTOWER.
...BUT I'M STILL LINKING WITH THE CAVE SYSTEMS.
PULLING UP THE DATA I UNCOVERED FROM THE CELL SAMPLE I TOOK WHEN WE DISCOVERED THE DERELICT.
SO, A SHAPE-SHIFTER. MAKES PERFECT SENSE.
CELLULAR ANALYSIS////NON-HUMAN//// CROSS-CHECKING JUSTICE LEAGUE DATA BANKS/////
HOW ELSE WOULD THOSE TERRORISTS HAVE INFILTRATED THE SHIP? THEY WERE POSING AS KRYPTONIANS.
DO WE HAVE ENOUGH REASON TO BELIEVE THIS SHAPE-SHIFTER IS NOW ON EARTH?

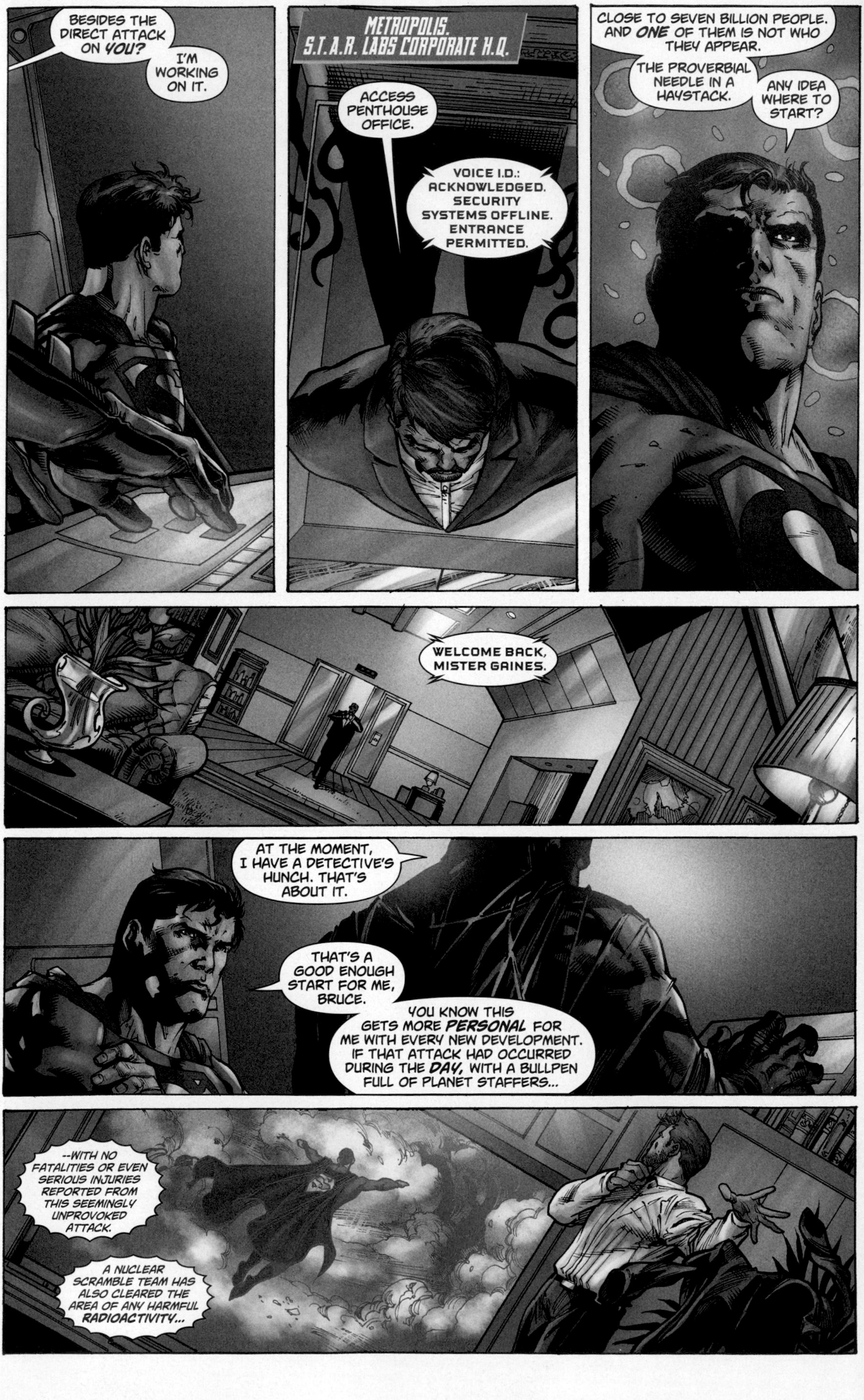
BESIDES THE DIRECT ATTACK ON YOU?
I'M WORKING ON IT.
METROPOLIS. S.T.A.R. LABS CORPORATE H.Q.
ACCESS PENTHOUSE OFFICE.
VOICE I.D.: ACKNOWLEDGED. SECURITY SYSTEMS OFFLINE. ENTRANCE PERMITTED.
CLOSE TO SEVEN BILLION PEOPLE. AND ONE OF THEM IS NOT WHO THEY APPEAR.
THE PROVERBIAL NEEDLE IN A HAYSTACK.
ANY IDEA WHERE TO START?
WELCOME BACK, MISTER GAINES.
AT THE MOMENT, I HAVE A DETECTIVE'S HUNCH. THAT'S ABOUT IT.
THAT'S A GOOD ENOUGH START FOR ME, BRUCE.
YOU KNOW THIS GETS MORE PERSONAL FOR ME WITH EVERY NEW DEVELOPMENT. IF THAT ATTACK HAD OCCURRED DURING THE DAY, WITH A BULLPEN FULL OF PLANET STAFFERS...
--WITH NO FATALITIES OR EVEN SERIOUS INJURIES REPORTED FROM THIS SEEMINGLY UNPROVOKED ATTACK.
A NUCLEAR SCRAMBLE TEAM HAS ALSO CLEARED THE AREA OF ANY HARMFUL RADIOACTIVITY...

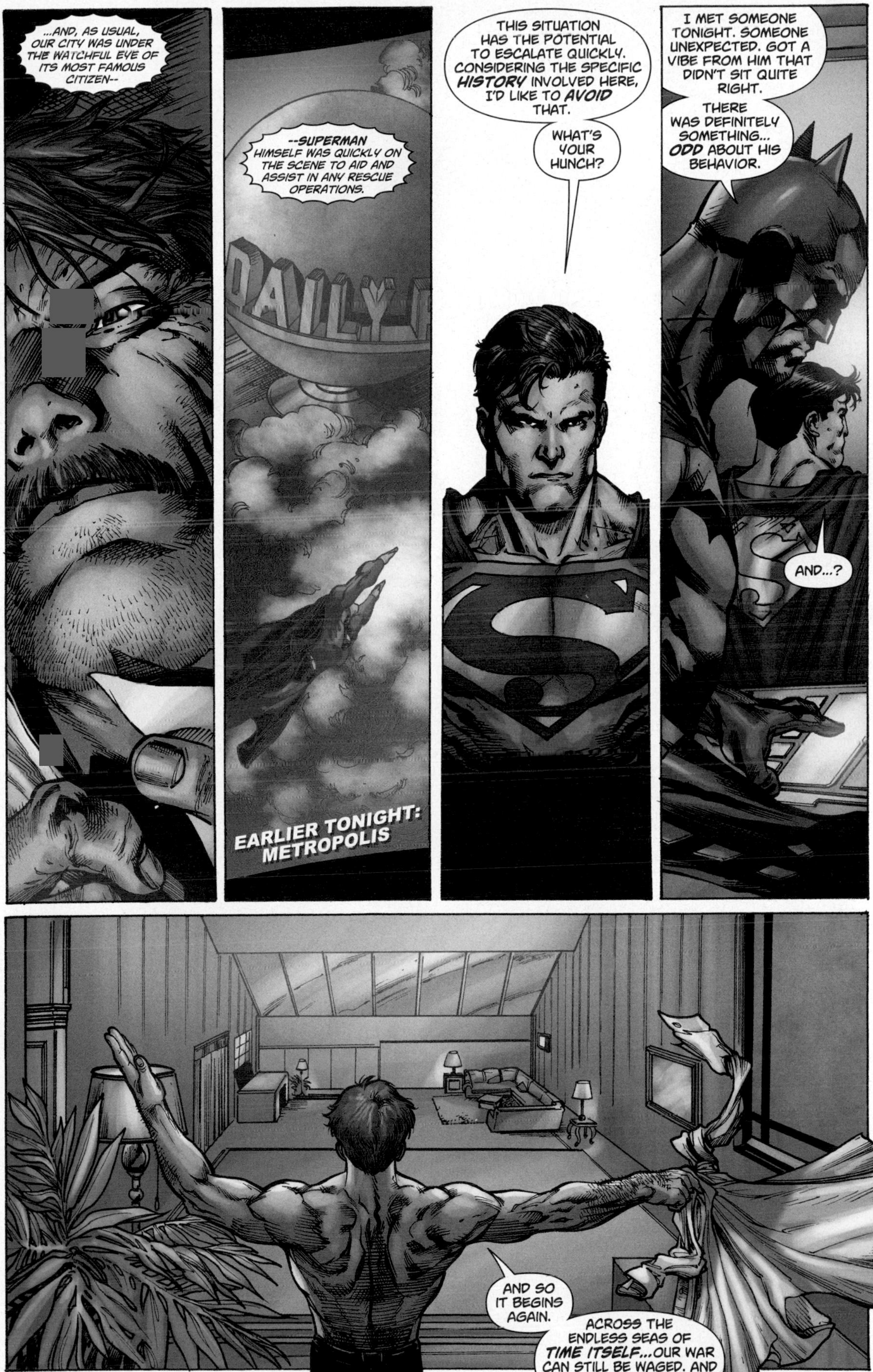
...AND, AS USUAL, OUR CITY WAS UNDER THE WATCHFUL EYE OF ITS MOST FAMOUS CITIZEN--
--SUPERMAN HIMSELF WAS QUICKLY ON THE SCENE TO AID AND ASSIST IN ANY RESCUE OPERATIONS.
DAILY
EARLIER TONIGHT: METROPOLIS
THIS SITUATION HAS THE POTENTIAL TO ESCALATE QUICKLY. CONSIDERING THE SPECIFIC HISTORY INVOLVED HERE, I'D LIKE TO AVOID THAT.
WHAT'S YOUR HUNCH?
I MET SOMEONE TONIGHT. SOMEONE UNEXPECTED. GOT A VIBE FROM HIM THAT DIDN'T SIT QUITE RIGHT.
THERE WAS DEFINITELY SOMETHING... ODD ABOUT HIS BEHAVIOR.
AND...?
AND SO IT BEGINS AGAIN.
ACROSS THE ENDLESS SEAS OF TIME ITSELF...OUR WAR CAN STILL BE WAGED. AND WE CAN STILL EMERGE VICTORIOUS.

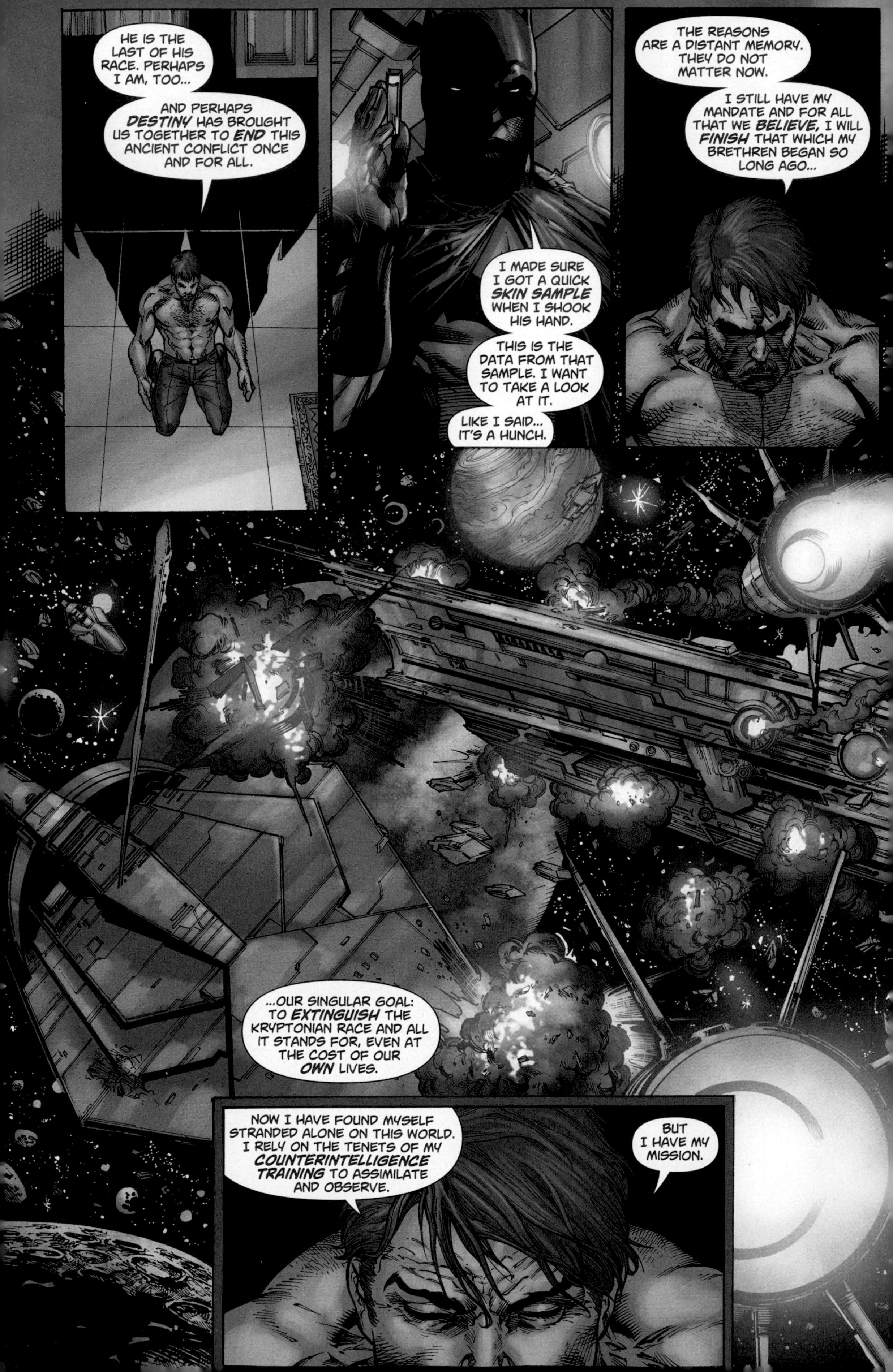
HE IS THE LAST OF HIS RACE. PERHAPS I AM, TOO...
AND PERHAPS DESTINY HAS BROUGHT US TOGETHER TO END THIS ANCIENT CONFLICT ONCE AND FOR ALL.
I MADE SURE I GOT A QUICK SKIN SAMPLE WHEN I SHOOK HIS HAND.
THIS IS THE DATA FROM THAT SAMPLE. I WANT TO TAKE A LOOK AT IT.
LIKE I SAID... IT'S A HUNCH.
THE REASONS ARE A DISTANT MEMORY. THEY DO NOT MATTER NOW.
I STILL HAVE MY MANDATE AND FOR ALL THAT WE BELIEVE, I WILL FINISH THAT WHICH MY BRETHREN BEGAN SO LONG AGO...
...OUR SINGULAR GOAL: TO EXTINGUISH THE KRYPTONIAN RACE AND ALL IT STANDS FOR, EVEN AT THE COST OF OUR OWN LIVES.
NOW I HAVE FOUND MYSELF STRANDED ALONE ON THIS WORLD. I RELY ON THE TENETS OF MY COUNTERINTELLIGENCE TRAINING TO ASSIMILATE AND OBSERVE.
BUT I HAVE MY MISSION.

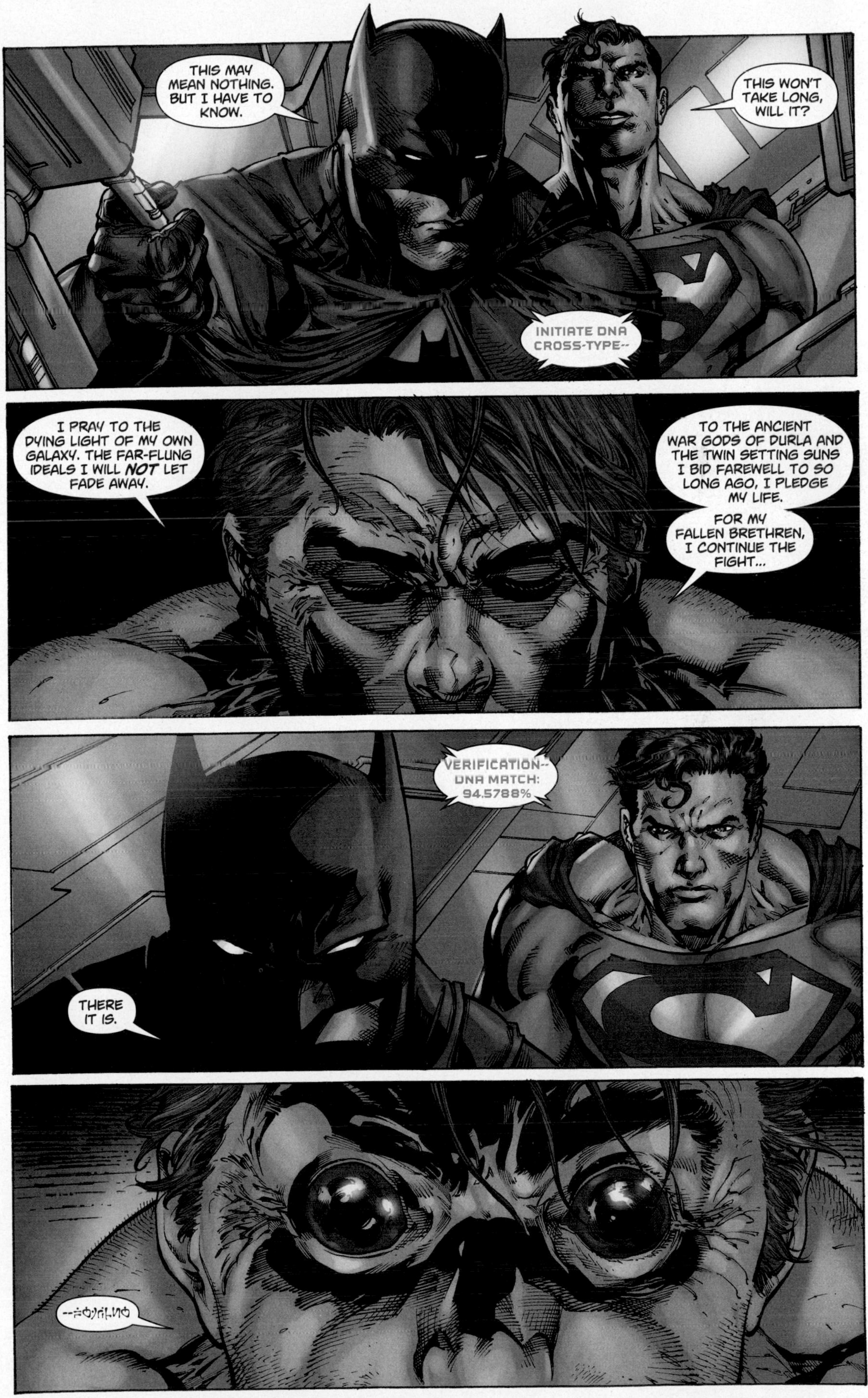

THIS MAY MEAN NOTHING. BUT I HAVE TO KNOW.
THIS WON'T TAKE LONG, WILL IT?
INITIATE DNA CROSS-TYPE--
I PRAY TO THE DYING LIGHT OF MY OWN GALAXY. THE FAR-FLUNG IDEALS I WILL NOT LET FADE AWAY.
TO THE ANCIENT WAR GODS OF DURLA AND THE TWIN SETTING SUNS I BID FAREWELL TO SO LONG AGO, I PLEDGE MY LIFE.
FOR MY FALLEN BRETHREN, I CONTINUE THE FIGHT...
VERIFICATION-- DNA MATCH: 94.5788%
THERE IT IS.

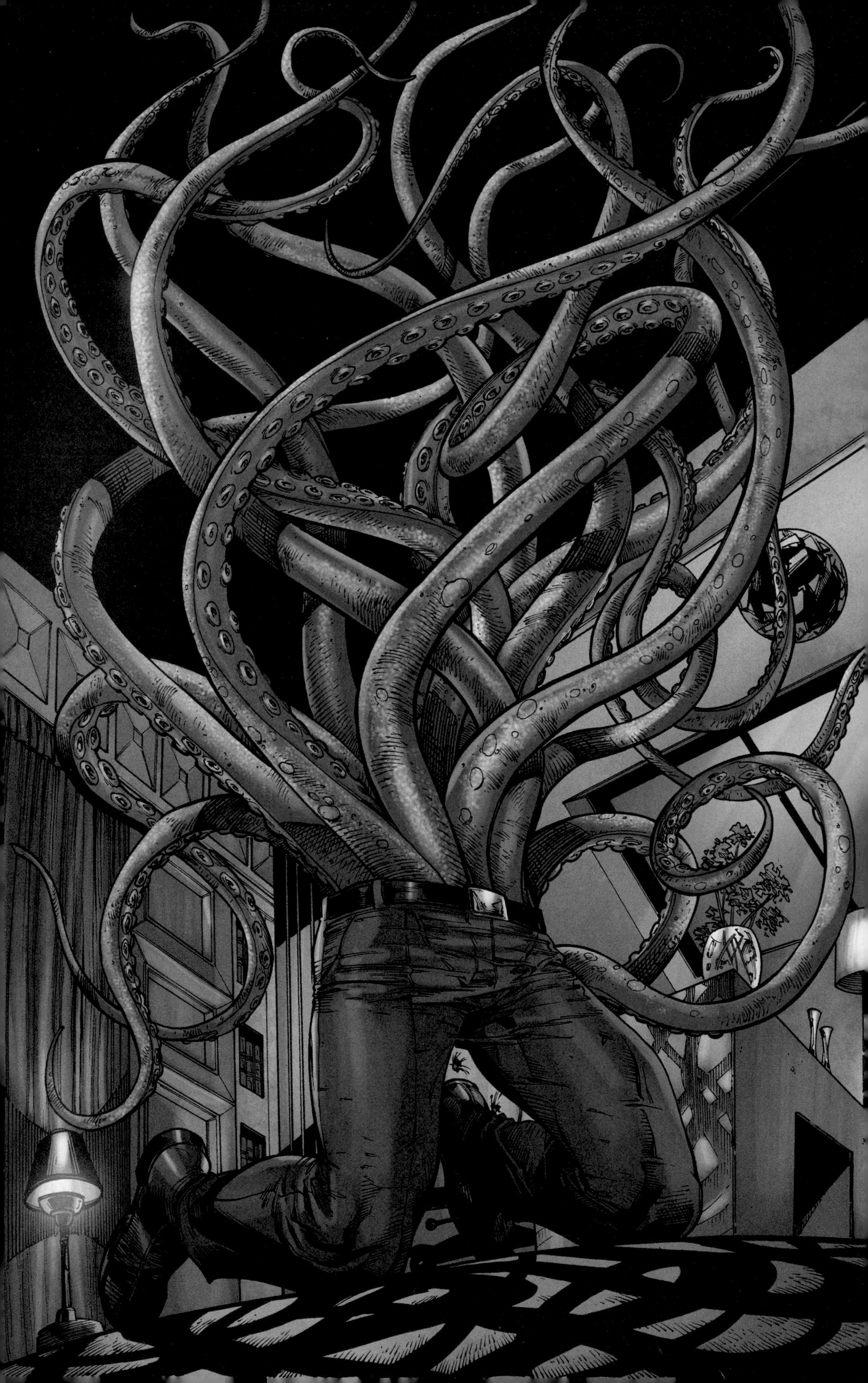

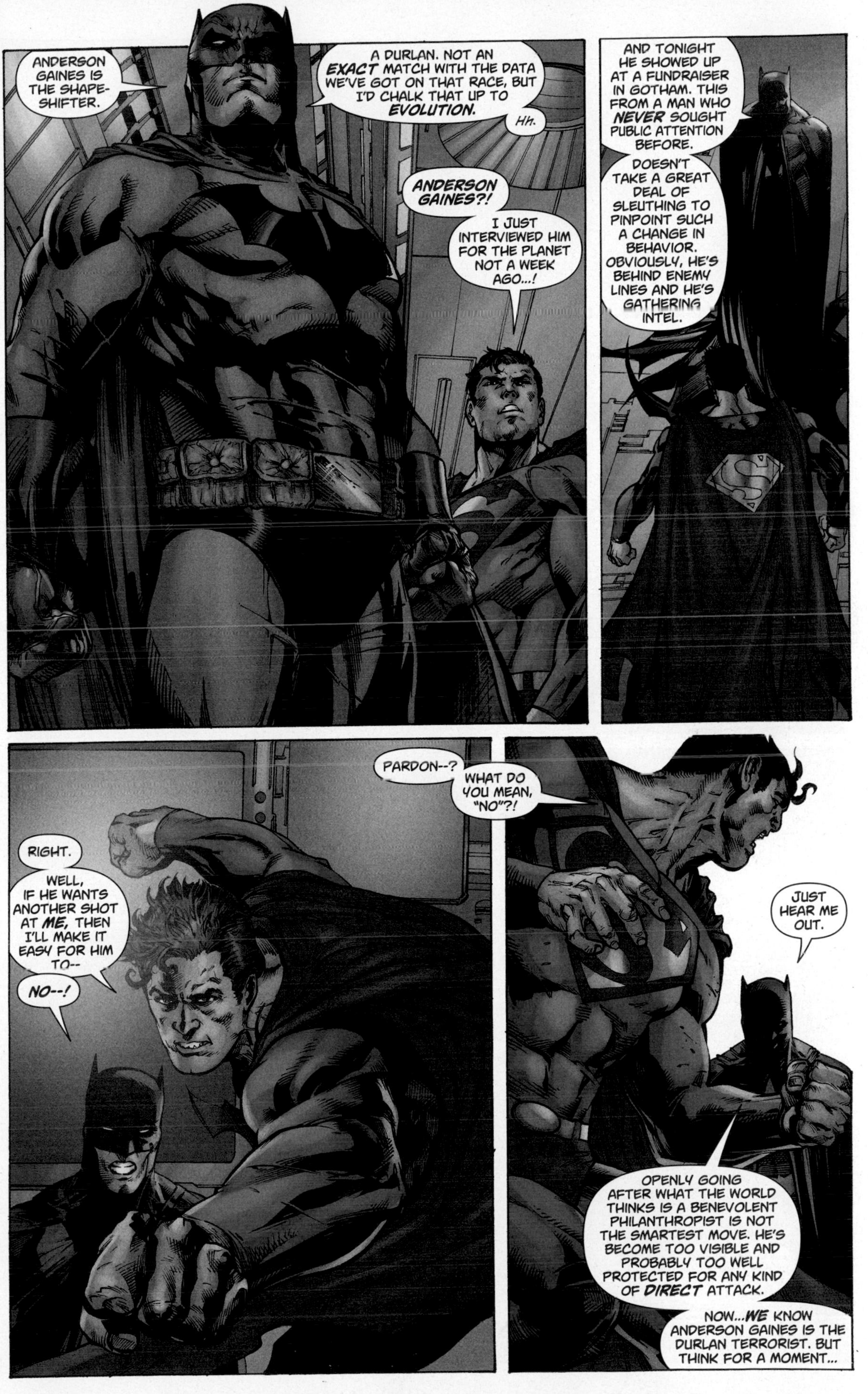

ANDERSON GAINES IS THE SHAPE-SHIFTER.
A DURLAN. NOT AN EXACT MATCH WITH THE DATA WE'VE GOT ON THAT RACE, BUT I'D CHALK THAT UP TO EVOLUTION.
Hh.
ANDERSON GAINES?!
I JUST INTERVIEWED HIM FOR THE PLANET NOT A WEEK AGO...!
AND TONIGHT HE SHOWED UP AT A FUNDRAISER IN GOTHAM. THIS FROM A MAN WHO NEVER SOUGHT PUBLIC ATTENTION BEFORE.
DOESN'T TAKE A GREAT DEAL OF SLEUTHING TO PINPOINT SUCH A CHANGE IN BEHAVIOR. OBVIOUSLY, HE'S BEHIND ENEMY LINES AND HE'S GATHERING INTEL.
RIGHT.
WELL, IF HE WANTS ANOTHER SHOT AT ME, THEN I'LL MAKE IT EASY FOR HIM TO--
NO--!
PARDON--?
WHAT DO YOU MEAN, "NO"?!
JUST HEAR ME OUT.
OPENLY GOING AFTER WHAT THE WORLD THINKS IS A BENEVOLENT PHILANTHROPIST IS NOT THE SMARTEST MOVE. HE'S BECOME TOO VISIBLE AND PROBABLY TOO WELL PROTECTED FOR ANY KIND OF DIRECT ATTACK.
NOW...WE KNOW ANDERSON GAINES IS THE DURLAN TERRORIST. BUT THINK FOR A MOMENT...

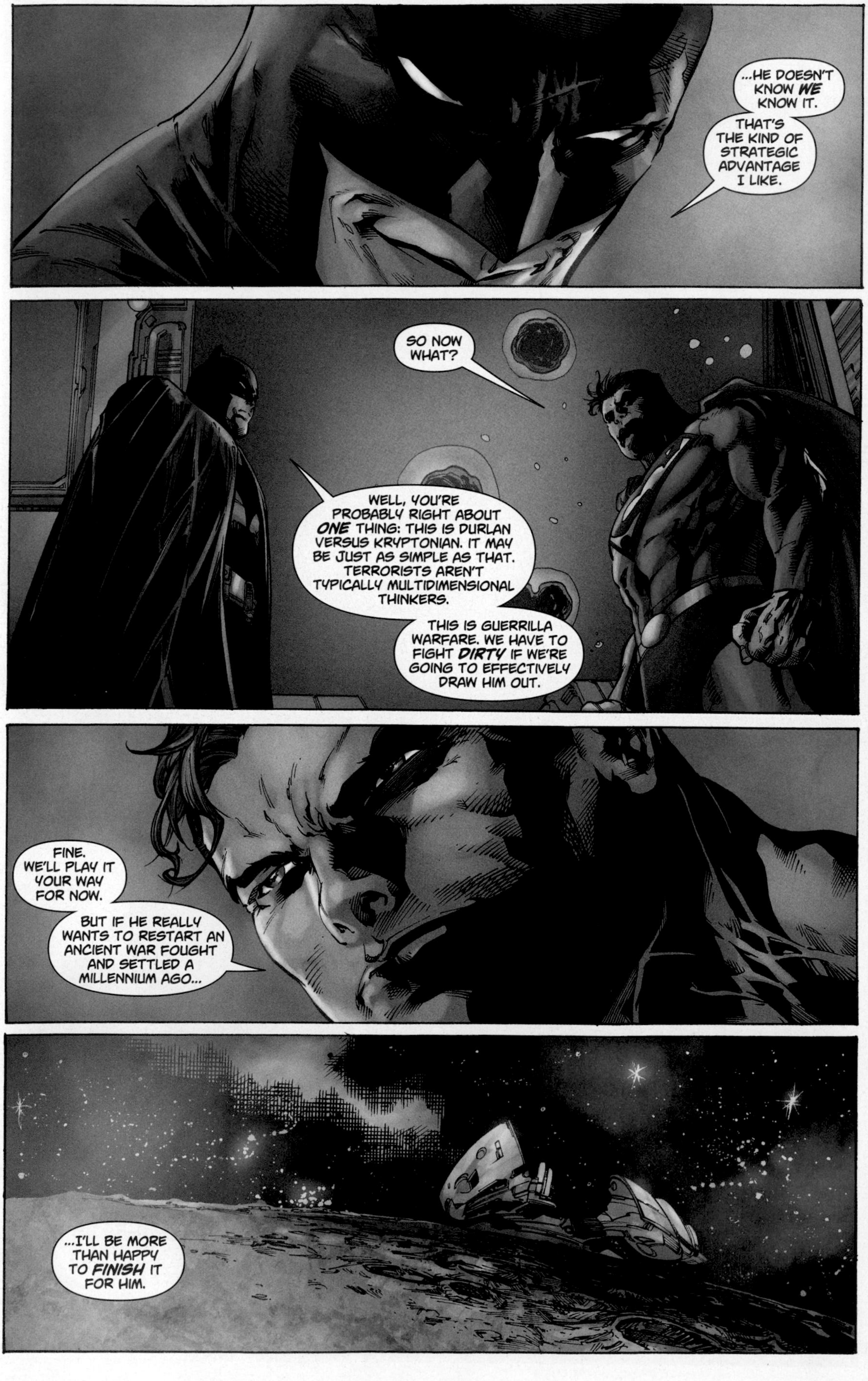
...HE DOESN'T KNOW WE KNOW IT.
THAT'S THE KIND OF STRATEGIC ADVANTAGE I LIKE.
SO NOW WHAT?
WELL, YOU'RE PROBABLY RIGHT ABOUT ONE THING: THIS IS DURLAN VERSUS KRYPTONIAN. IT MAY BE JUST AS SIMPLE AS THAT. TERRORISTS AREN'T TYPICALLY MULTIDIMENSIONAL THINKERS.
THIS IS GUERRILLA WARFARE. WE HAVE TO FIGHT DIRTY IF WE'RE GOING TO EFFECTIVELY DRAW HIM OUT.
FINE. WE'LL PLAY IT YOUR WAY FOR NOW.
BUT IF HE REALLY WANTS TO RESTART AN ANCIENT WAR FOUGHT AND SETTLED A MILLENNIUM AGO...
...I'LL BE MORE THAN HAPPY TO FINISH IT FOR HIM.

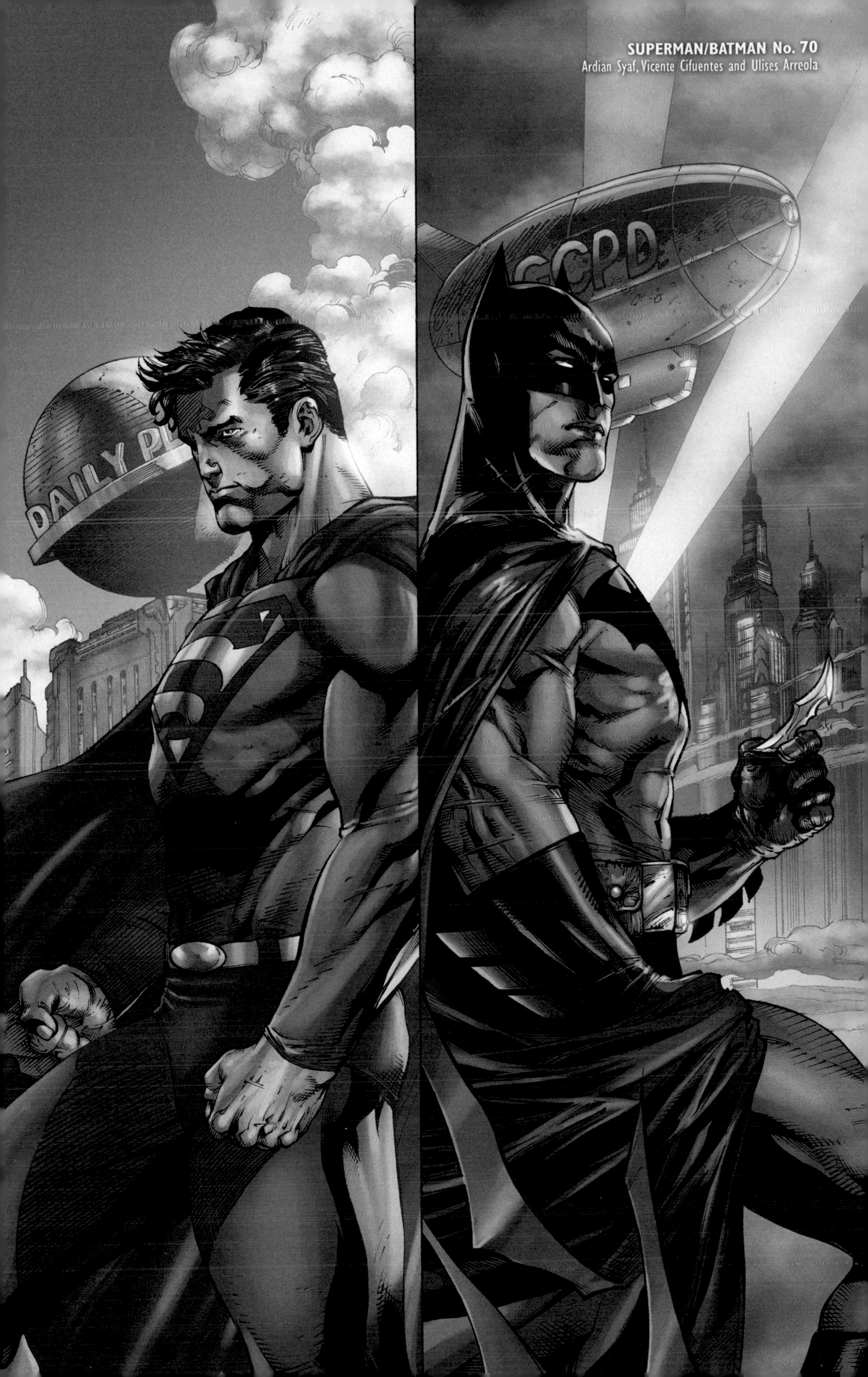
DAILY PL
GCPD

SUPERMAN/BATMAN No. 70
Ardian Syaf, Vicente Cifuentes and Ulises Arreola

THE BIG NOISE PART 3: RIGHTEOUS DESTROYER

Pencillers: Ardian Syaf and Jason Fabok

Inkers: Vicente Cifuentes, Norm Rapmund and Marlo Alquiza

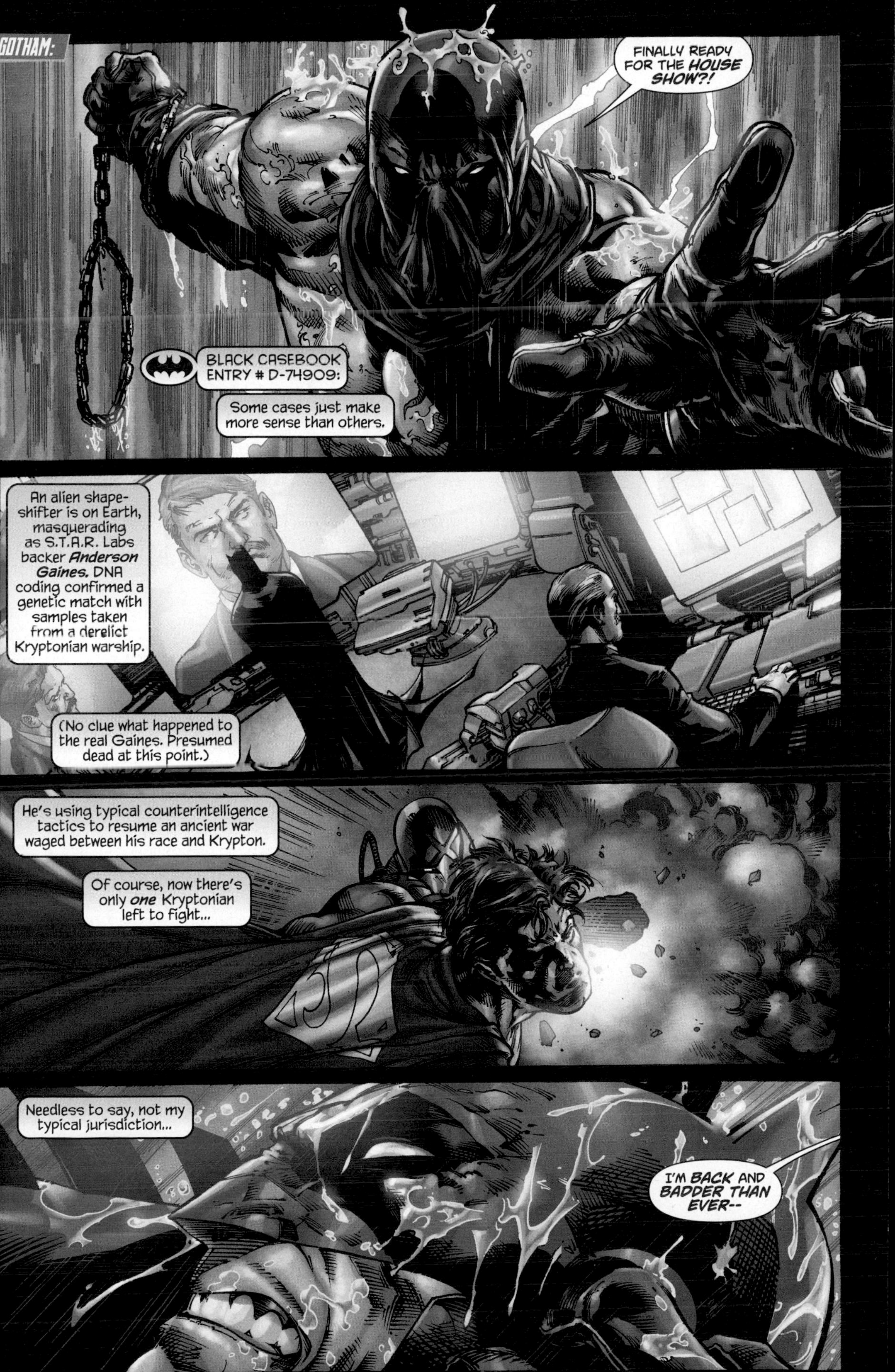
GOTHAM:
FINALLY READY FOR THE HOUSE SHOW?!
BLACK CASEBOOK ENTRY # D-74909:
Some cases just make more sense than others.
An alien shape-shifter is on Earth, masquerading as S.T.A.R. Labs backer Anderson Gaines. DNA coding confirmed a genetic match with samples taken from a derelict Kryptonian warship.
(No clue what happened to the real Gaines. Presumed dead at this point.)
He's using typical counterintelligence tactics to resume an ancient war waged between his race and Krypton.
Of course, now there's only one Kryptonian left to fight...
Needless to say, not my typical jurisdiction...
I'M BACK AND BADDER THAN EVER--

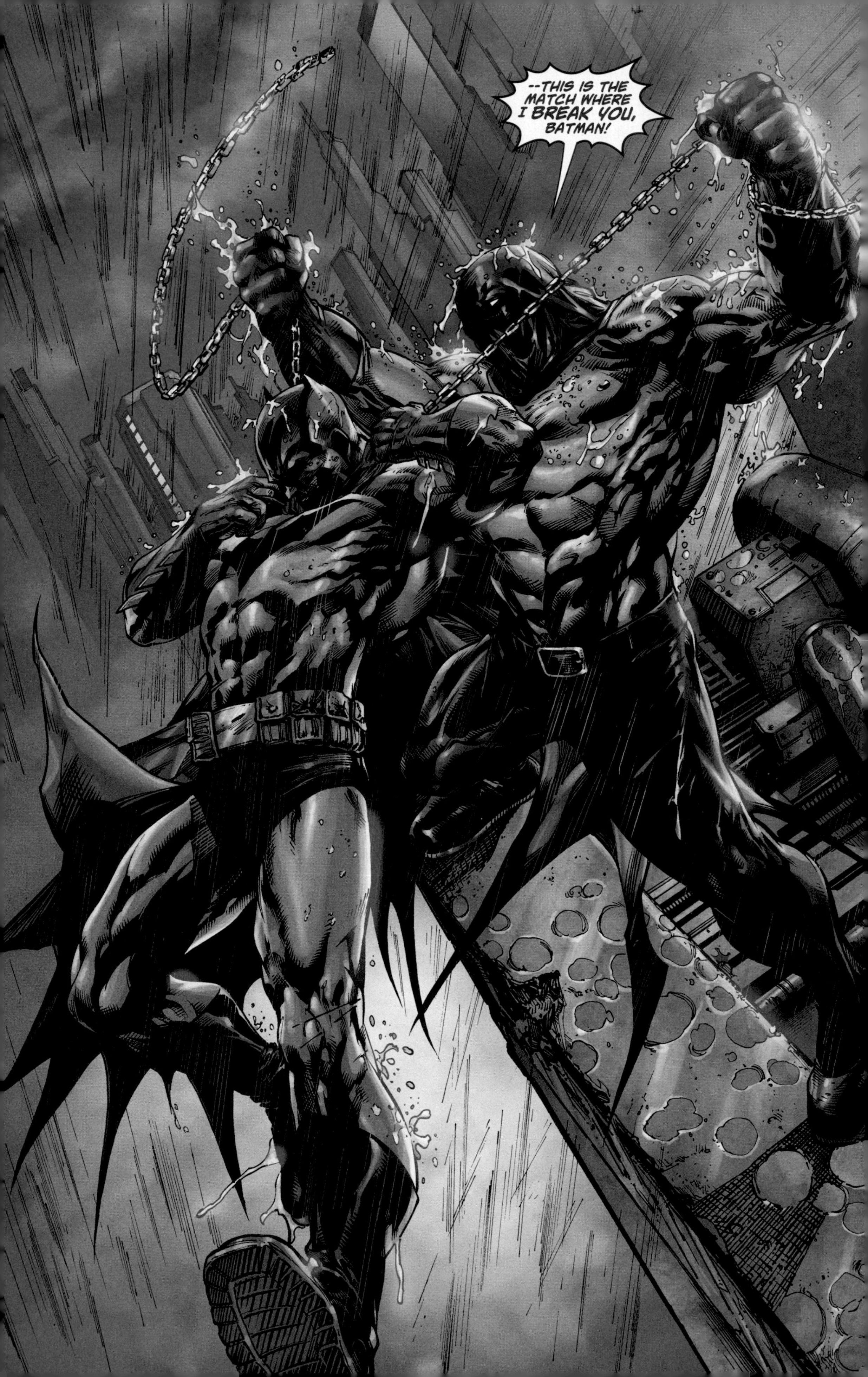
--THIS IS THE MATCH WHERE I BREAK YOU, BATMAN!

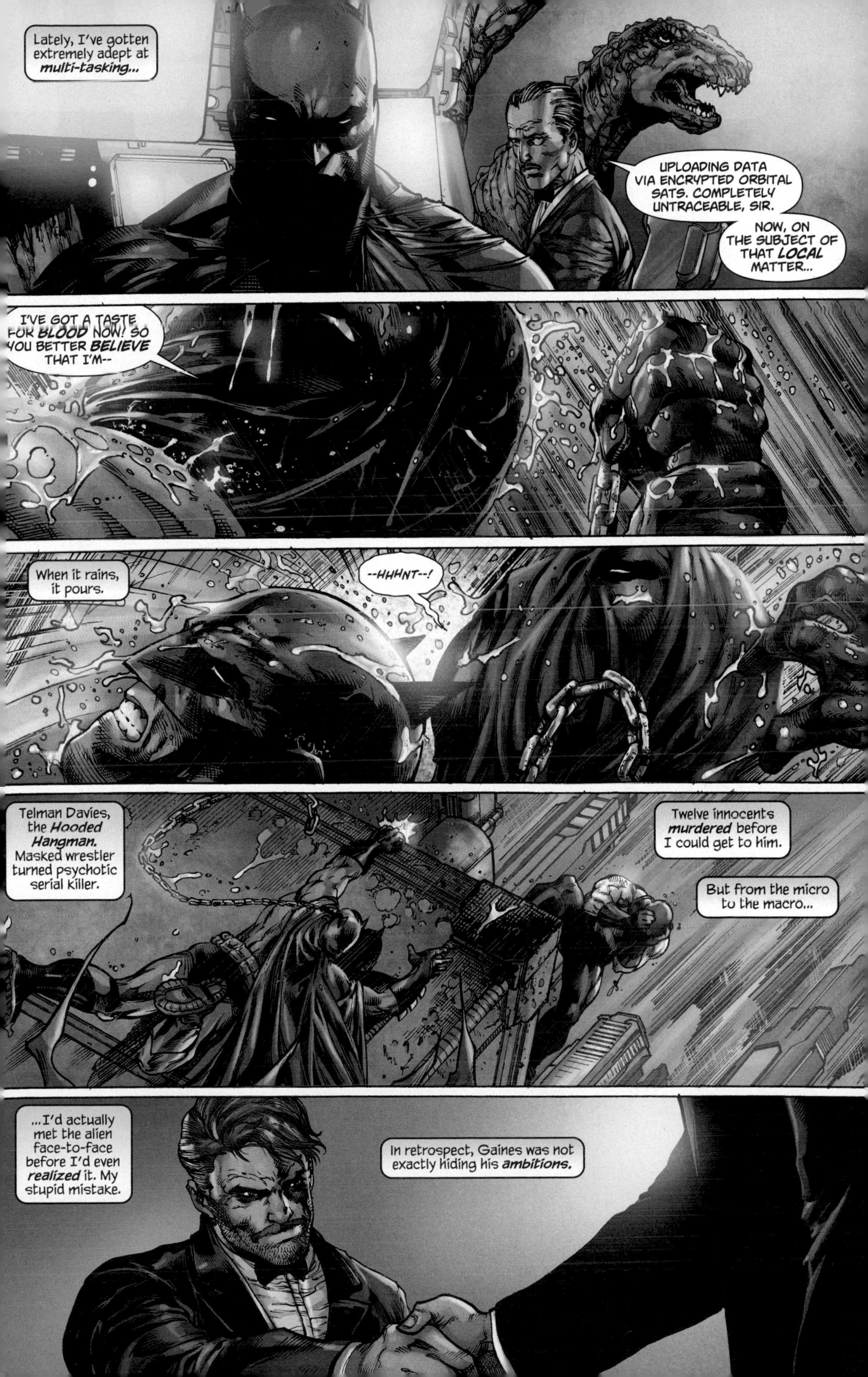
Lately, I've gotten extremely adept at *multi-tasking...*
UPLOADING DATA VIA ENCRYPTED ORBITAL SATS. COMPLETELY UNTRACEABLE, SIR.
NOW, ON THE SUBJECT OF THAT *LOCAL* MATTER...
I'VE GOT A TASTE FOR *BLOOD* NOW! SO YOU BETTER *BELIEVE* THAT I'M--
When it rains, it pours.
--HHHNT--!
Telman Davies, the *Hooded Hangman.* Masked wrestler turned psychotic serial killer.
Twelve innocents *murdered* before I could get to him.
But from the micro to the macro...
...I'd actually met the alien face-to-face before I'd even *realized* it. My stupid mistake.
In retrospect, Gaines was not exactly hiding his *ambitions.*

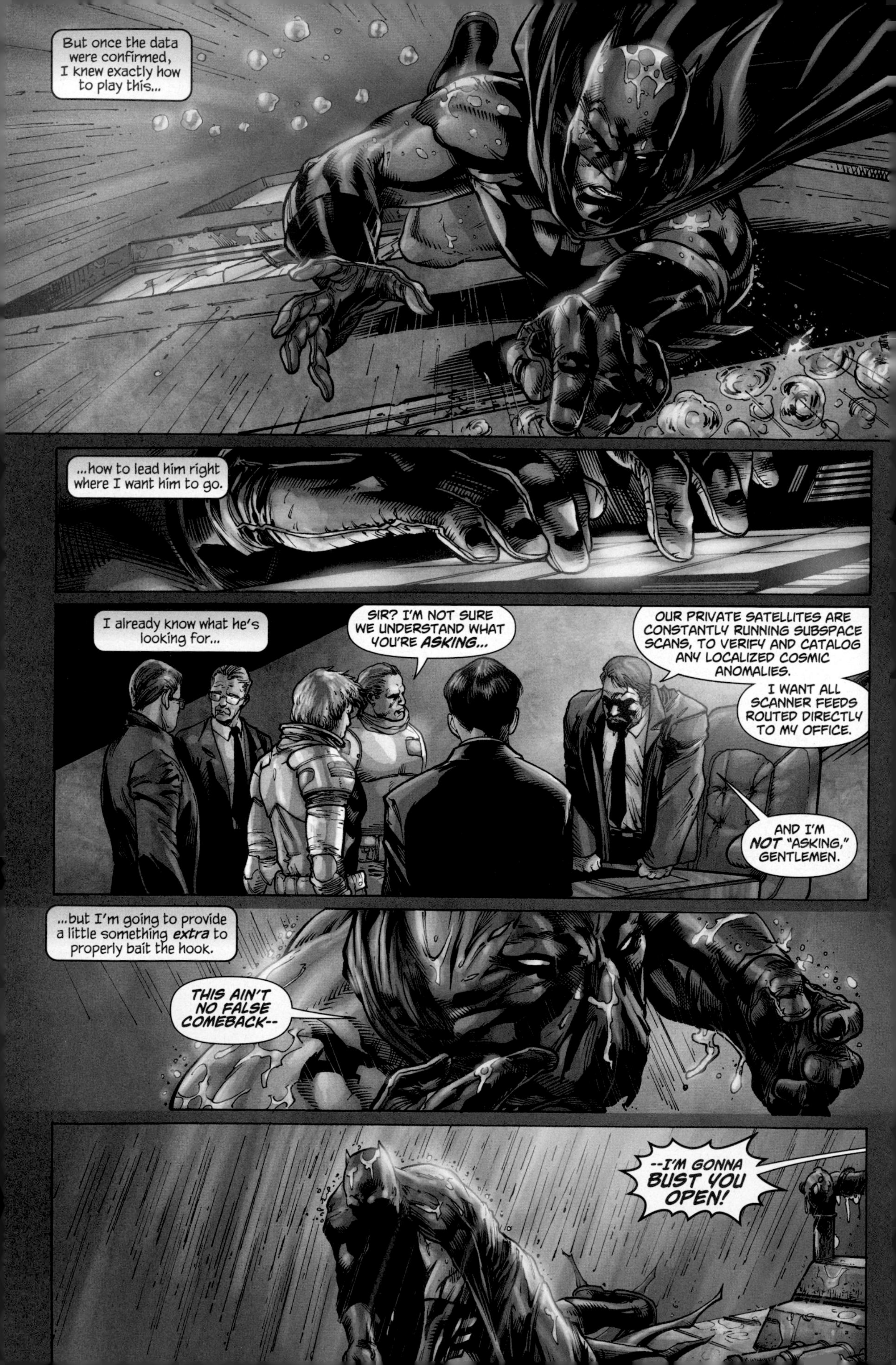
But once the data were confirmed, I knew exactly how to play this...
...how to lead him right where I want him to go.
I already know what he's looking for...
SIR? I'M NOT SURE WE UNDERSTAND WHAT YOU'RE *ASKING*...
OUR PRIVATE SATELLITES ARE CONSTANTLY RUNNING SUBSPACE SCANS, TO VERIFY AND CATALOG ANY LOCALIZED COSMIC ANOMALIES.
I WANT ALL SCANNER FEEDS ROUTED DIRECTLY TO MY OFFICE.
AND I'M *NOT* "ASKING," GENTLEMEN.
...but I'm going to provide a little something *extra* to properly bait the hook.
THIS AIN'T NO FALSE COMEBACK--
--I'M GONNA **BUST YOU OPEN!**

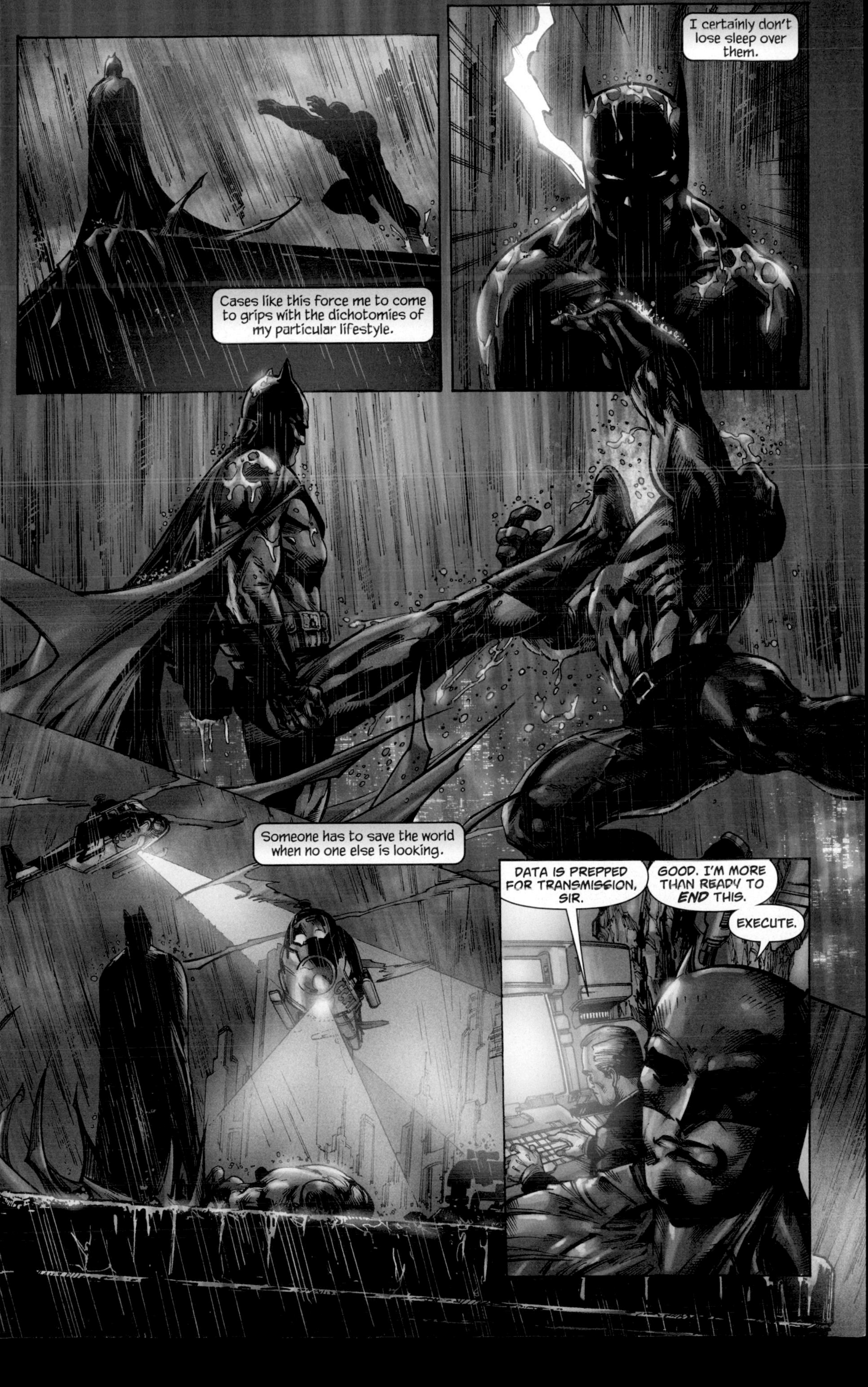
Cases like this force me to come to grips with the dichotomies of my particular lifestyle.
I certainly don't lose sleep over them.
Someone has to save the world when no one else is looking.
DATA IS PREPPED FOR TRANSMISSION, SIR.
GOOD. I'M MORE THAN READY TO END THIS.
EXECUTE.

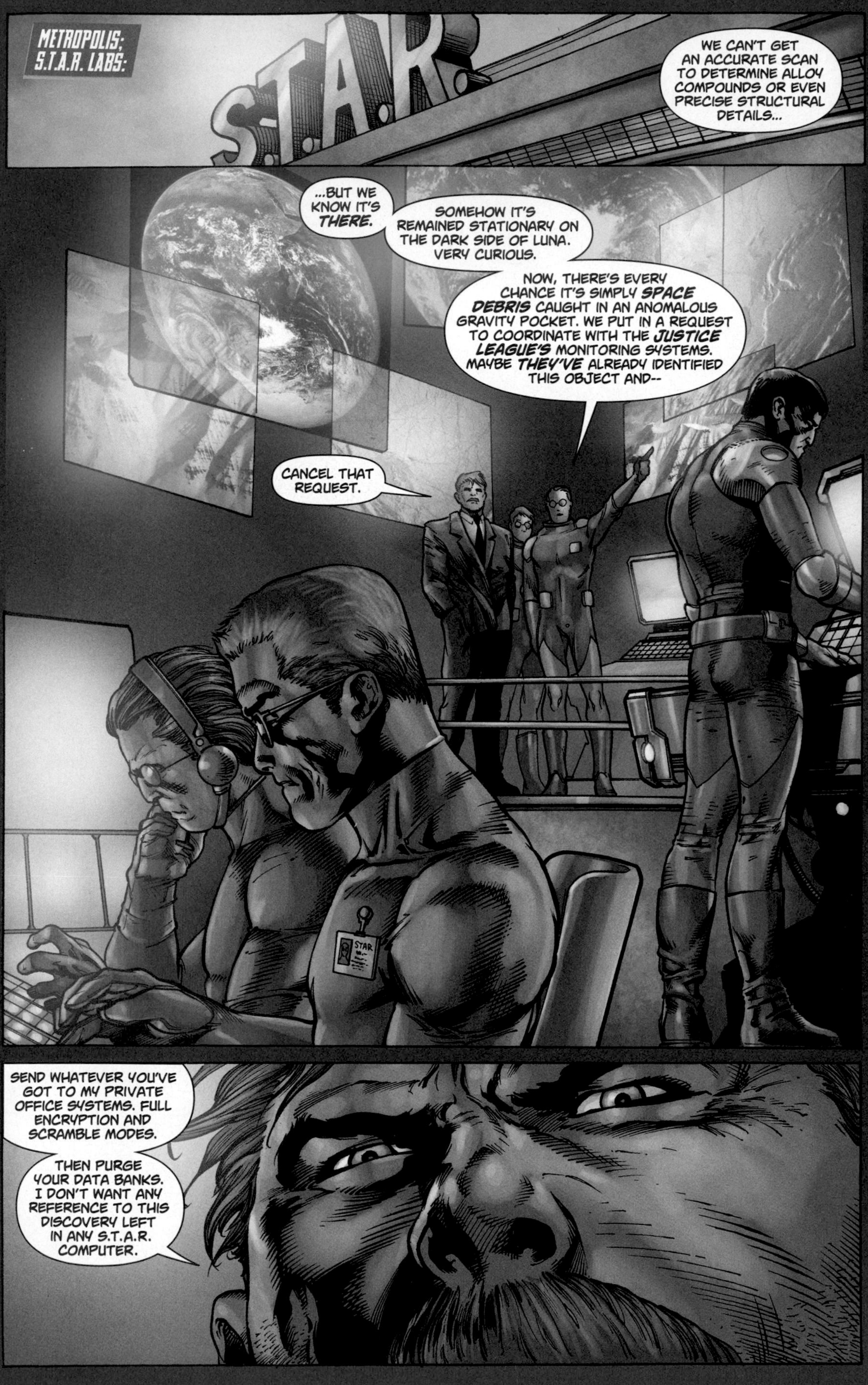
METROPOLIS: S.T.A.R. LABS:
S.T.A.R.
WE CAN'T GET AN ACCURATE SCAN TO DETERMINE ALLOY COMPOUNDS OR EVEN PRECISE STRUCTURAL DETAILS...
...BUT WE KNOW IT'S THERE.
SOMEHOW IT'S REMAINED STATIONARY ON THE DARK SIDE OF LUNA. VERY CURIOUS.
NOW, THERE'S EVERY CHANCE IT'S SIMPLY SPACE DEBRIS CAUGHT IN AN ANOMALOUS GRAVITY POCKET. WE PUT IN A REQUEST TO COORDINATE WITH THE JUSTICE LEAGUE'S MONITORING SYSTEMS. MAYBE THEY'VE ALREADY IDENTIFIED THIS OBJECT AND--
CANCEL THAT REQUEST.
STAR
SEND WHATEVER YOU'VE GOT TO MY PRIVATE OFFICE SYSTEMS. FULL ENCRYPTION AND SCRAMBLE MODES.
THEN PURGE YOUR DATA BANKS. I DON'T WANT ANY REFERENCE TO THIS DISCOVERY LEFT IN ANY S.T.A.R. COMPUTER.

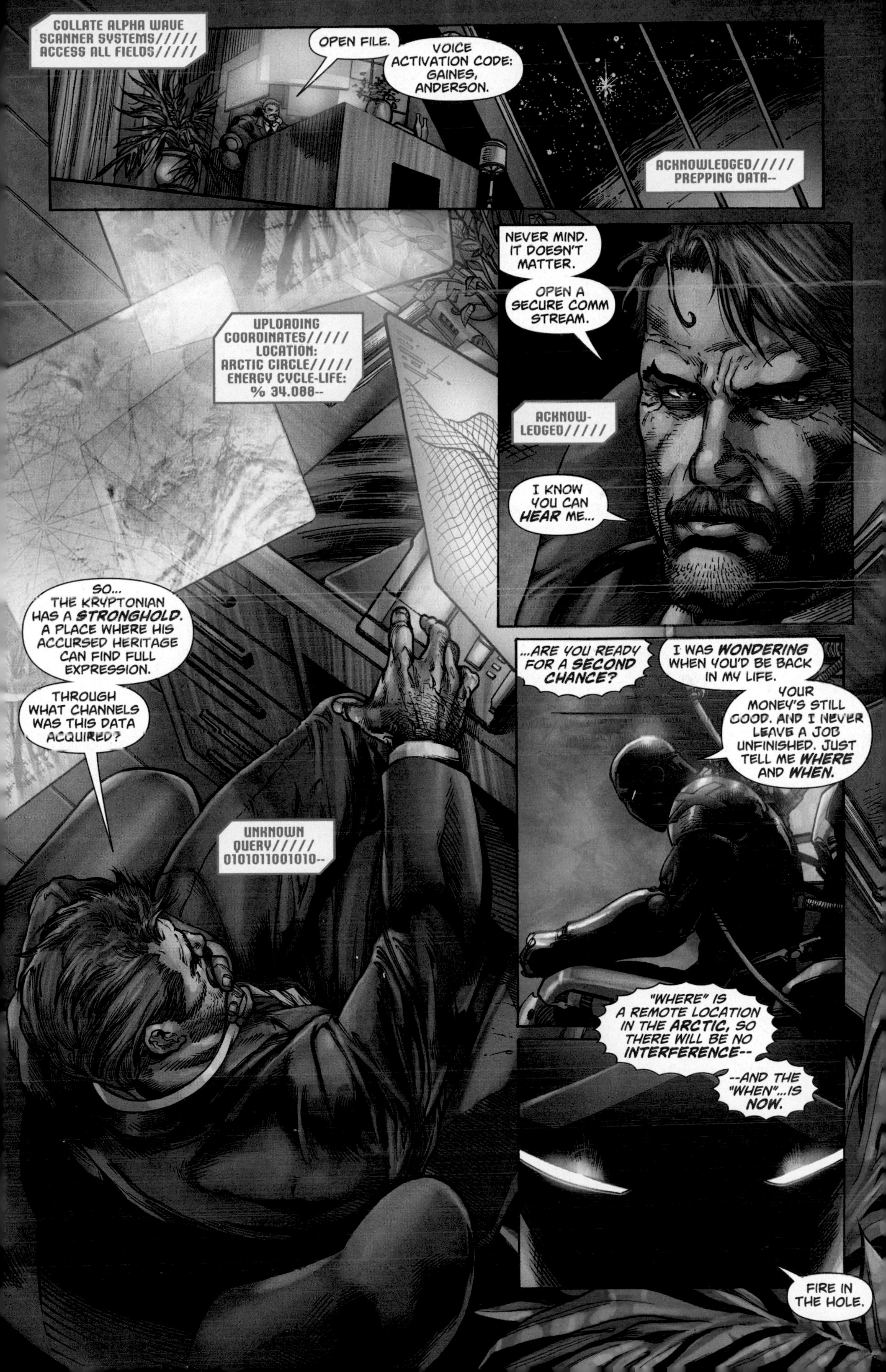

COLLATE ALPHA WAVE SCANNER SYSTEMS////// ACCESS ALL FIELDS//////
OPEN FILE.
VOICE ACTIVATION CODE: GAINES, ANDERSON.
ACKNOWLEDGED////// PREPPING DATA--
UPLOADING COORDINATES////// LOCATION: ARCTIC CIRCLE////// ENERGY CYCLE-LIFE: % 34.088--
SO... THE KRYPTONIAN HAS A STRONGHOLD. A PLACE WHERE HIS ACCURSED HERITAGE CAN FIND FULL EXPRESSION.
THROUGH WHAT CHANNELS WAS THIS DATA ACQUIRED?
UNKNOWN QUERY////// 0101011001010--
NEVER MIND. IT DOESN'T MATTER.
OPEN A SECURE COMM STREAM.
ACKNOW-LEDGED//////
I KNOW YOU CAN HEAR ME...
...ARE YOU READY FOR A SECOND CHANCE?
I WAS WONDERING WHEN YOU'D BE BACK IN MY LIFE.
YOUR MONEY'S STILL GOOD. AND I NEVER LEAVE A JOB UNFINISHED. JUST TELL ME WHERE AND WHEN.
"WHERE" IS A REMOTE LOCATION IN THE ARCTIC, SO THERE WILL BE NO INTERFERENCE--
--AND THE "WHEN"...IS NOW.
FIRE IN THE HOLE.

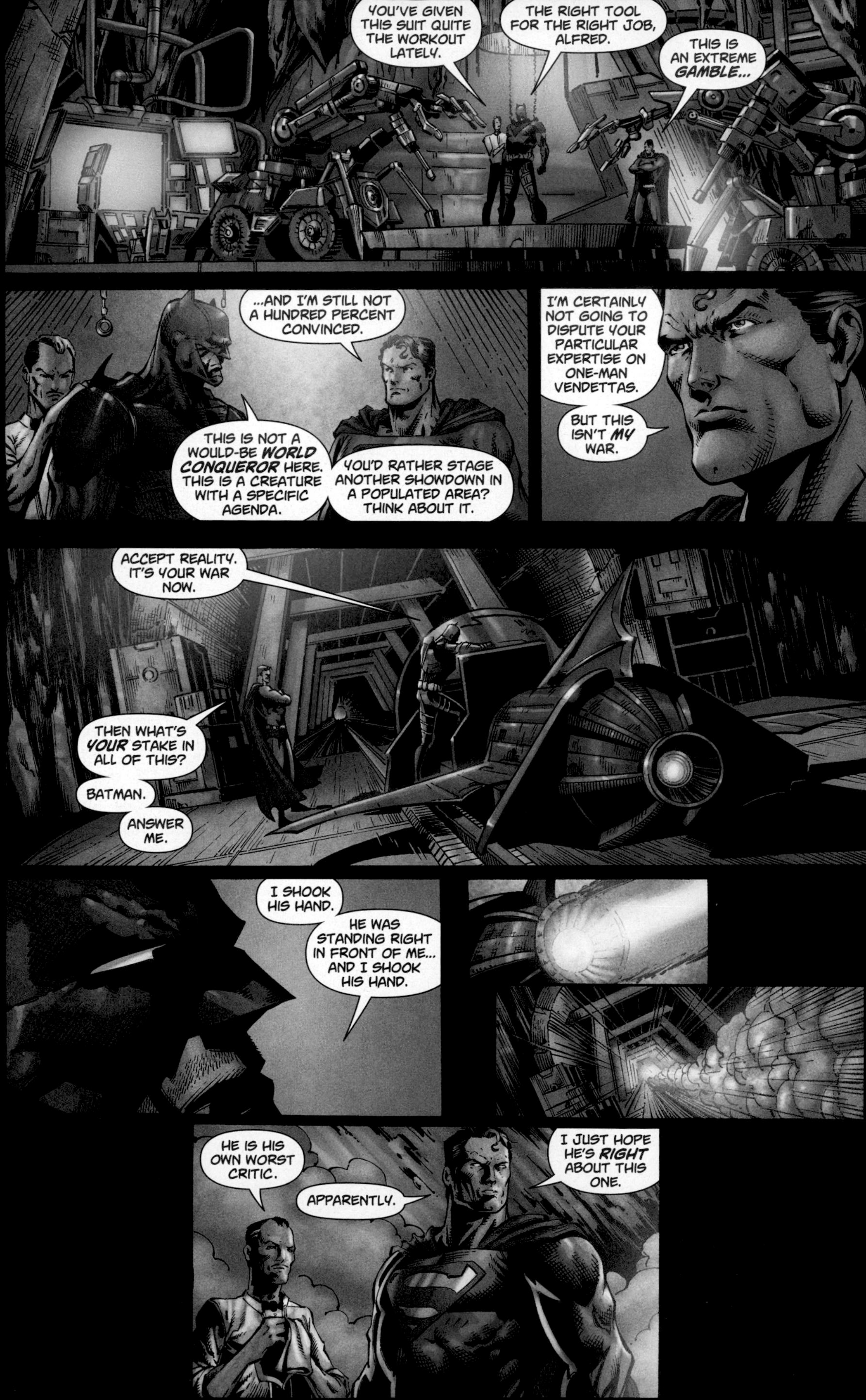

YOU'VE GIVEN THIS SUIT QUITE THE WORKOUT LATELY.
THE RIGHT TOOL FOR THE RIGHT JOB, ALFRED.
THIS IS AN EXTREME GAMBLE...
...AND I'M STILL NOT A HUNDRED PERCENT CONVINCED.
THIS IS NOT A WOULD-BE WORLD CONQUEROR HERE. THIS IS A CREATURE WITH A SPECIFIC AGENDA.
YOU'D RATHER STAGE ANOTHER SHOWDOWN IN A POPULATED AREA? THINK ABOUT IT.
I'M CERTAINLY NOT GOING TO DISPUTE YOUR PARTICULAR EXPERTISE ON ONE-MAN VENDETTAS.
BUT THIS ISN'T MY WAR.
ACCEPT REALITY. IT'S YOUR WAR NOW.
THEN WHAT'S YOUR STAKE IN ALL OF THIS?
BATMAN.
ANSWER ME.
I SHOOK HIS HAND.
HE WAS STANDING RIGHT IN FRONT OF ME... AND I SHOOK HIS HAND.
HE IS HIS OWN WORST CRITIC.
APPARENTLY.
I JUST HOPE HE'S RIGHT ABOUT THIS ONE.

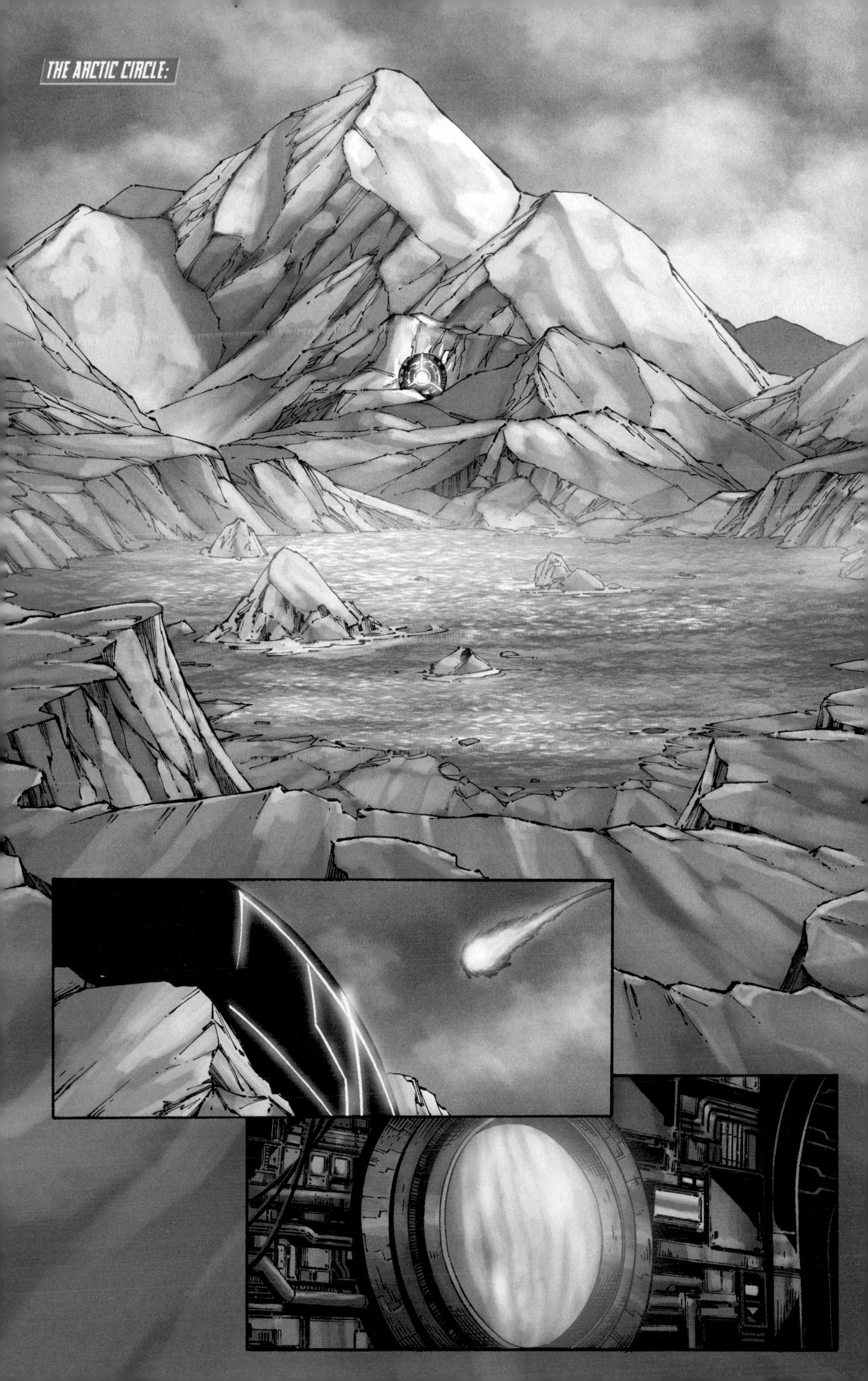
THE ARCTIC CIRCLE:

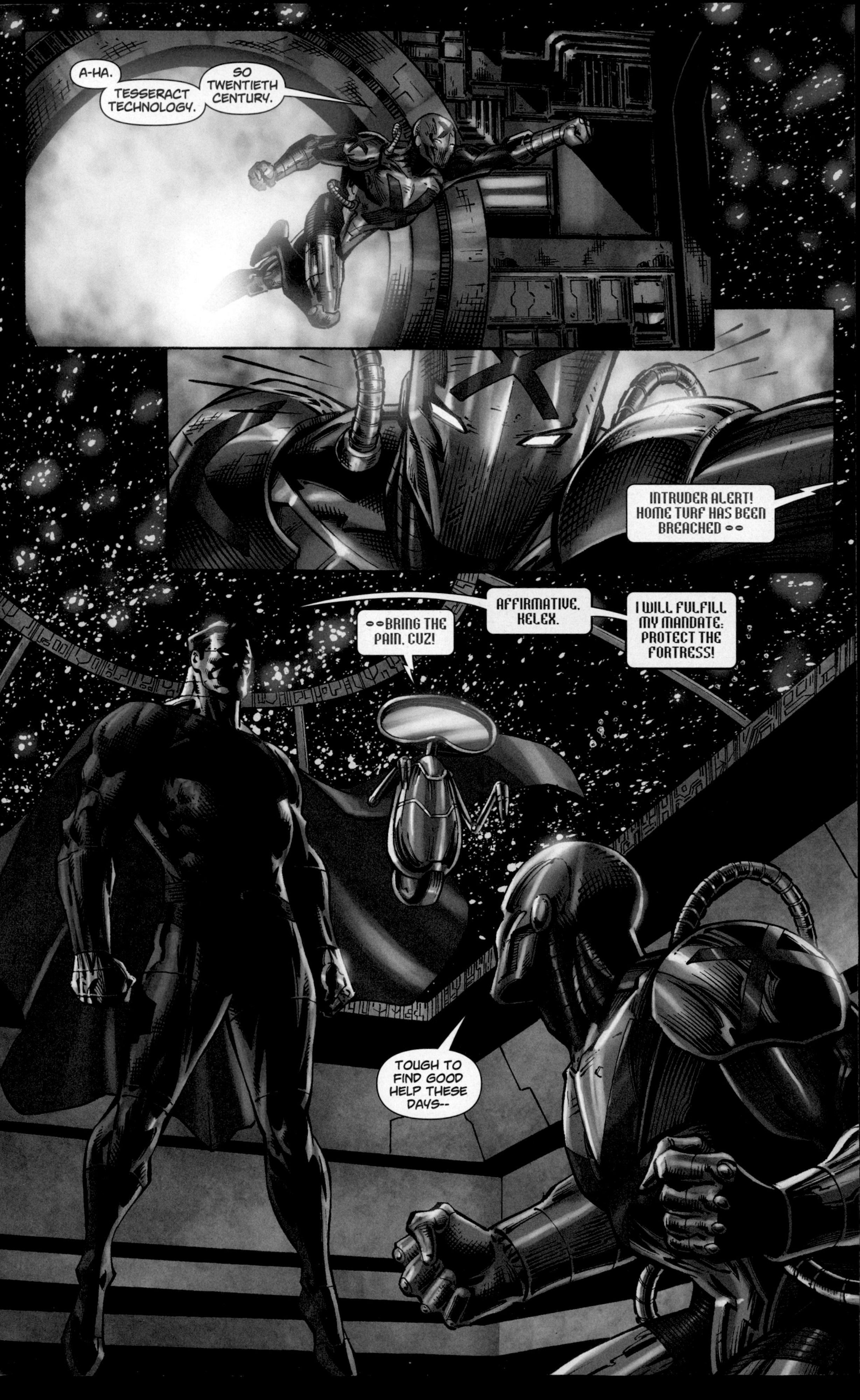
A-HA.
TESSERACT TECHNOLOGY.
SO TWENTIETH CENTURY.
INTRUDER ALERT! HOME TURF HAS BEEN BREACHED --
--BRING THE PAIN, CUZ!
AFFIRMATIVE, KELEX.
I WILL FULFILL MY MANDATE: PROTECT THE FORTRESS!
TOUGH TO FIND GOOD HELP THESE DAYS--

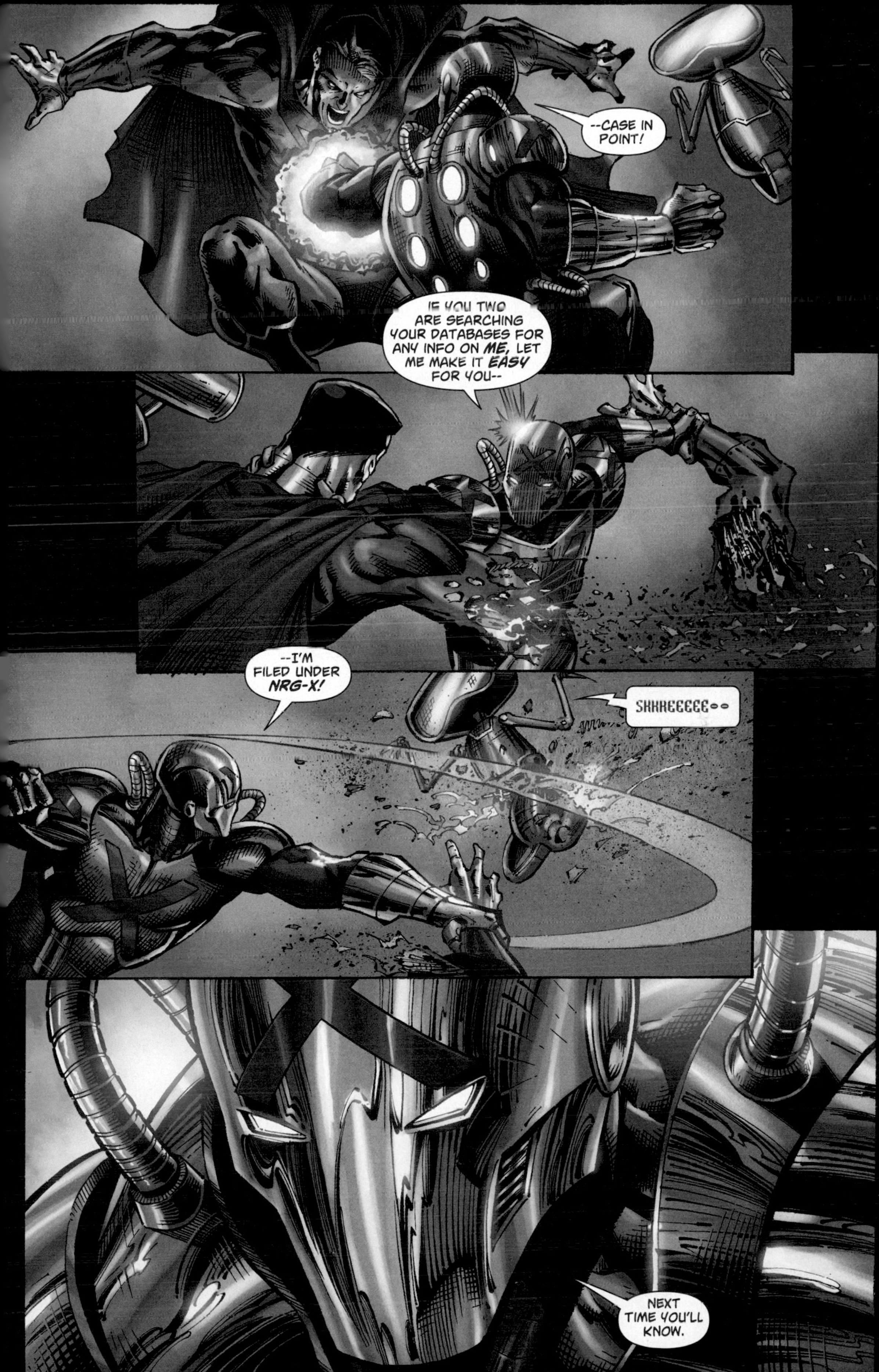
--CASE IN POINT!
IF YOU TWO ARE SEARCHING YOUR DATABASES FOR ANY INFO ON **ME,** LET ME MAKE IT **EASY** FOR YOU--
--I'M FILED UNDER **NRG-X!**
SKKREEEEE--
NEXT TIME YOU'LL KNOW.

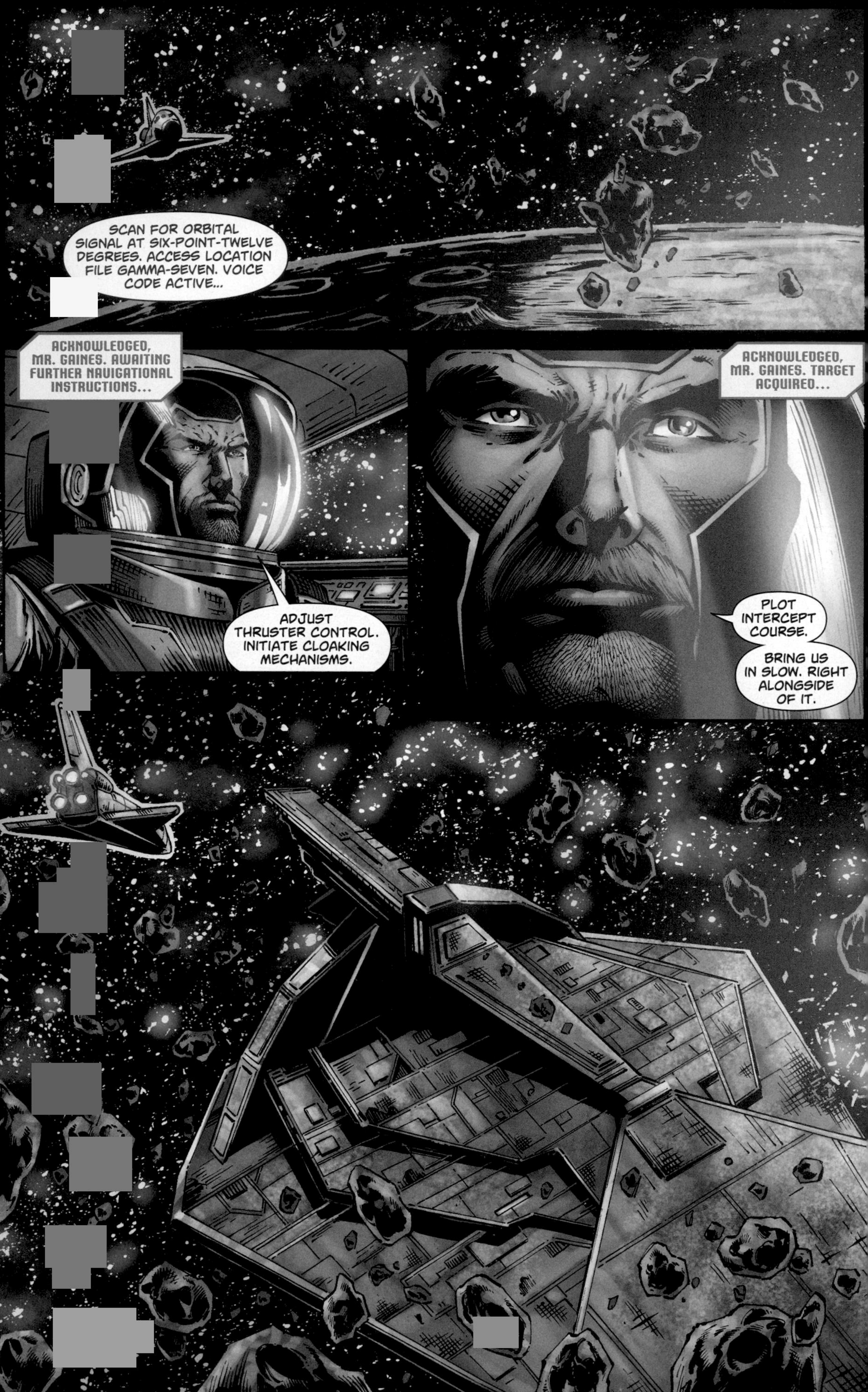
SCAN FOR ORBITAL SIGNAL AT SIX-POINT-TWELVE DEGREES. ACCESS LOCATION FILE GAMMA-SEVEN. VOICE CODE ACTIVE...
ACKNOWLEDGED, MR. GAINES. AWAITING FURTHER NAVIGATIONAL INSTRUCTIONS...
ADJUST THRUSTER CONTROL. INITIATE CLOAKING MECHANISMS.
ACKNOWLEDGED, MR. GAINES. TARGET ACQUIRED...
PLOT INTERCEPT COURSE.
BRING US IN SLOW. RIGHT ALONGSIDE OF IT.

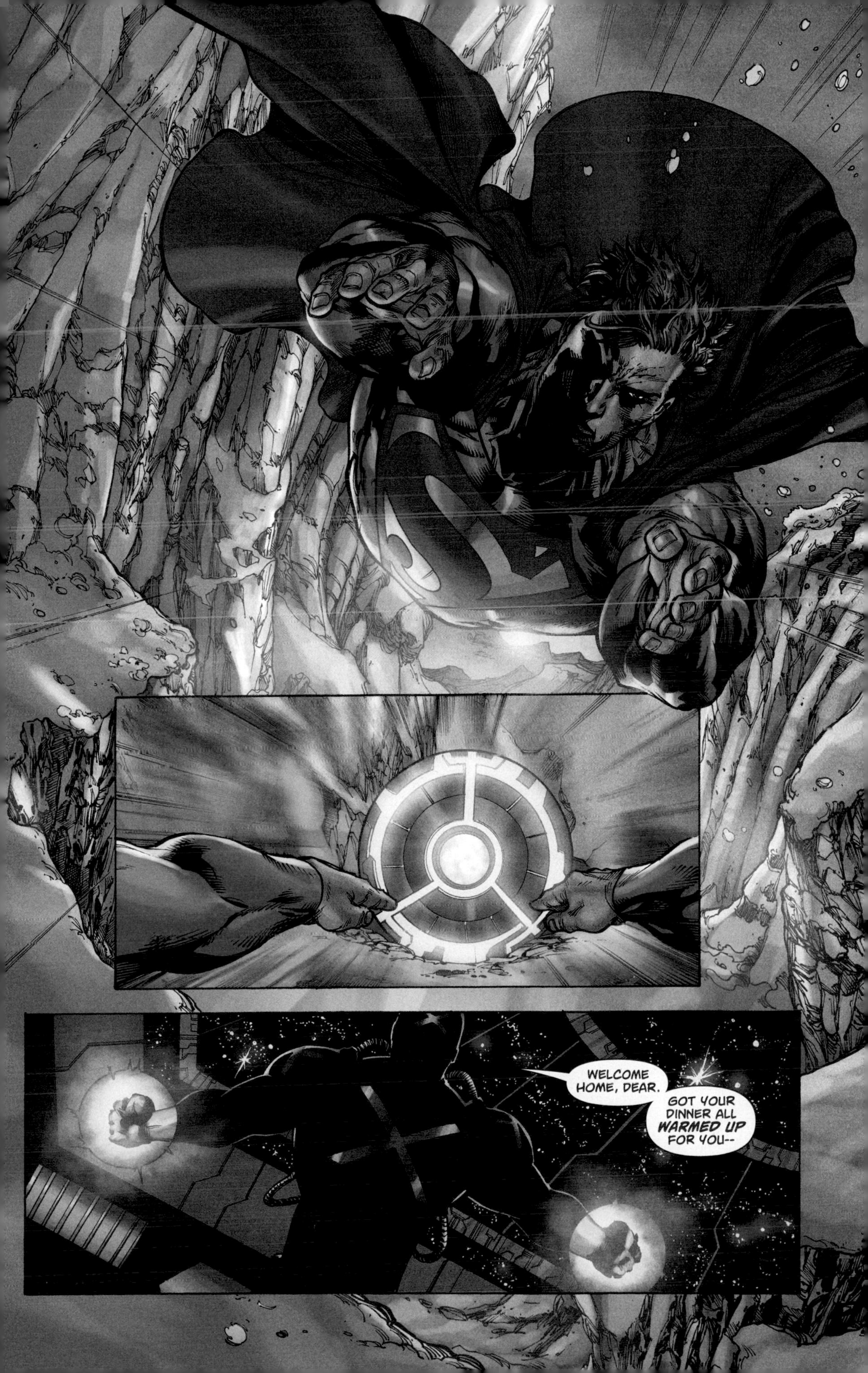
WELCOME HOME, DEAR.
GOT YOUR DINNER ALL WARMED UP FOR YOU--

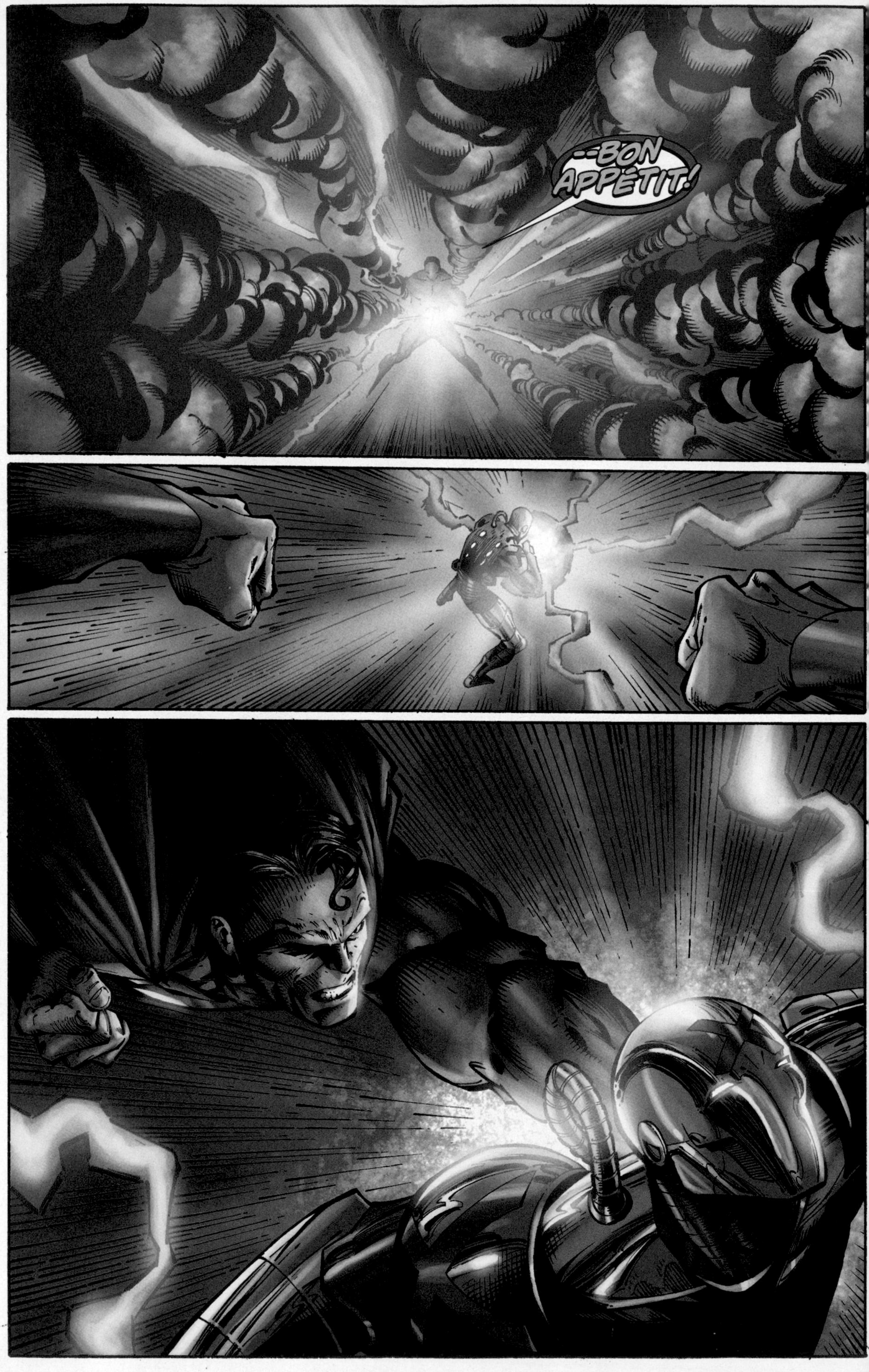
--BON APPÉTIT!

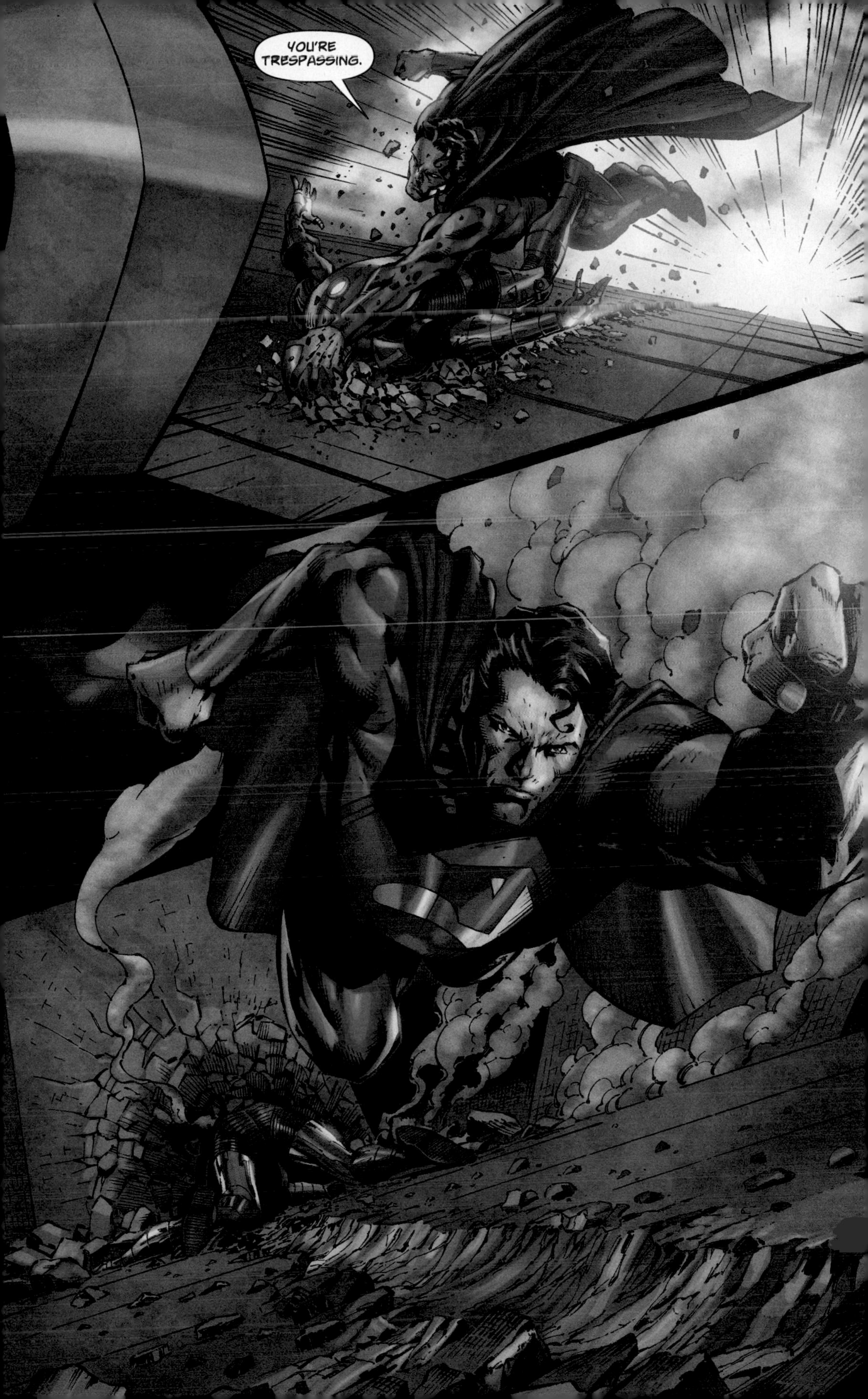
YOU'RE TRESPASSING.

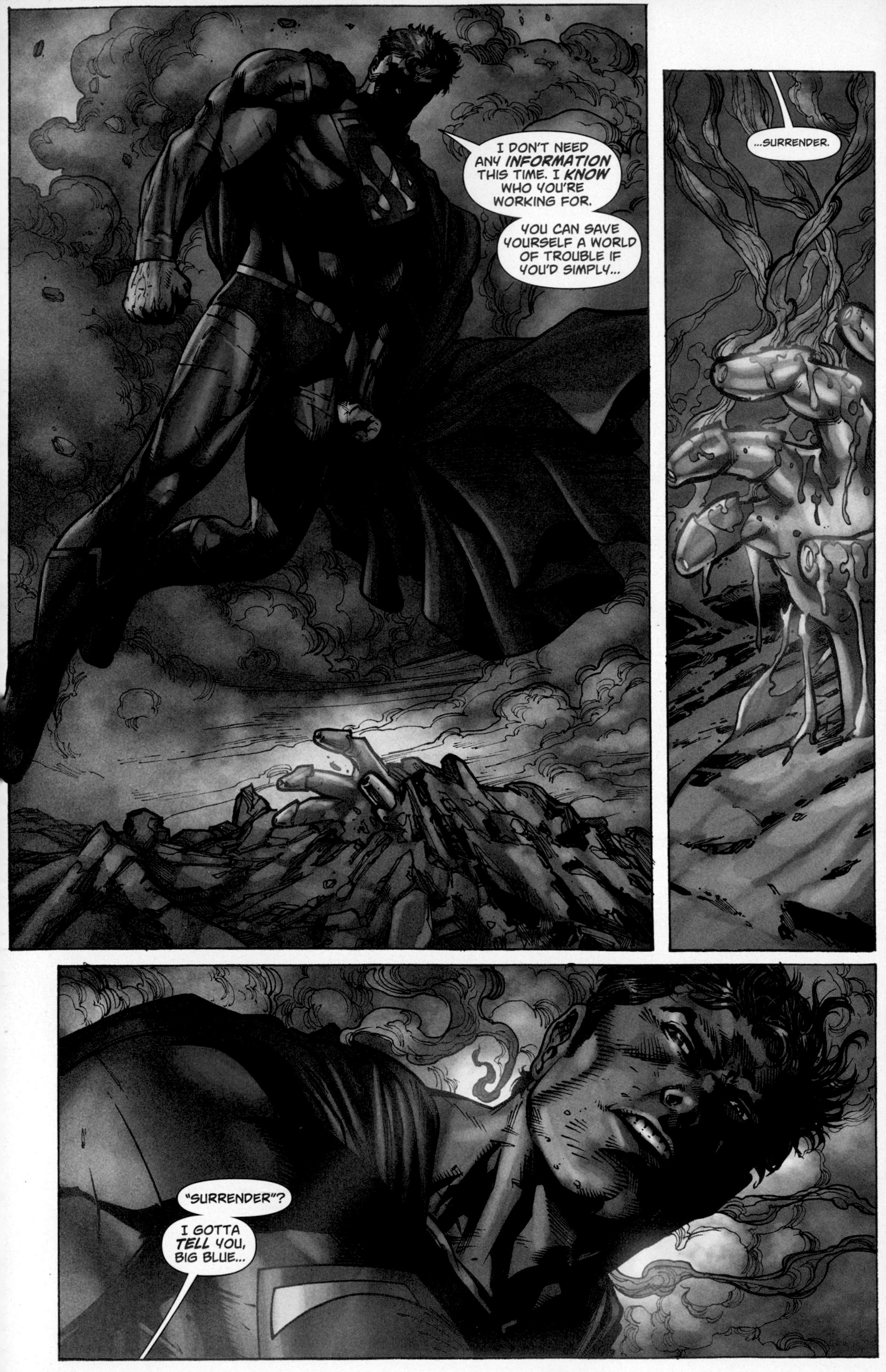
I DON'T NEED ANY INFORMATION THIS TIME. I KNOW WHO YOU'RE WORKING FOR.
YOU CAN SAVE YOURSELF A WORLD OF TROUBLE IF YOU'D SIMPLY...
...SURRENDER.
"SURRENDER"?
I GOTTA TELL YOU, BIG BLUE...

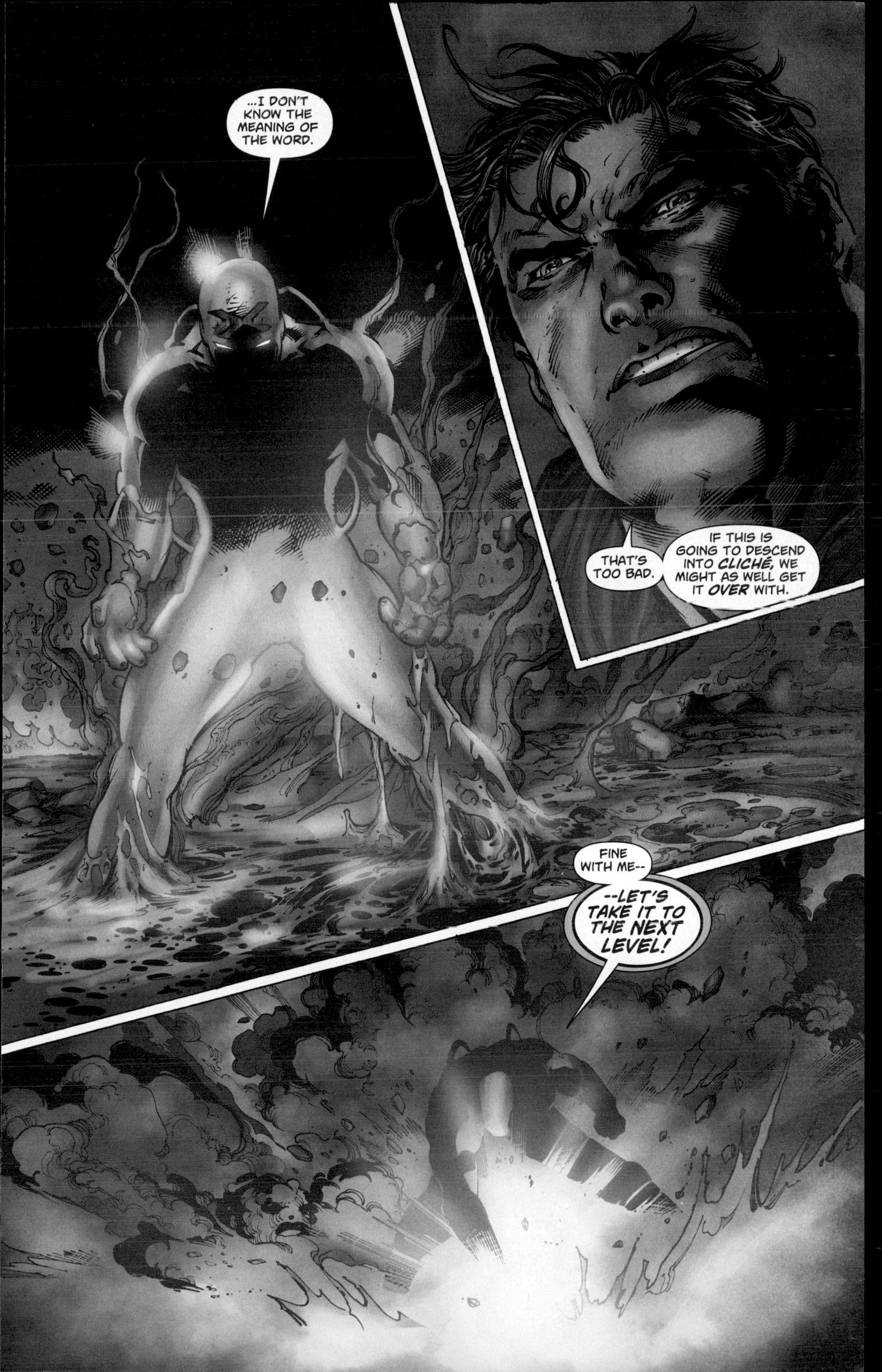
...I DON'T KNOW THE MEANING OF THE WORD.
THAT'S TOO BAD.
IF THIS IS GOING TO DESCEND INTO CLICHÉ, WE MIGHT AS WELL GET IT OVER WITH.
FINE WITH ME--
--LET'S TAKE IT TO THE NEXT LEVEL!

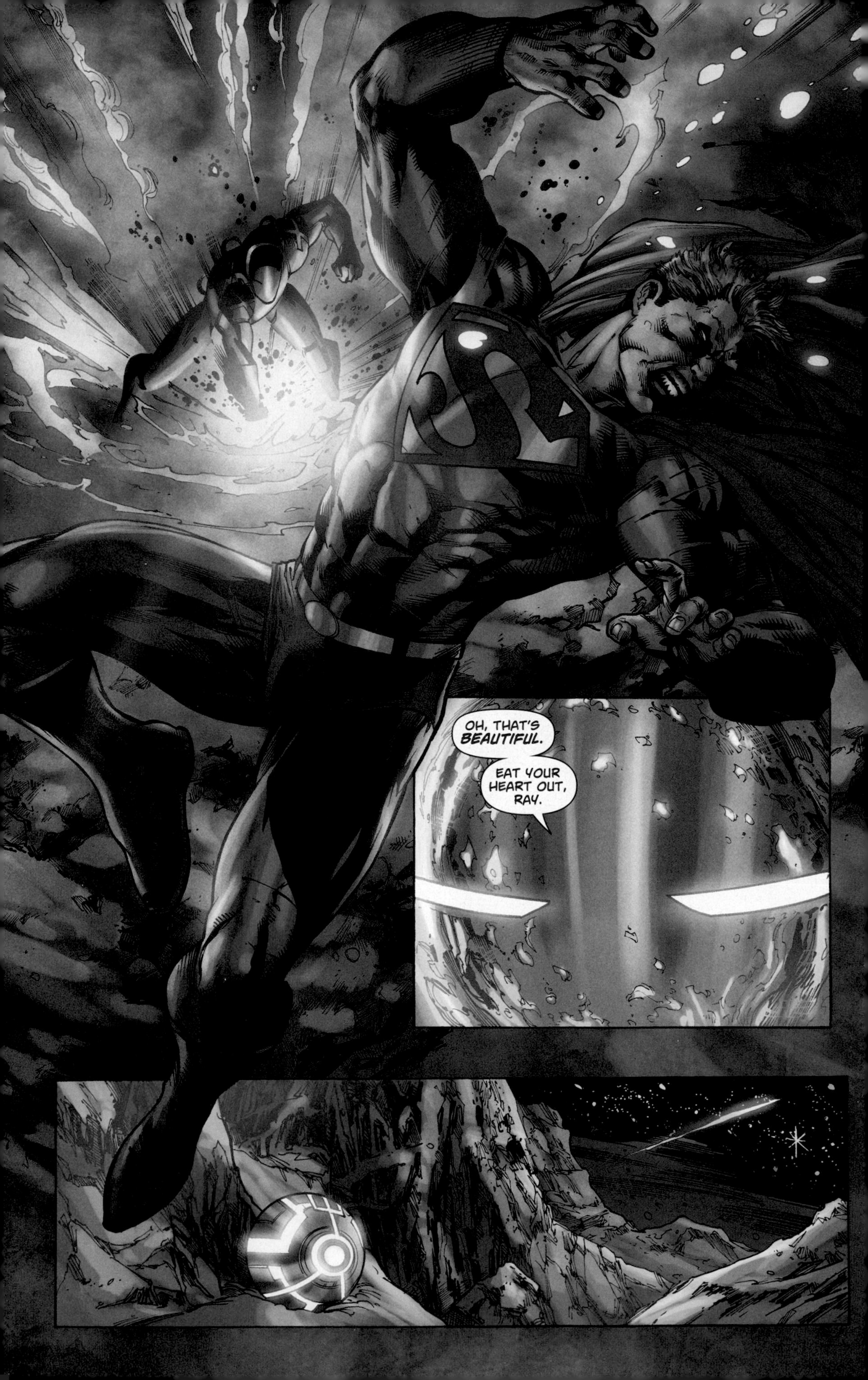

OH, THAT'S *BEAUTIFUL.*
EAT YOUR HEART OUT, RAY.

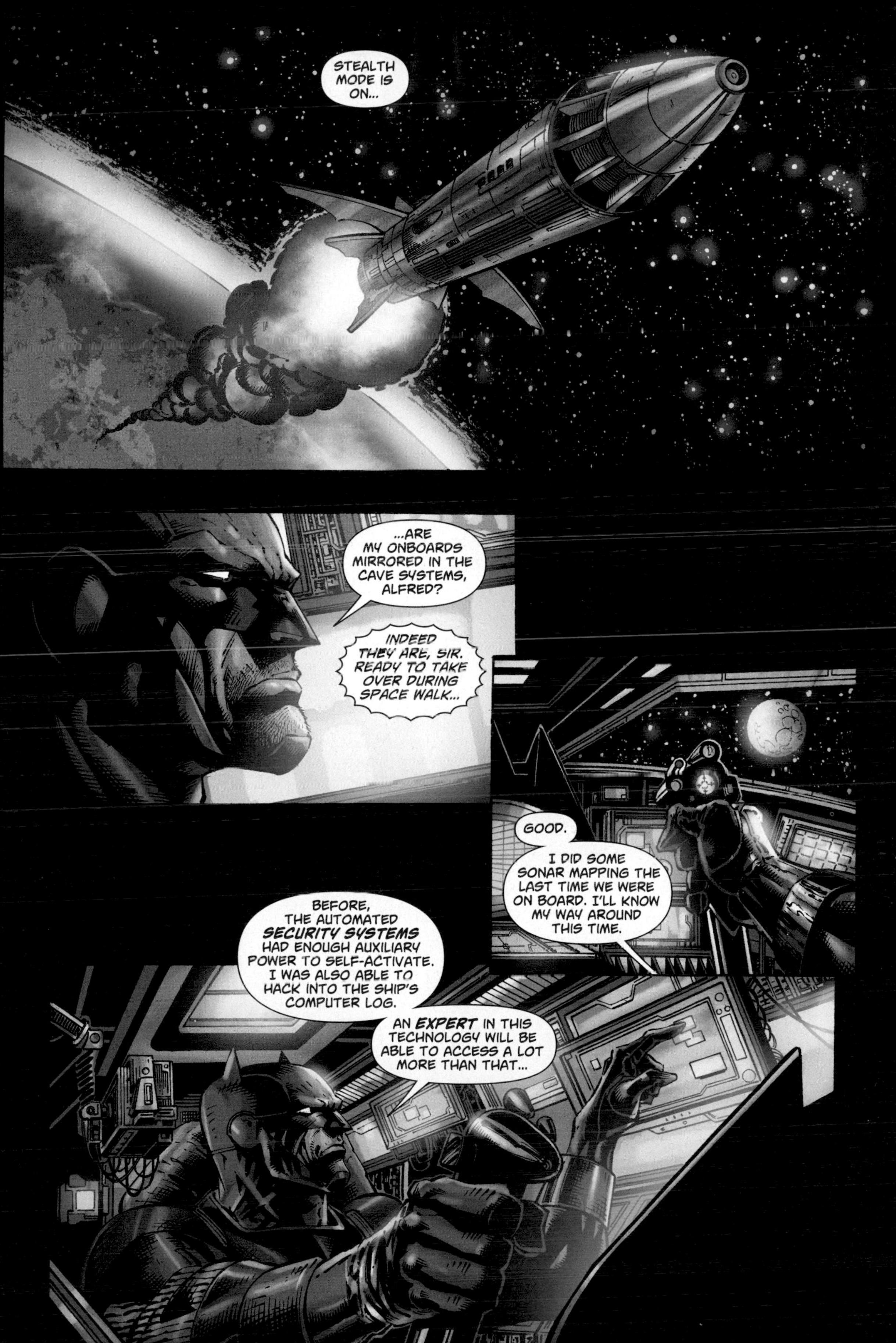
STEALTH MODE IS ON...
...ARE MY ONBOARDS MIRRORED IN THE CAVE SYSTEMS, ALFRED?
INDEED THEY ARE, SIR. READY TO TAKE OVER DURING SPACE WALK...
GOOD.
I DID SOME SONAR MAPPING THE LAST TIME WE WERE ON BOARD. I'LL KNOW MY WAY AROUND THIS TIME.
BEFORE, THE AUTOMATED SECURITY SYSTEMS HAD ENOUGH AUXILIARY POWER TO SELF-ACTIVATE. I WAS ALSO ABLE TO HACK INTO THE SHIP'S COMPUTER LOG.
AN EXPERT IN THIS TECHNOLOGY WILL BE ABLE TO ACCESS A LOT MORE THAN THAT...

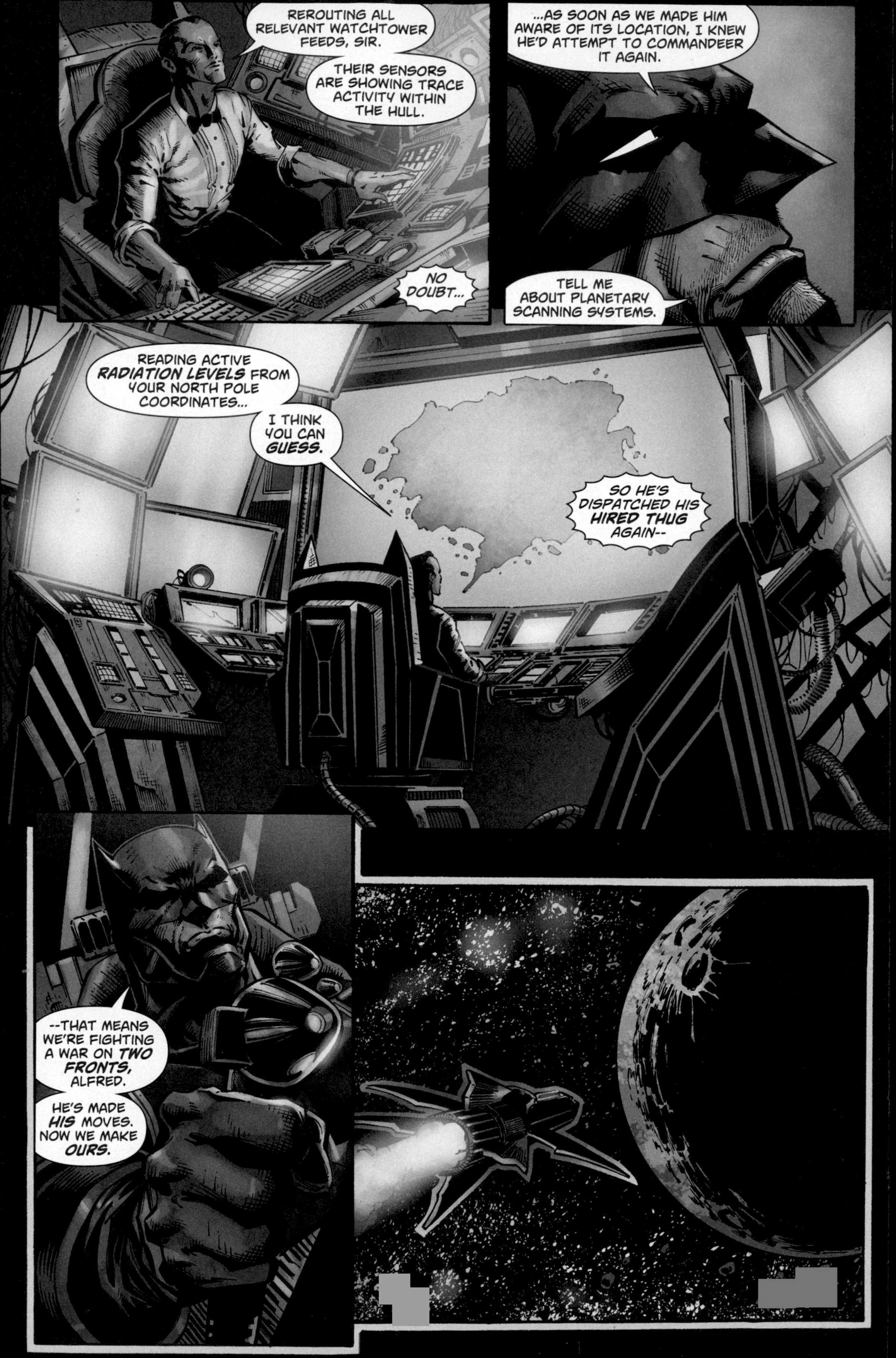
REROUTING ALL RELEVANT WATCHTOWER FEEDS, SIR.
THEIR SENSORS ARE SHOWING TRACE ACTIVITY WITHIN THE HULL.
NO DOUBT...
...AS SOON AS WE MADE HIM AWARE OF ITS LOCATION, I KNEW HE'D ATTEMPT TO COMMANDEER IT AGAIN.
TELL ME ABOUT PLANETARY SCANNING SYSTEMS.
READING ACTIVE *RADIATION LEVELS* FROM YOUR NORTH POLE COORDINATES...
I THINK YOU CAN *GUESS.*
SO HE'S DISPATCHED HIS *HIRED THUG* AGAIN--
--THAT MEANS WE'RE FIGHTING A WAR ON *TWO FRONTS,* ALFRED.
HE'S MADE *HIS* MOVES. NOW WE MAKE *OURS.*

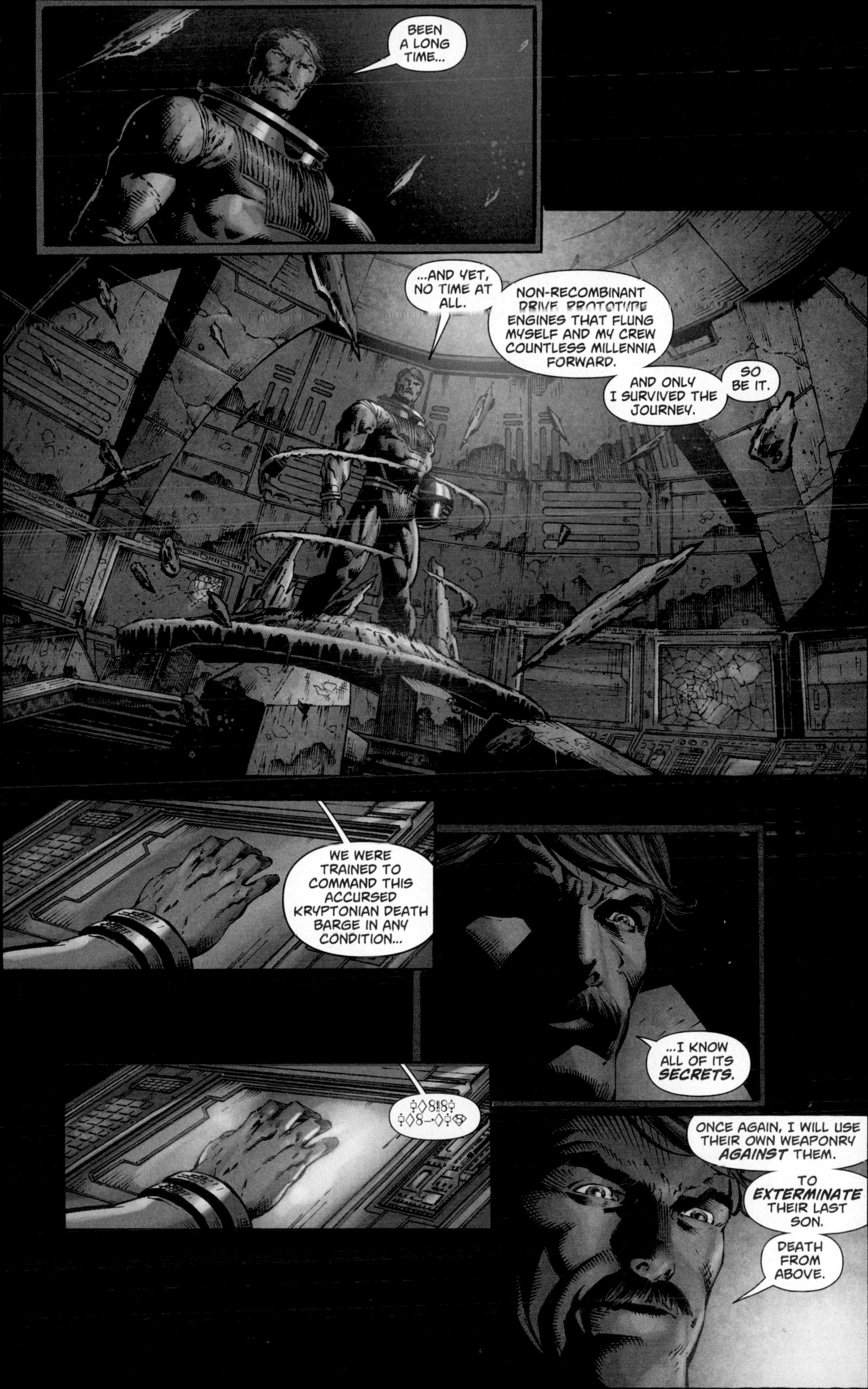

BEEN A LONG TIME...
...AND YET, NO TIME AT ALL.
NON-RECOMBINANT DRIVE PROTOTYPE ENGINES THAT FLUNG MYSELF AND MY CREW COUNTLESS MILLENNIA FORWARD.
AND ONLY I SURVIVED THE JOURNEY.
SO BE IT.
WE WERE TRAINED TO COMMAND THIS ACCURSED KRYPTONIAN DEATH BARGE IN ANY CONDITION...
...I KNOW ALL OF ITS *SECRETS*.
ONCE AGAIN, I WILL USE THEIR OWN WEAPONRY *AGAINST* THEM.
TO *EXTERMINATE* THEIR LAST SON.
DEATH FROM ABOVE.

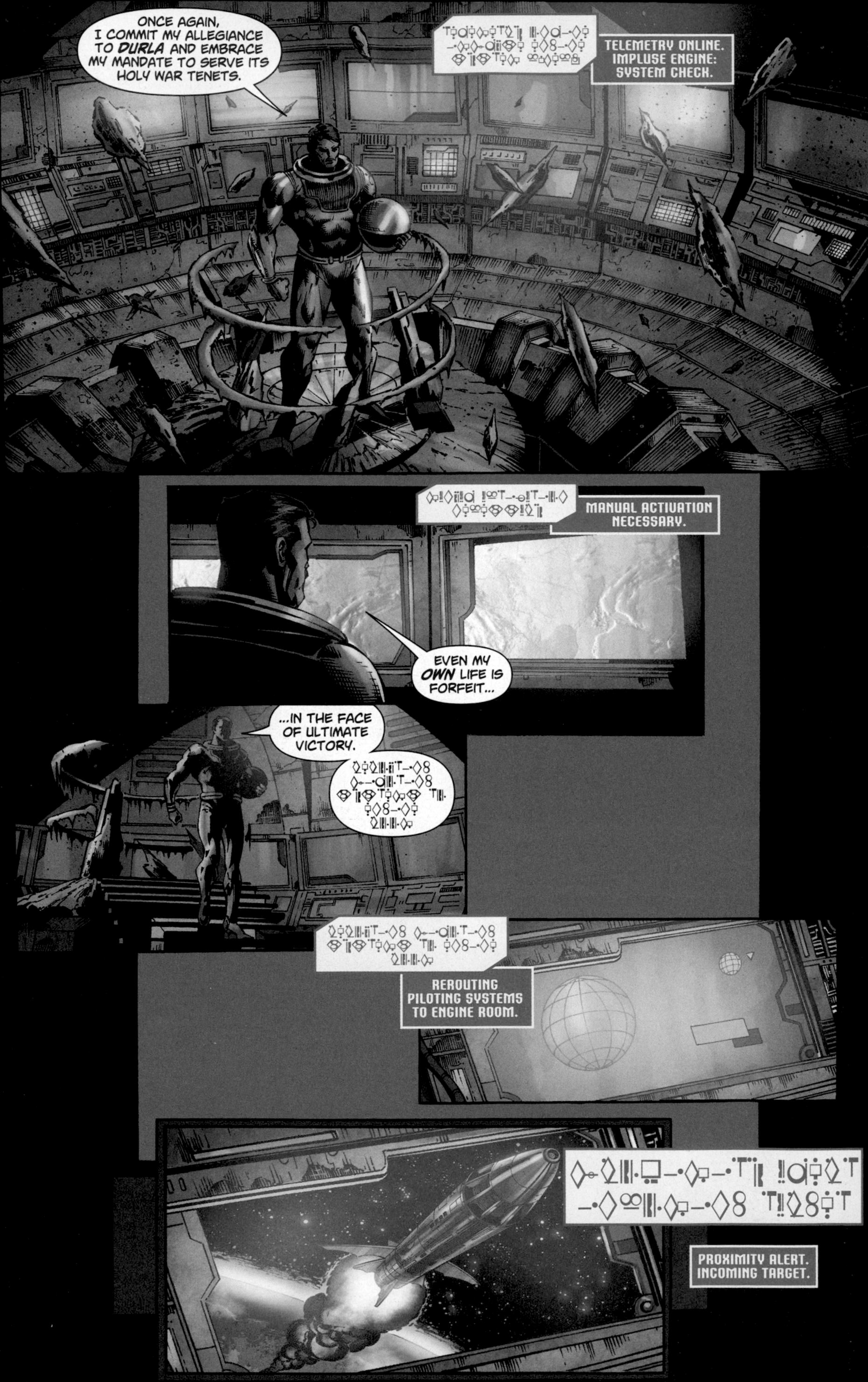
ONCE AGAIN, I COMMIT MY ALLEGIANCE TO DURLA AND EMBRACE MY MANDATE TO SERVE ITS HOLY WAR TENETS.
TELEMETRY ONLINE. IMPLUSE ENGINE: SYSTEM CHECK.
MANUAL ACTIVATION NECESSARY.
EVEN MY OWN LIFE IS FORFEIT...
...IN THE FACE OF ULTIMATE VICTORY.
REROUTING PILOTING SYSTEMS TO ENGINE ROOM.
PROXIMITY ALERT. INCOMING TARGET.

SUPERMAN/BATMAN No. 71
Ardian Syaf, Vicente Cifuentes and Ulises Arreola

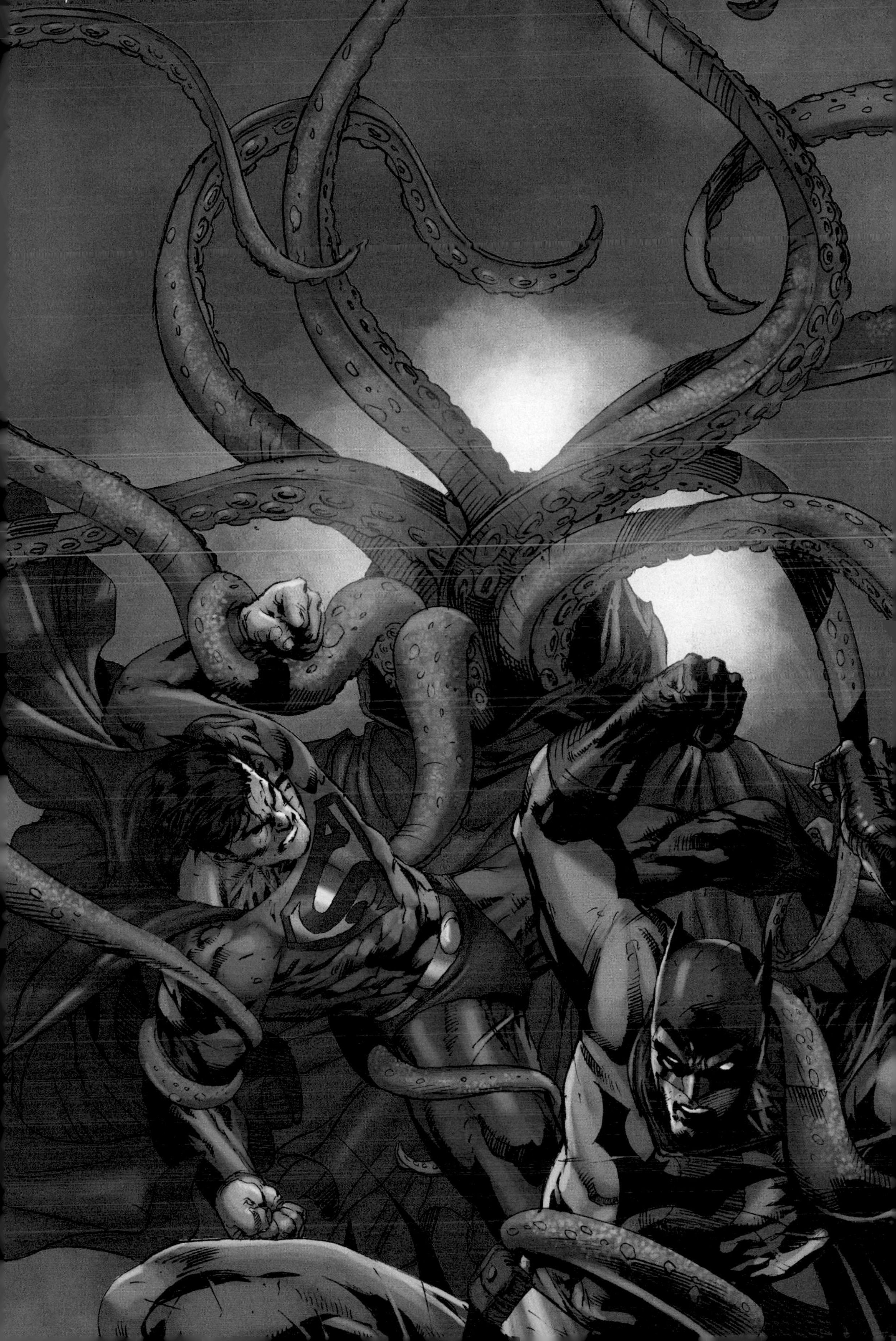

THE BIG NOISE PART 4: THE FINAL SOLUTION

Penciller: Jason Fabok

Inkers: Prentis Rollins, Rebecca Buchman,
Derek Fridolfs and Walden Wong

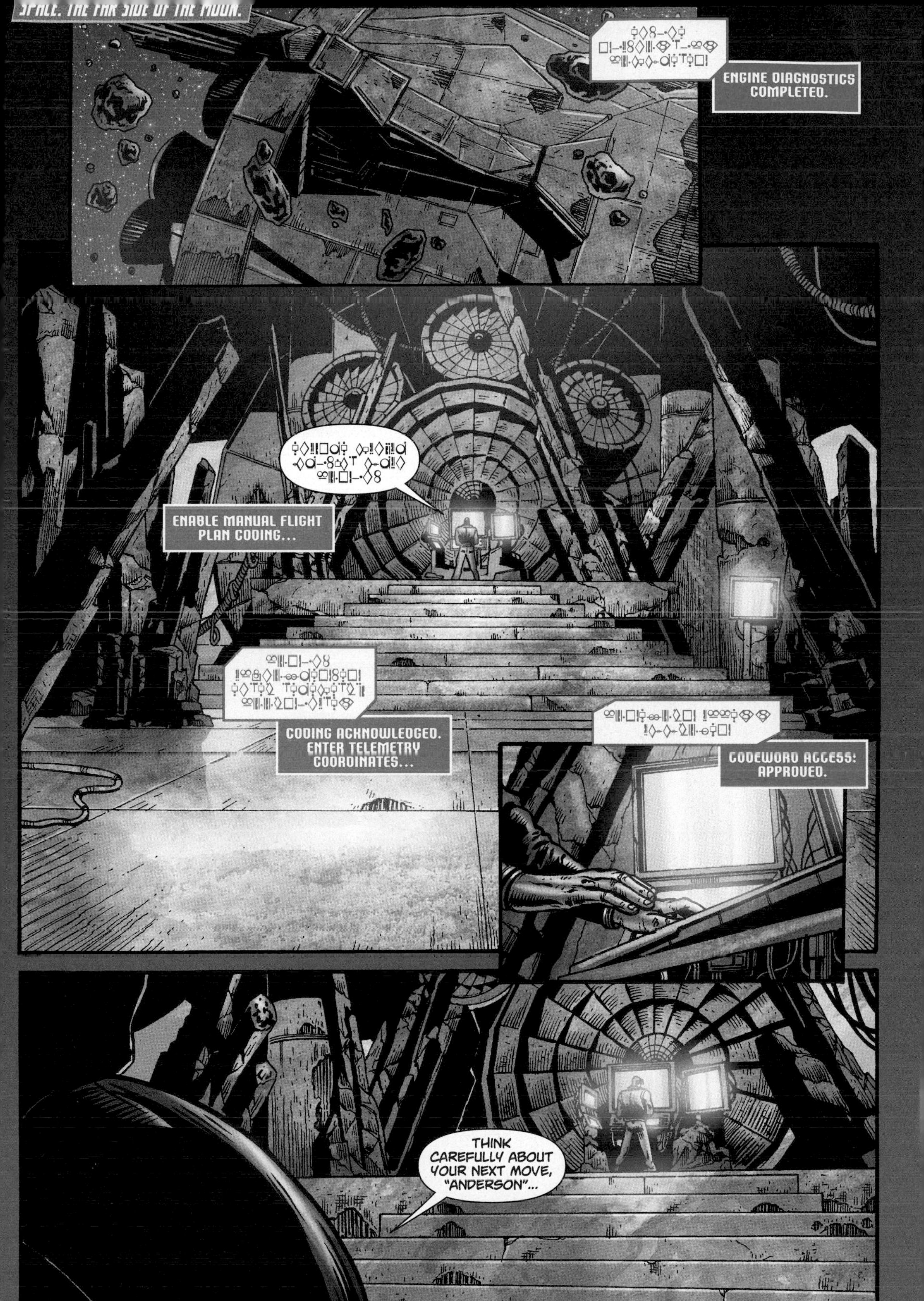
SPACE. THE FAR SIDE OF THE MOON.
ENGINE DIAGNOSTICS COMPLETED.
ENABLE MANUAL FLIGHT PLAN CODING...
CODING ACKNOWLEDGED. ENTER TELEMETRY COORDINATES...
CODEWORD ACCESS: APPROVED.
THINK CAREFULLY ABOUT YOUR NEXT MOVE, "ANDERSON"...

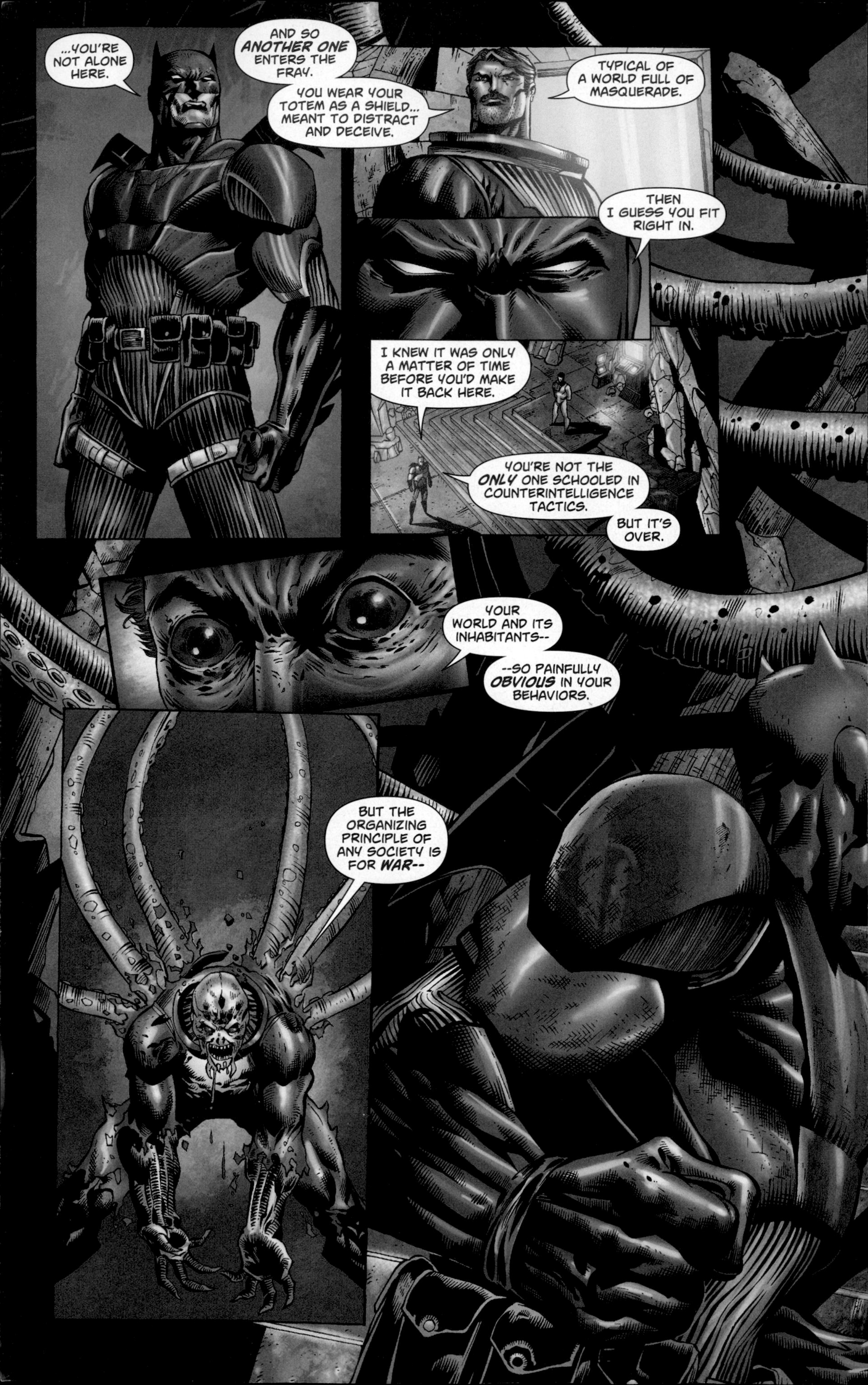
...YOU'RE NOT ALONE HERE.
AND SO ANOTHER ONE ENTERS THE FRAY.
YOU WEAR YOUR TOTEM AS A SHIELD... MEANT TO DISTRACT AND DECEIVE.
TYPICAL OF A WORLD FULL OF MASQUERADE.
THEN I GUESS YOU FIT RIGHT IN.
I KNEW IT WAS ONLY A MATTER OF TIME BEFORE YOU'D MAKE IT BACK HERE.
YOU'RE NOT THE ONLY ONE SCHOOLED IN COUNTERINTELLIGENCE TACTICS.
BUT IT'S OVER.
YOUR WORLD AND ITS INHABITANTS--
--SO PAINFULLY OBVIOUS IN YOUR BEHAVIORS.
BUT THE ORGANIZING PRINCIPLE OF ANY SOCIETY IS FOR WAR--

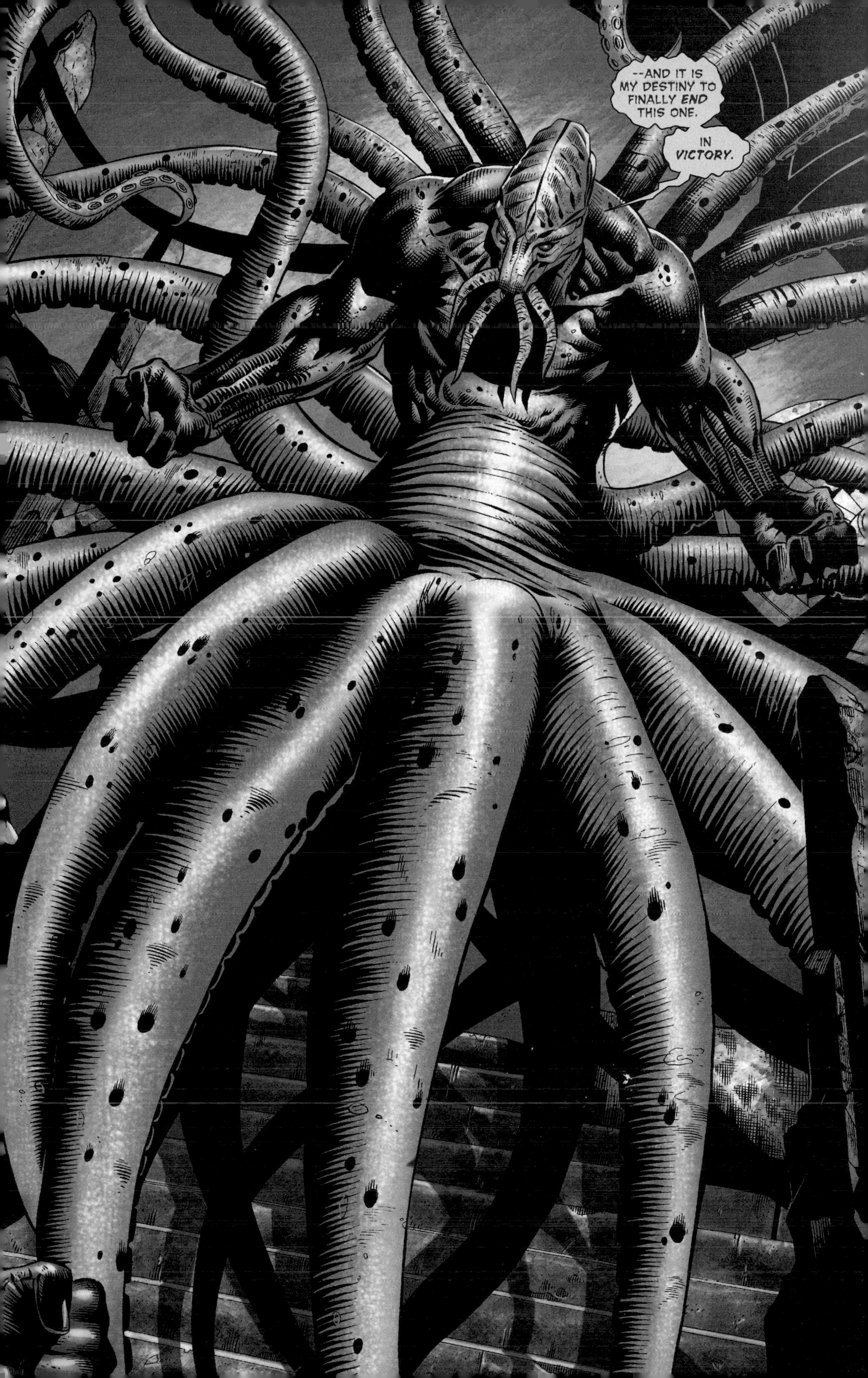

--AND IT IS MY DESTINY TO FINALLY END THIS ONE.
IN VICTORY.

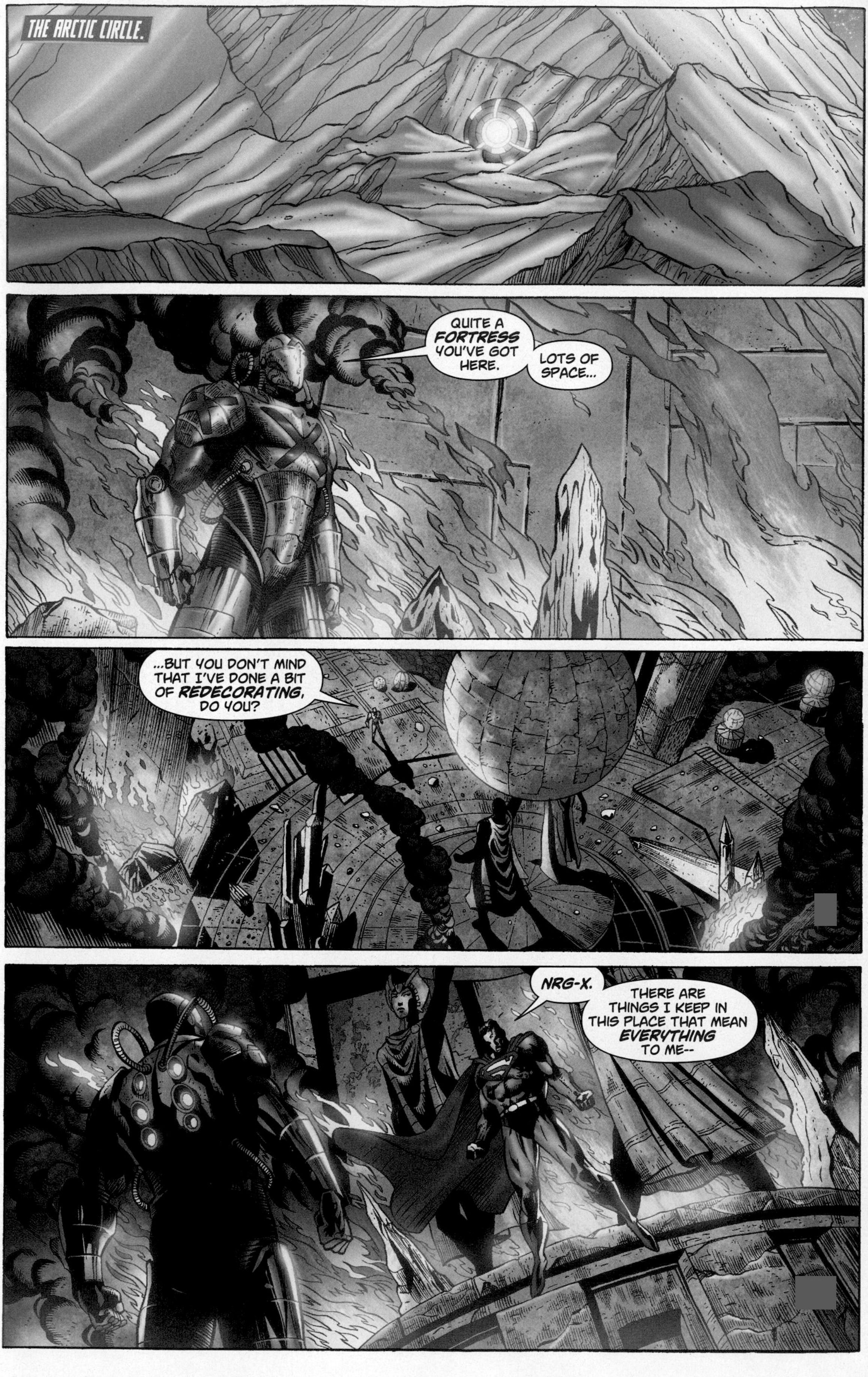
THE ARCTIC CIRCLE.
QUITE A FORTRESS YOU'VE GOT HERE.
LOTS OF SPACE...
...BUT YOU DON'T MIND THAT I'VE DONE A BIT OF REDECORATING, DO YOU?
NRG-X.
THERE ARE THINGS I KEEP IN THIS PLACE THAT MEAN EVERYTHING TO ME--

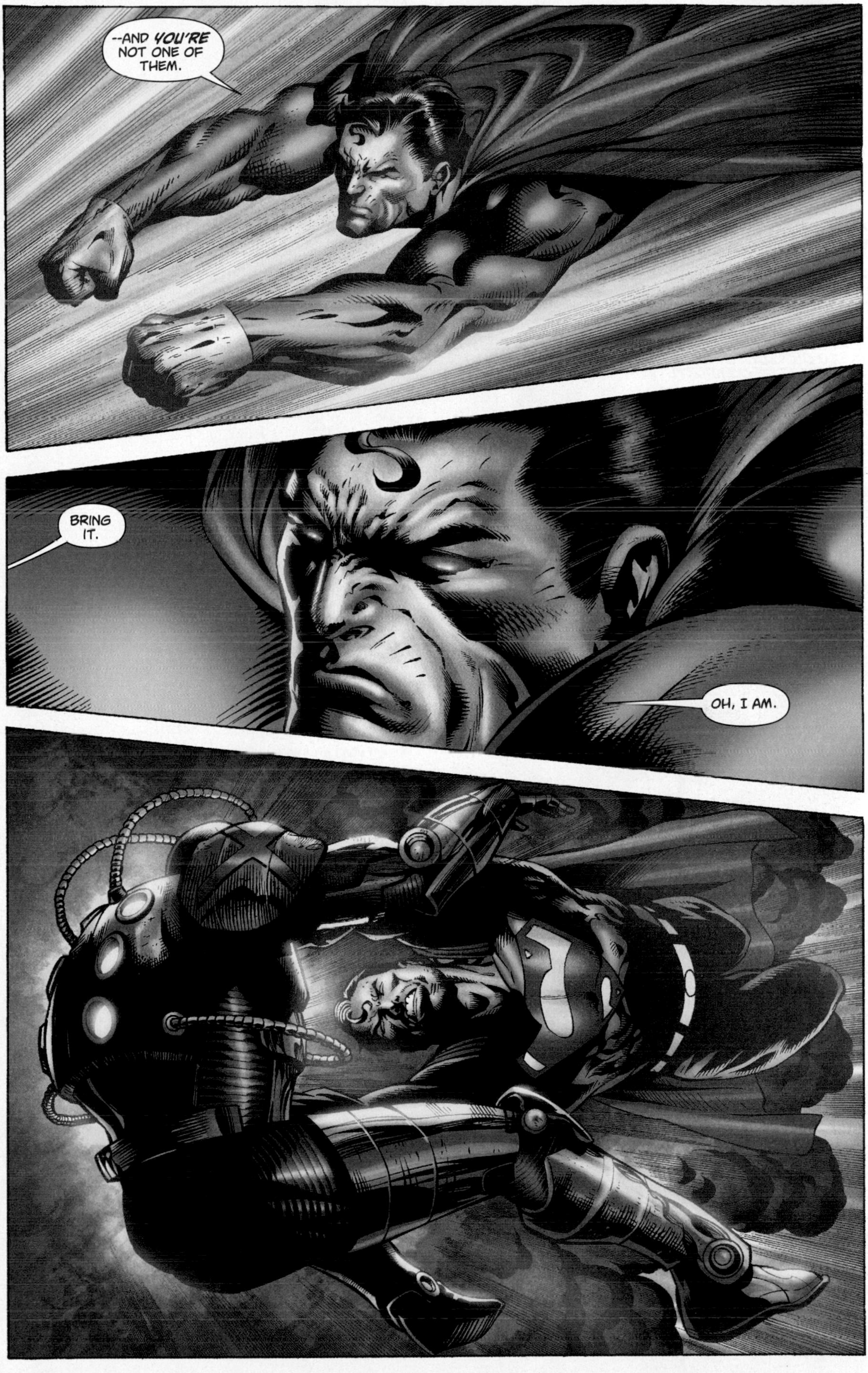
--AND YOU'RE NOT ONE OF THEM.
BRING IT.
OH, I AM.

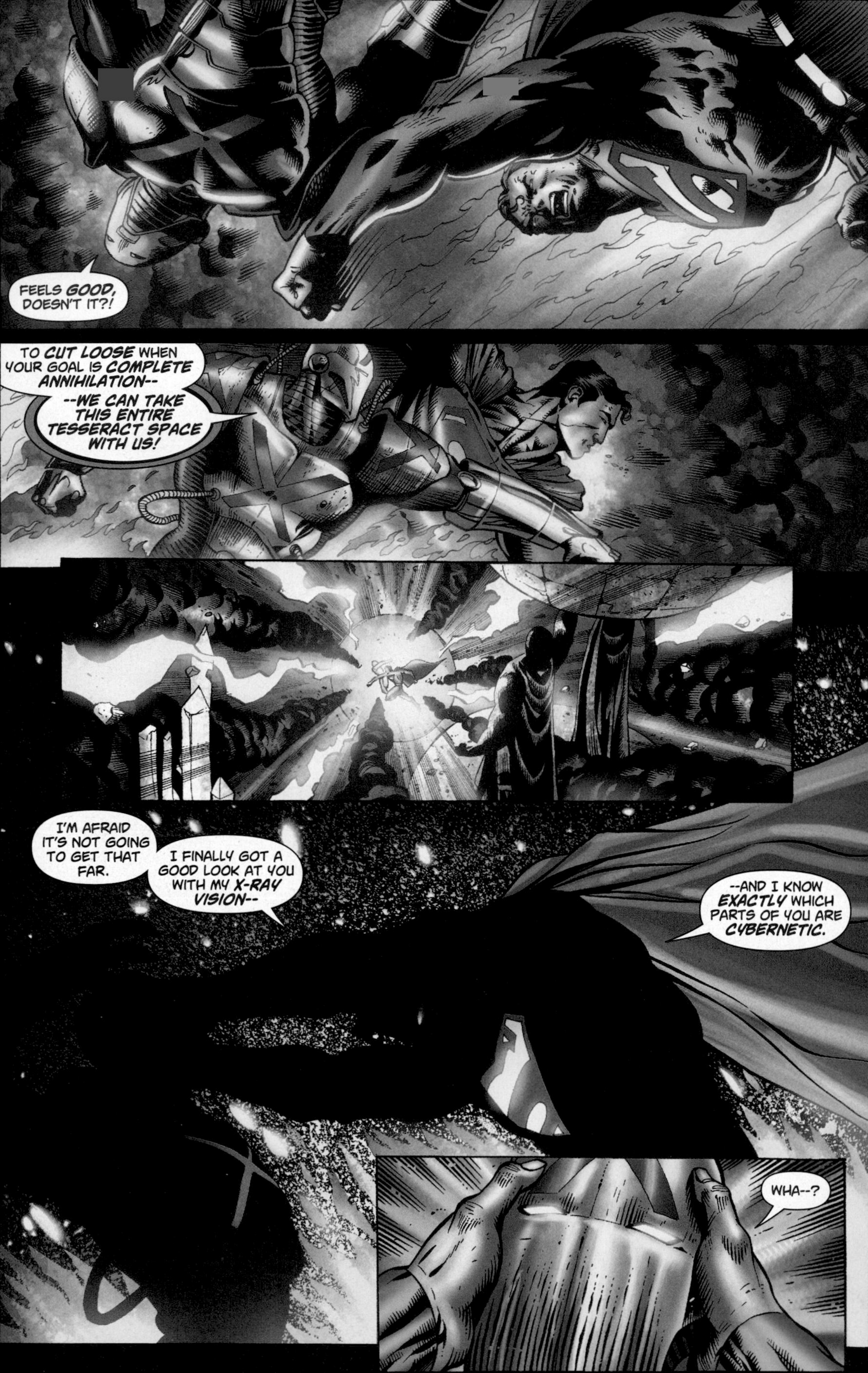
FEELS GOOD, DOESN'T IT?!
TO CUT LOOSE WHEN YOUR GOAL IS COMPLETE ANNIHILATION--
--WE CAN TAKE THIS ENTIRE TESSERACT SPACE WITH US!
I'M AFRAID IT'S NOT GOING TO GET THAT FAR.
I FINALLY GOT A GOOD LOOK AT YOU WITH MY X-RAY VISION--
--AND I KNOW EXACTLY WHICH PARTS OF YOU ARE CYBERNETIC.
WHA--?

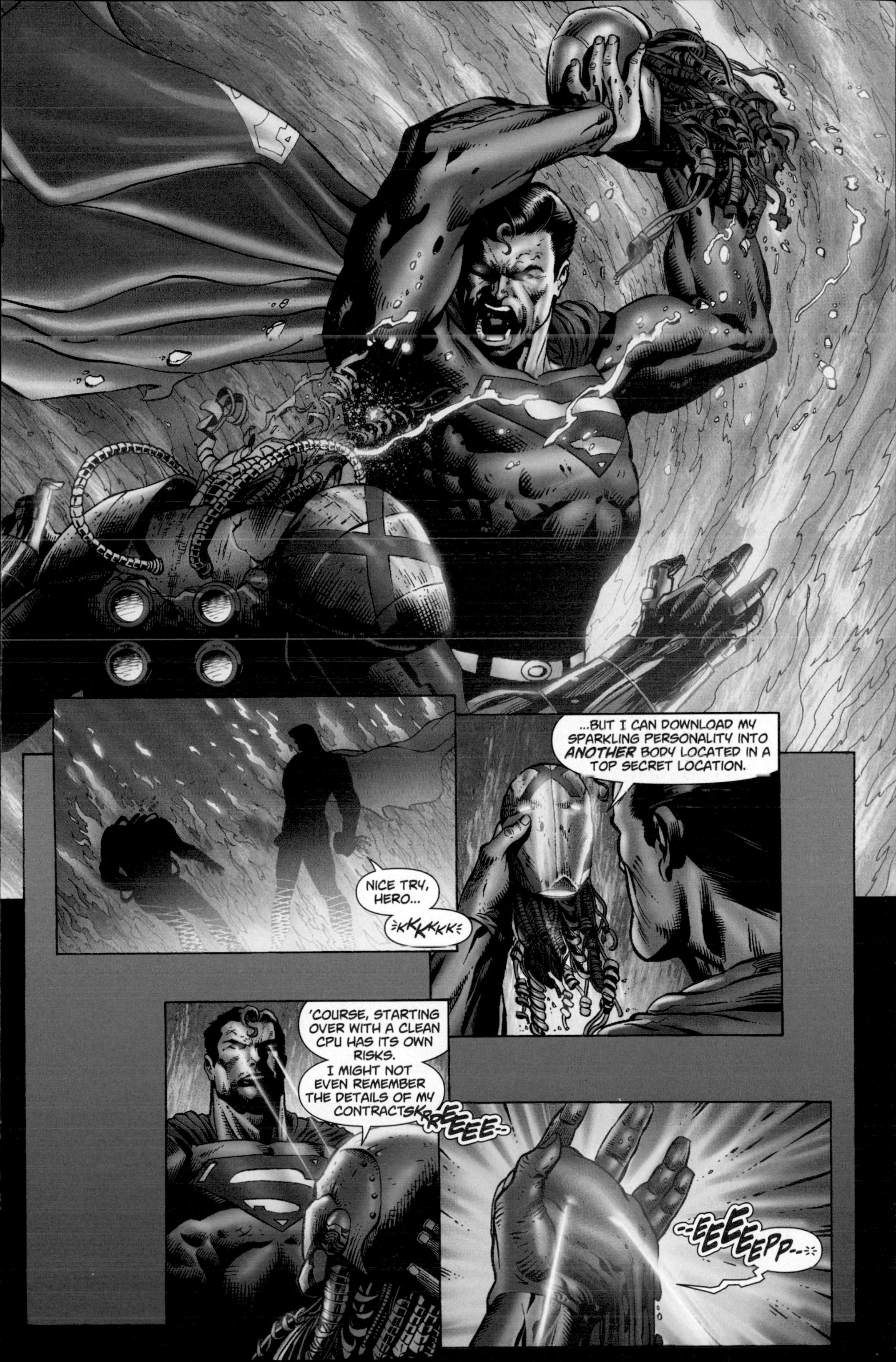
NICE TRY, HERO...
KKKKKKK
...BUT I CAN DOWNLOAD MY SPARKLING PERSONALITY INTO ANOTHER BODY LOCATED IN A TOP SECRET LOCATION.
'COURSE, STARTING OVER WITH A CLEAN CPU HAS ITS OWN RISKS.
I MIGHT NOT EVEN REMEMBER THE DETAILS OF MY CONTRACTSKRREEEEE-
--EEEEEPP--

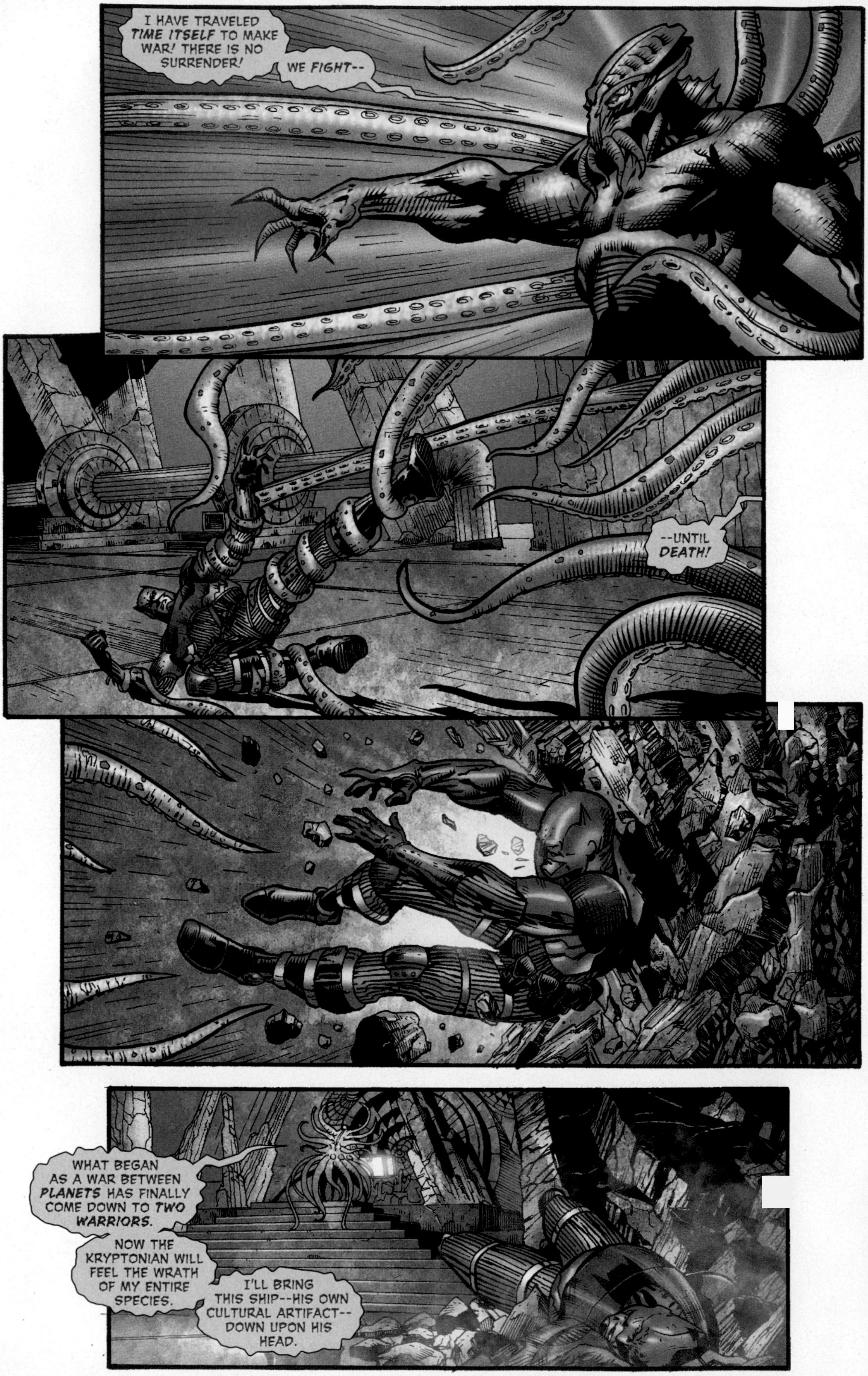
I HAVE TRAVELED TIME ITSELF TO MAKE WAR! THERE IS NO SURRENDER!
WE FIGHT--
--UNTIL DEATH!
WHAT BEGAN AS A WAR BETWEEN PLANETS HAS FINALLY COME DOWN TO TWO WARRIORS.
NOW THE KRYPTONIAN WILL FEEL THE WRATH OF MY ENTIRE SPECIES.
I'LL BRING THIS SHIP--HIS OWN CULTURAL ARTIFACT--DOWN UPON HIS HEAD.

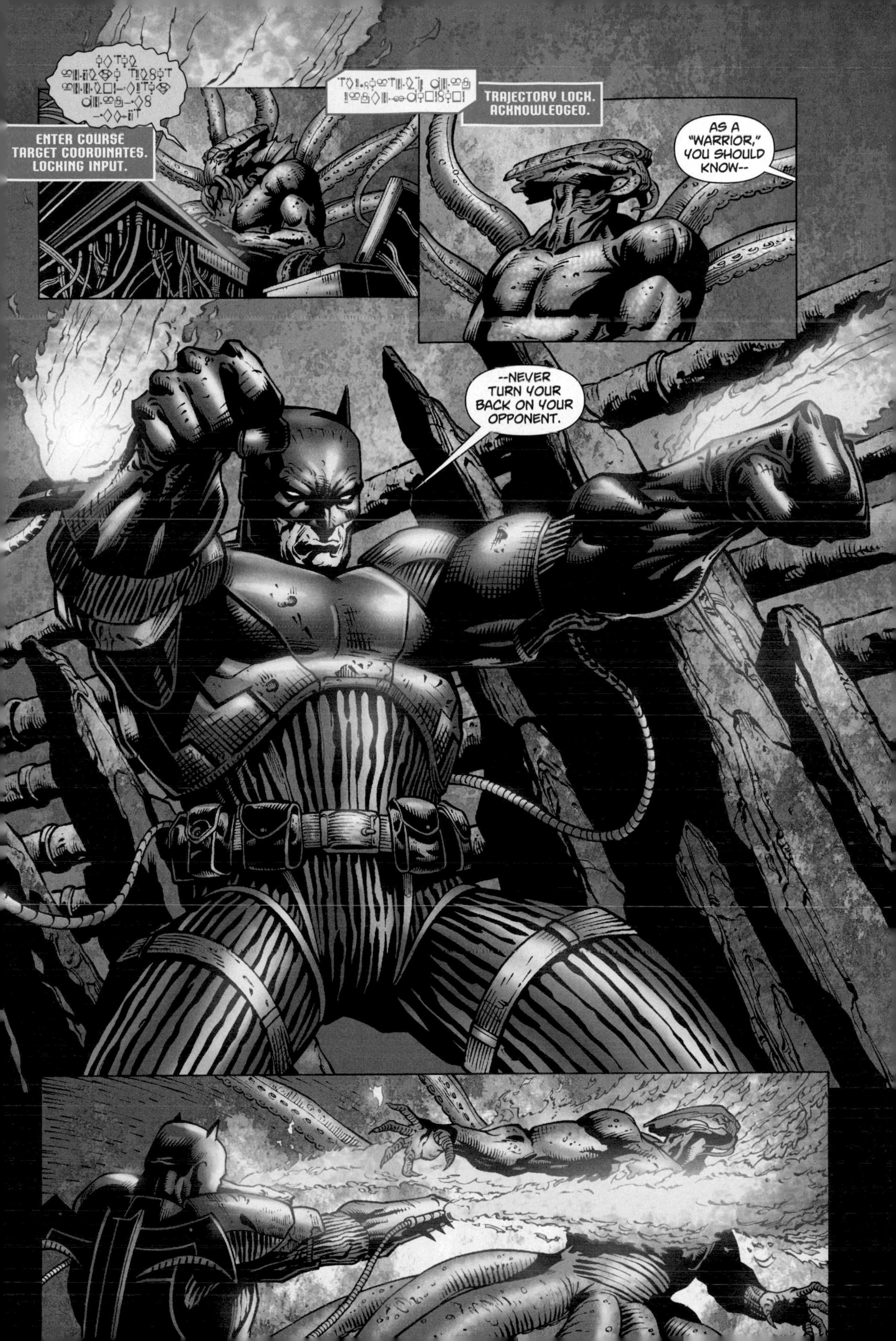
ENTER COURSE TARGET COORDINATES. LOCKING INPUT.
TRAJECTORY LOCK. ACKNOWLEDGED.
AS A "WARRIOR," YOU SHOULD KNOW--
--NEVER TURN YOUR BACK ON YOUR OPPONENT.

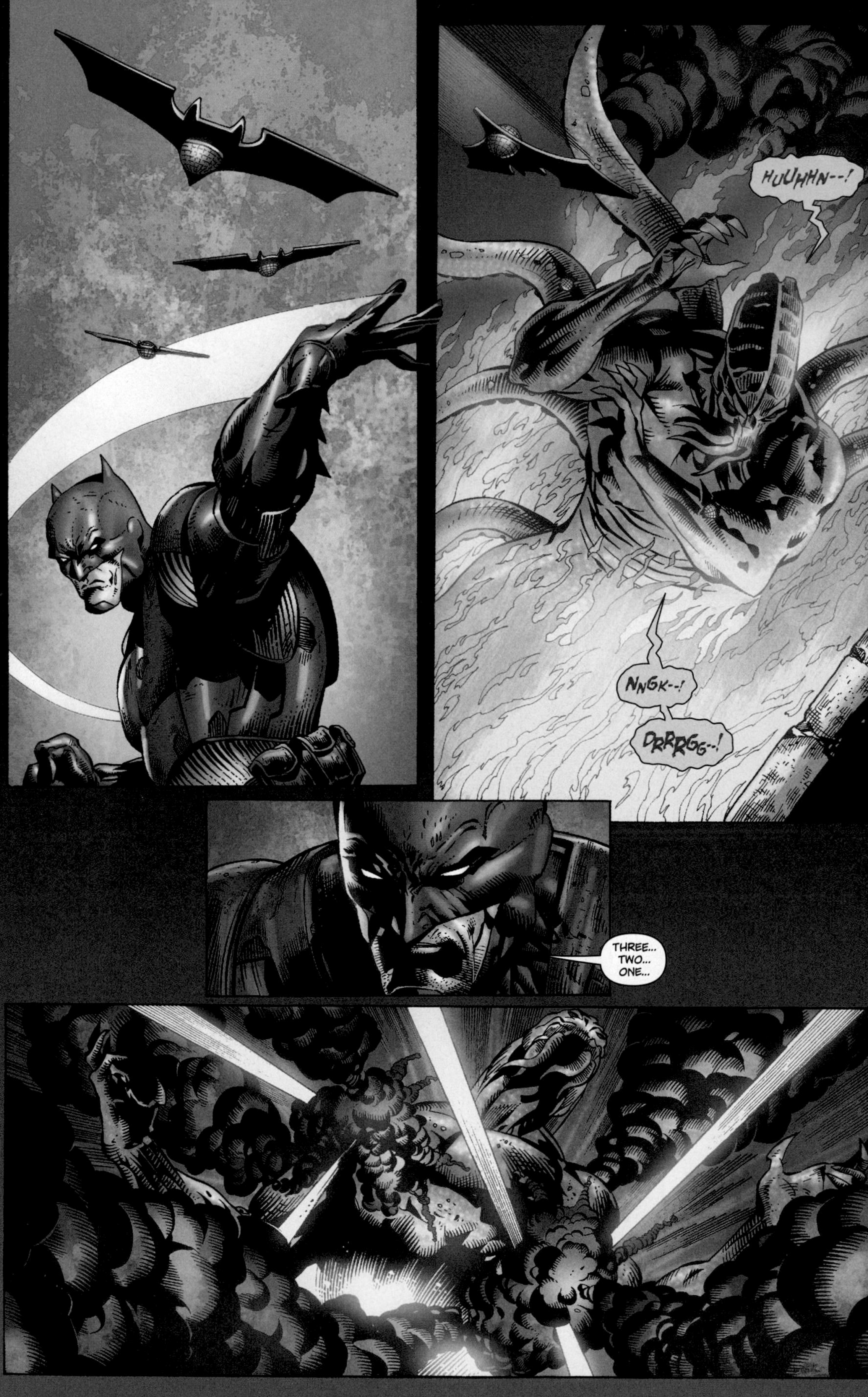
HUUHHN--!
NNGK--!
DRRRGG--!
THREE... TWO... ONE...

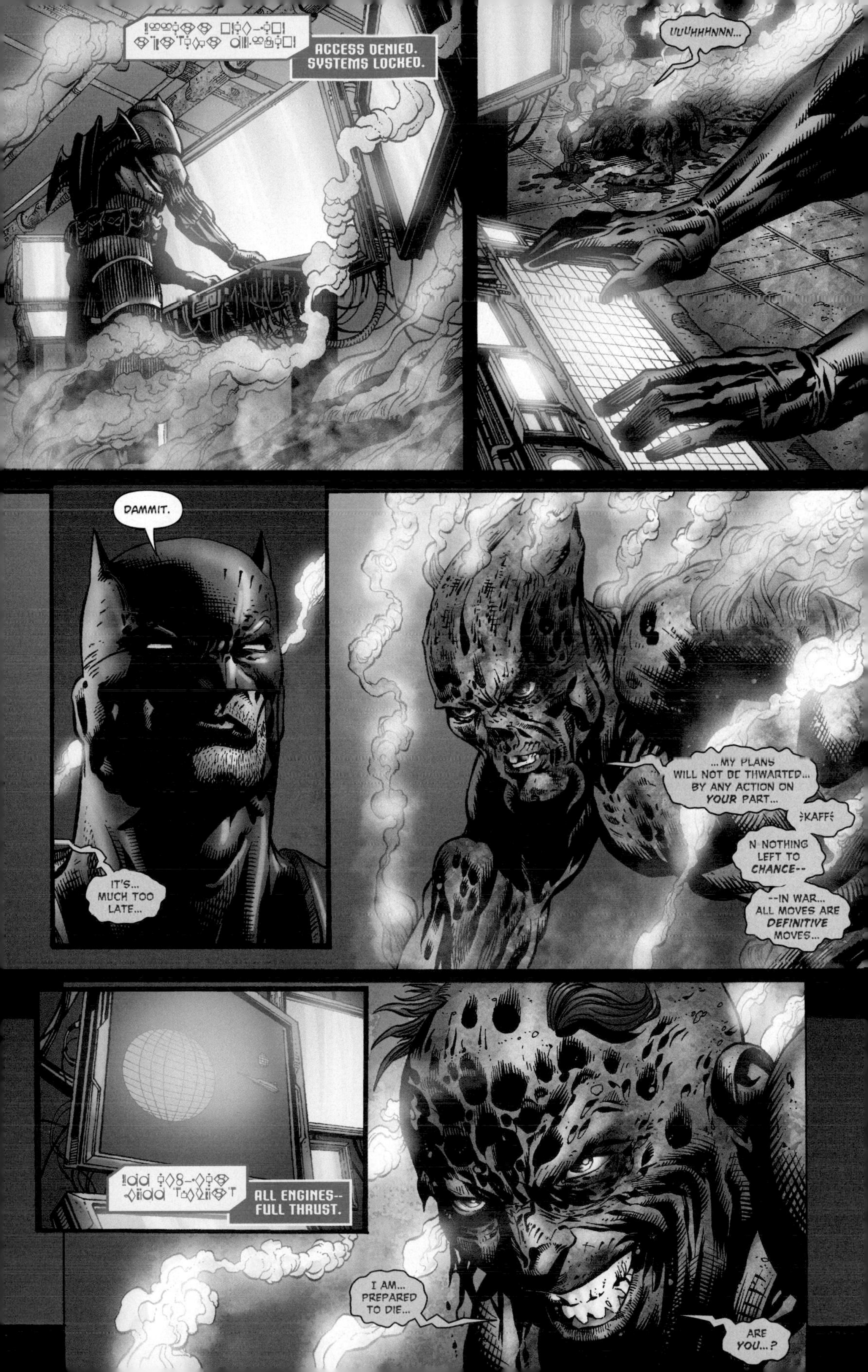
ACCESS DENIED. SYSTEMS LOCKED.
UUUHHHNNN...
DAMMIT.
IT'S... MUCH TOO LATE...
...MY PLANS WILL NOT BE THWARTED... BY ANY ACTION ON *YOUR* PART...
KAFF
N NOTHING LEFT TO *CHANCE*--
--IN WAR... ALL MOVES ARE *DEFINITIVE* MOVES...
ALL ENGINES-- FULL THRUST.
I AM... PREPARED TO DIE...
ARE *YOU*...?

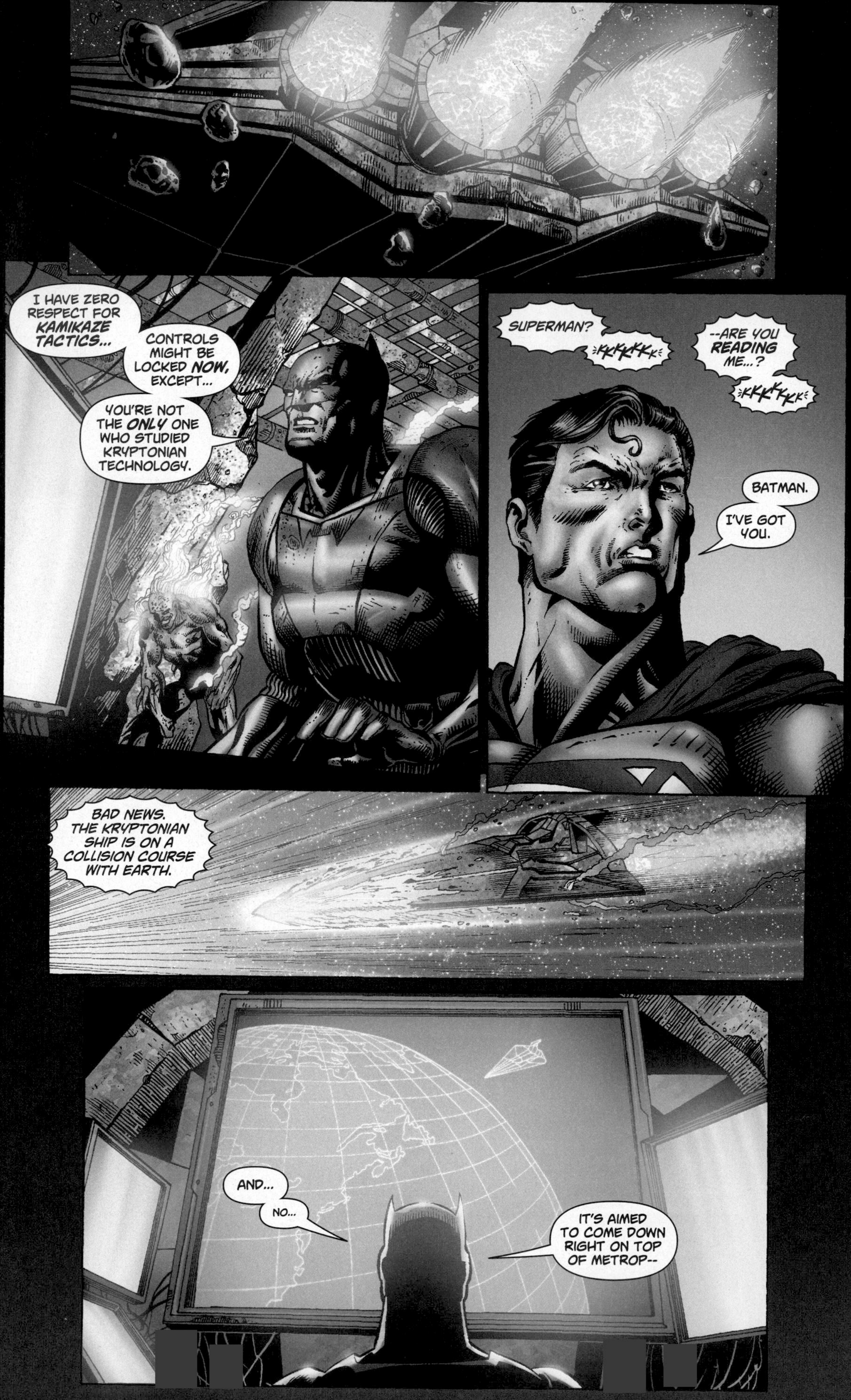
I HAVE ZERO RESPECT FOR KAMIKAZE TACTICS...
CONTROLS MIGHT BE LOCKED NOW, EXCEPT...
YOU'RE NOT THE ONLY ONE WHO STUDIED KRYPTONIAN TECHNOLOGY.
SUPERMAN?
KKKKKKK
--ARE YOU READING ME...?
KKKKKKK
BATMAN.
I'VE GOT YOU.
BAD NEWS. THE KRYPTONIAN SHIP IS ON A COLLISION COURSE WITH EARTH.
AND...
NO...
IT'S AIMED TO COME DOWN RIGHT ON TOP OF METROP--

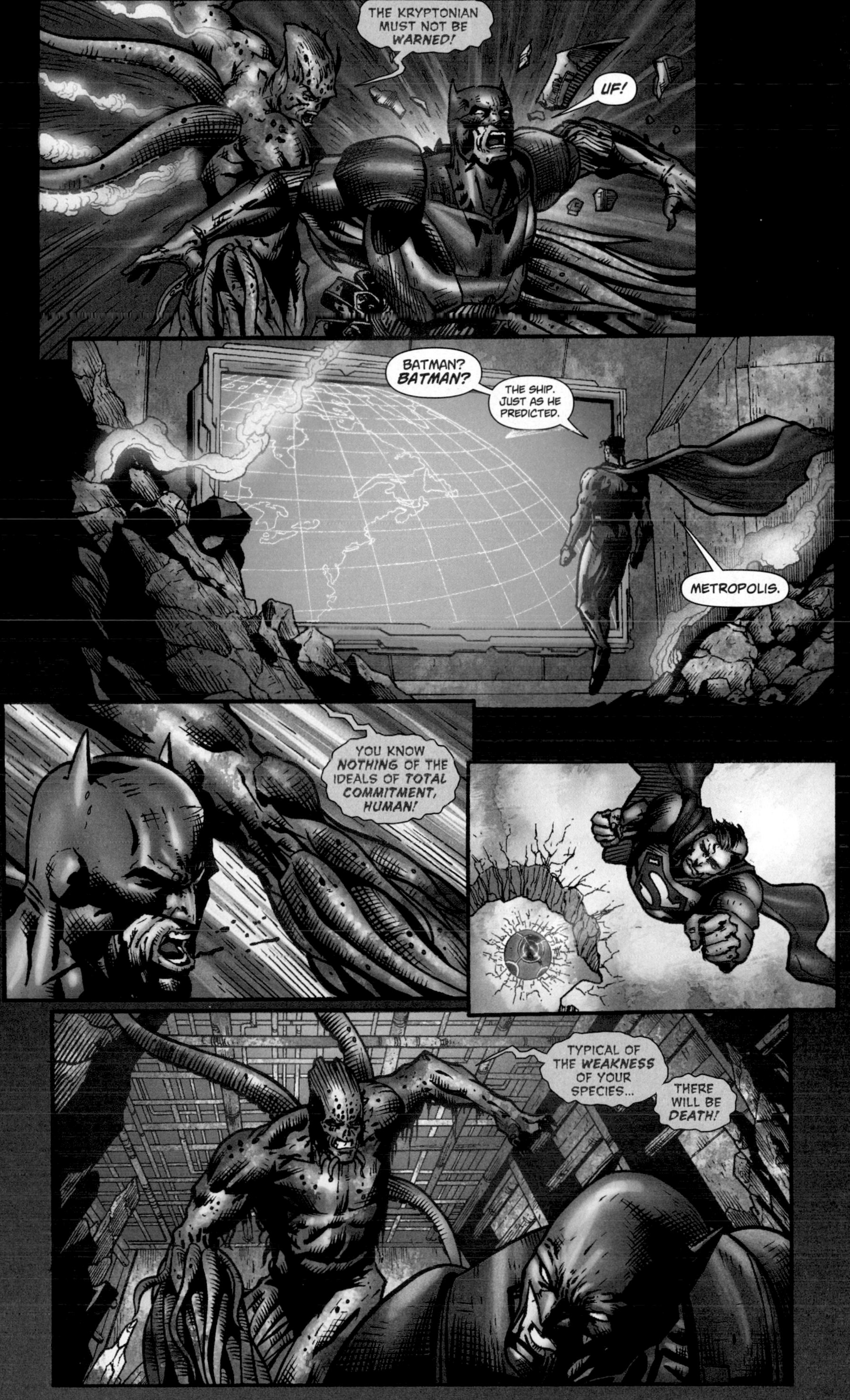
THE KRYPTONIAN MUST NOT BE WARNED!
UF!
BATMAN? BATMAN?
THE SHIP. JUST AS HE PREDICTED.
METROPOLIS.
YOU KNOW NOTHING OF THE IDEALS OF TOTAL COMMITMENT, HUMAN!
TYPICAL OF THE WEAKNESS OF YOUR SPECIES...
THERE WILL BE DEATH!

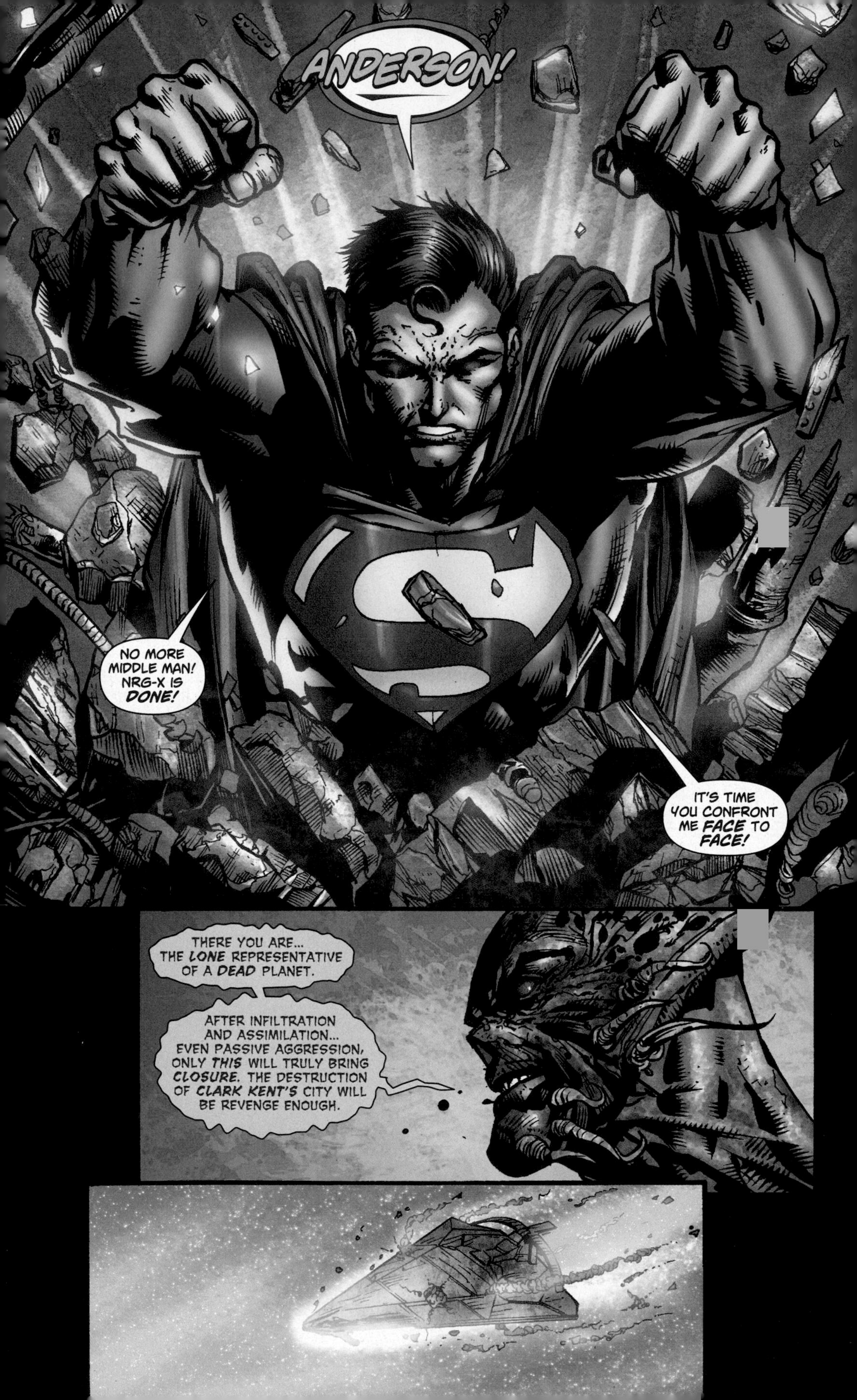
ANDERSON!
NO MORE MIDDLE MAN! NRG-X IS DONE!
IT'S TIME YOU CONFRONT ME FACE TO FACE!
THERE YOU ARE... THE LONE REPRESENTATIVE OF A DEAD PLANET.
AFTER INFILTRATION AND ASSIMILATION... EVEN PASSIVE AGGRESSION, ONLY THIS WILL TRULY BRING CLOSURE. THE DESTRUCTION OF CLARK KENT'S CITY WILL BE REVENGE ENOUGH.

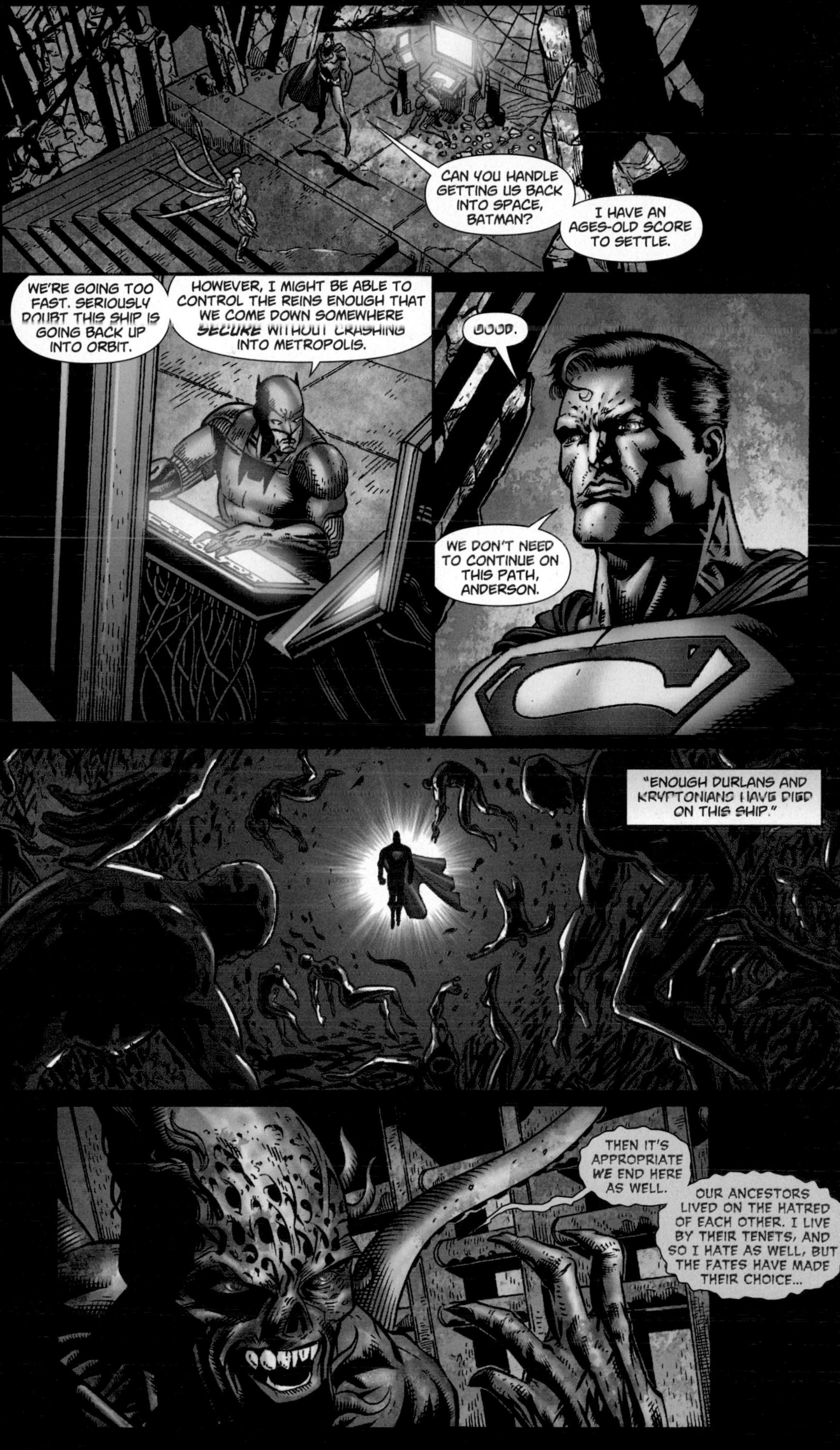

CAN YOU HANDLE GETTING US BACK INTO SPACE, BATMAN?
I HAVE AN AGES-OLD SCORE TO SETTLE.
WE'RE GOING TOO FAST. SERIOUSLY DOUBT THIS SHIP IS GOING BACK UP INTO ORBIT.
HOWEVER, I MIGHT BE ABLE TO CONTROL THE REINS ENOUGH THAT WE COME DOWN SOMEWHERE SECURE WITHOUT CRASHING INTO METROPOLIS.
GOOD.
WE DON'T NEED TO CONTINUE ON THIS PATH, ANDERSON.
"ENOUGH DURLANS AND KRYPTONIANS HAVE DIED ON THIS SHIP."
THEN IT'S APPROPRIATE WE END HERE AS WELL.
OUR ANCESTORS LIVED ON THE HATRED OF EACH OTHER. I LIVE BY THEIR TENETS, AND SO I HATE AS WELL, BUT THE FATES HAVE MADE THEIR CHOICE...

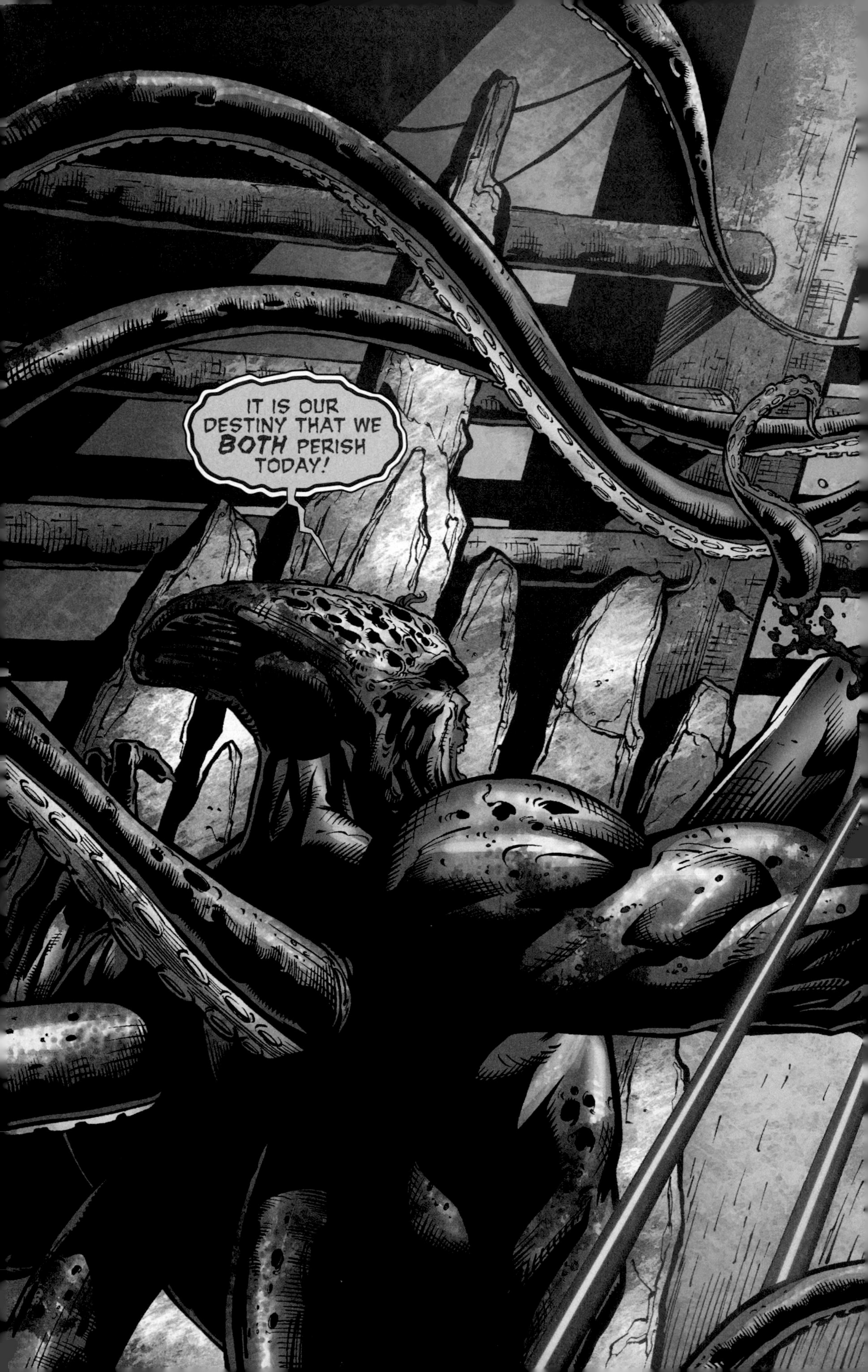
IT IS OUR DESTINY THAT WE BOTH PERISH TODAY!

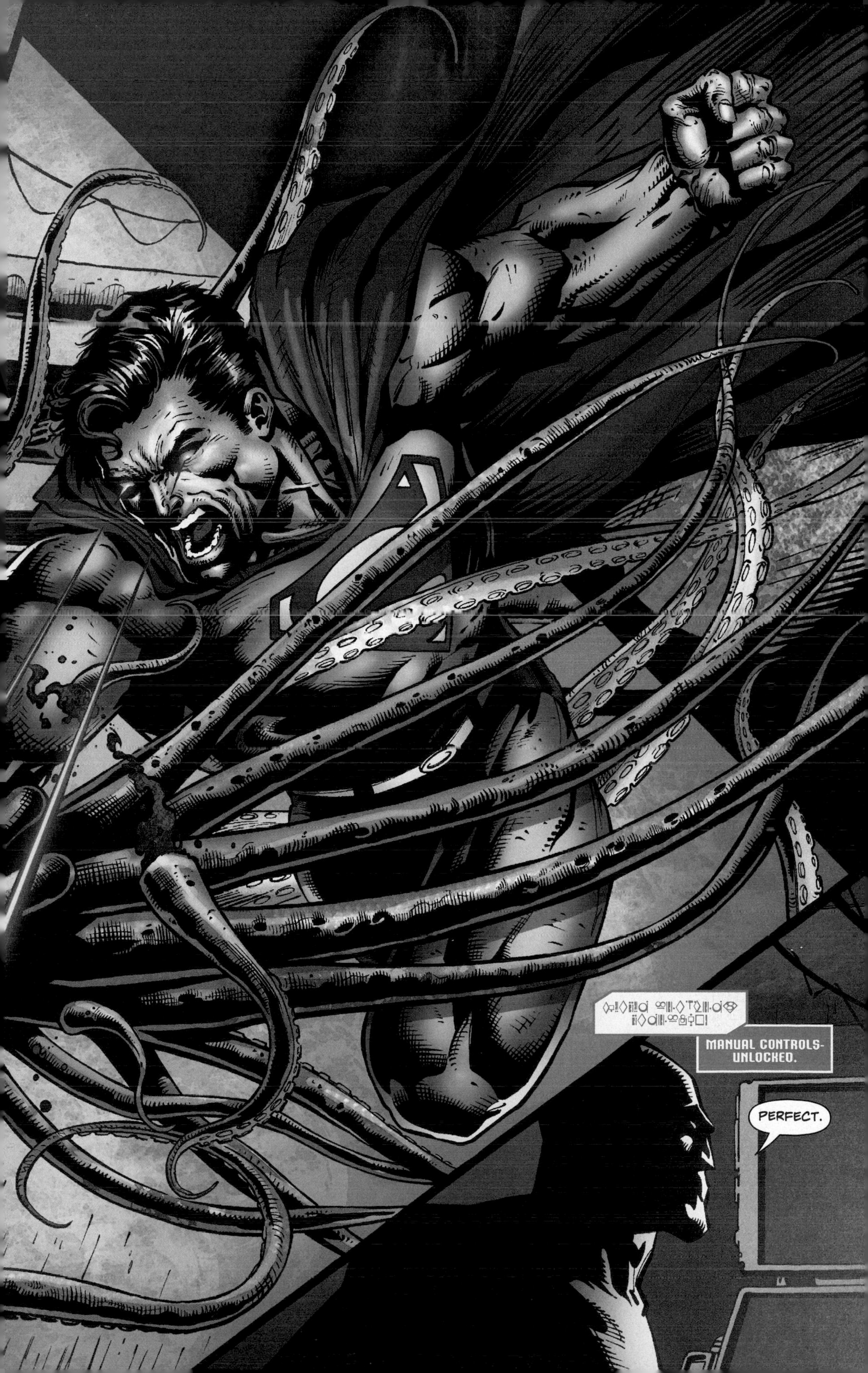
MANUAL CONTROLS-
UNLOCKED.
PERFECT.

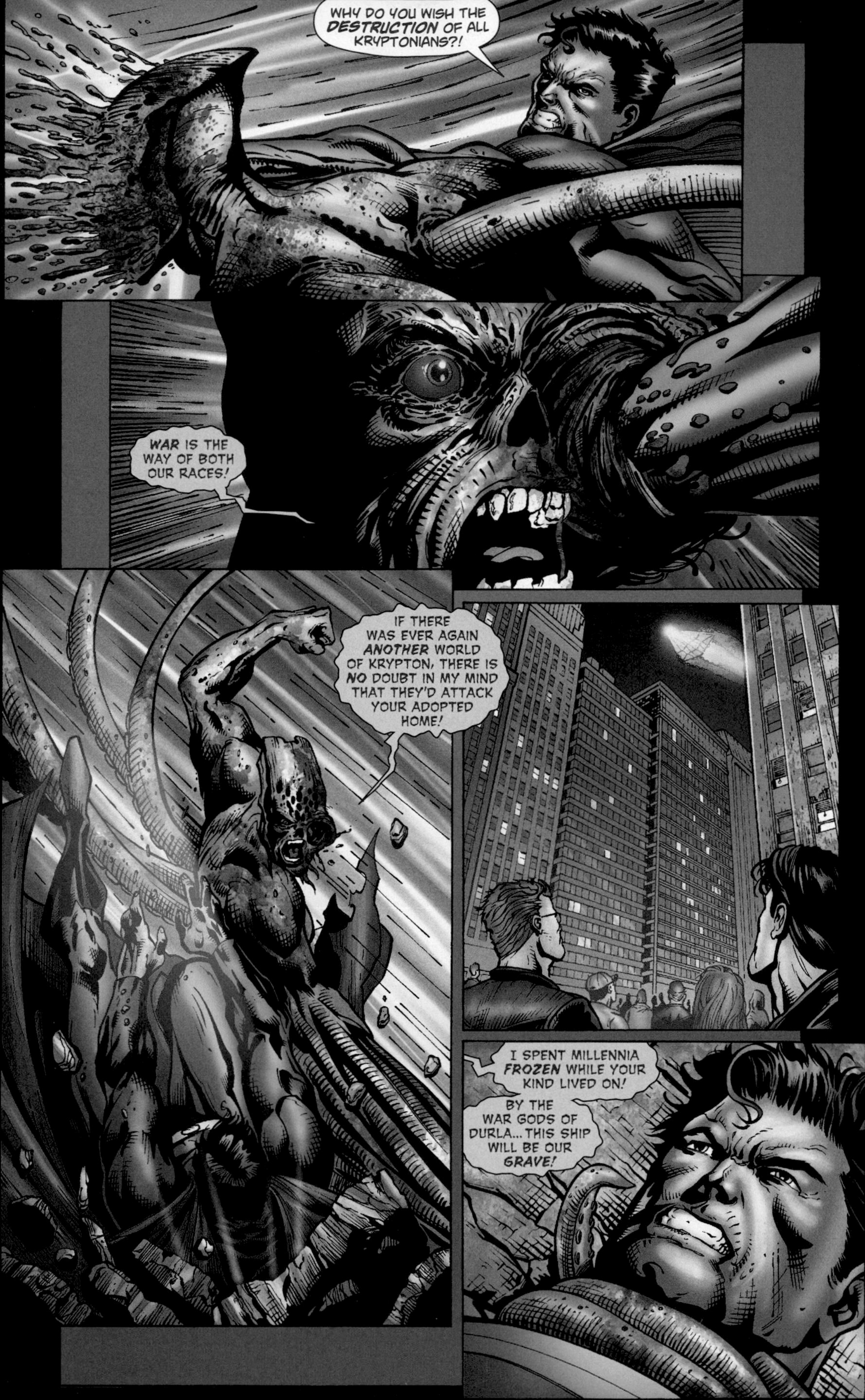
WHY DO YOU WISH THE DESTRUCTION OF ALL KRYPTONIANS?!
WAR IS THE WAY OF BOTH OUR RACES!
IF THERE WAS EVER AGAIN ANOTHER WORLD OF KRYPTON, THERE IS NO DOUBT IN MY MIND THAT THEY'D ATTACK YOUR ADOPTED HOME!
I SPENT MILLENNIA FROZEN WHILE YOUR KIND LIVED ON!
BY THE WAR GODS OF DURLA... THIS SHIP WILL BE OUR GRAVE!

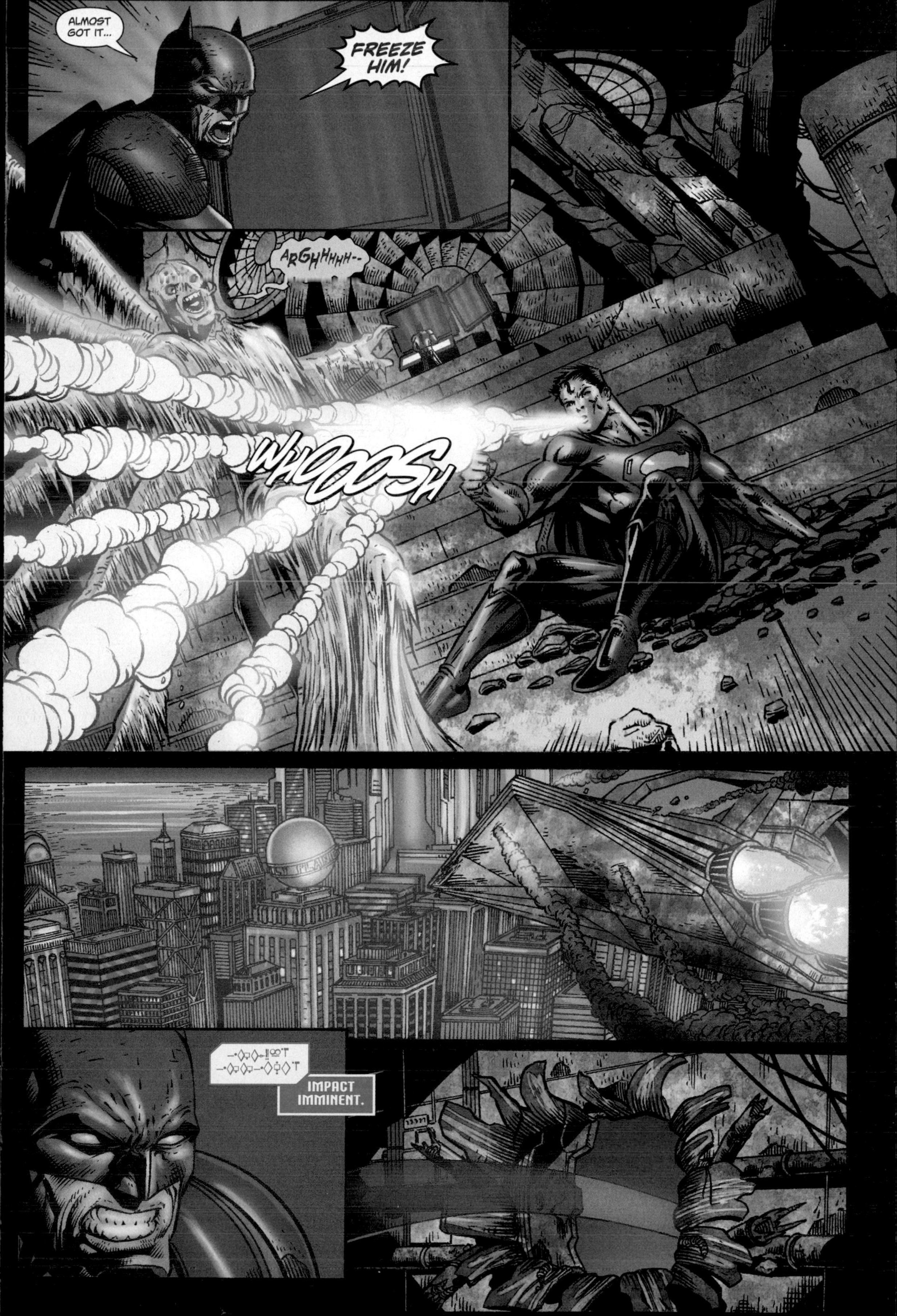
ALMOST GOT IT...
FREEZE HIM!
ARGHHHHH--
WHOOOOSH
IMPACT IMMINENT.

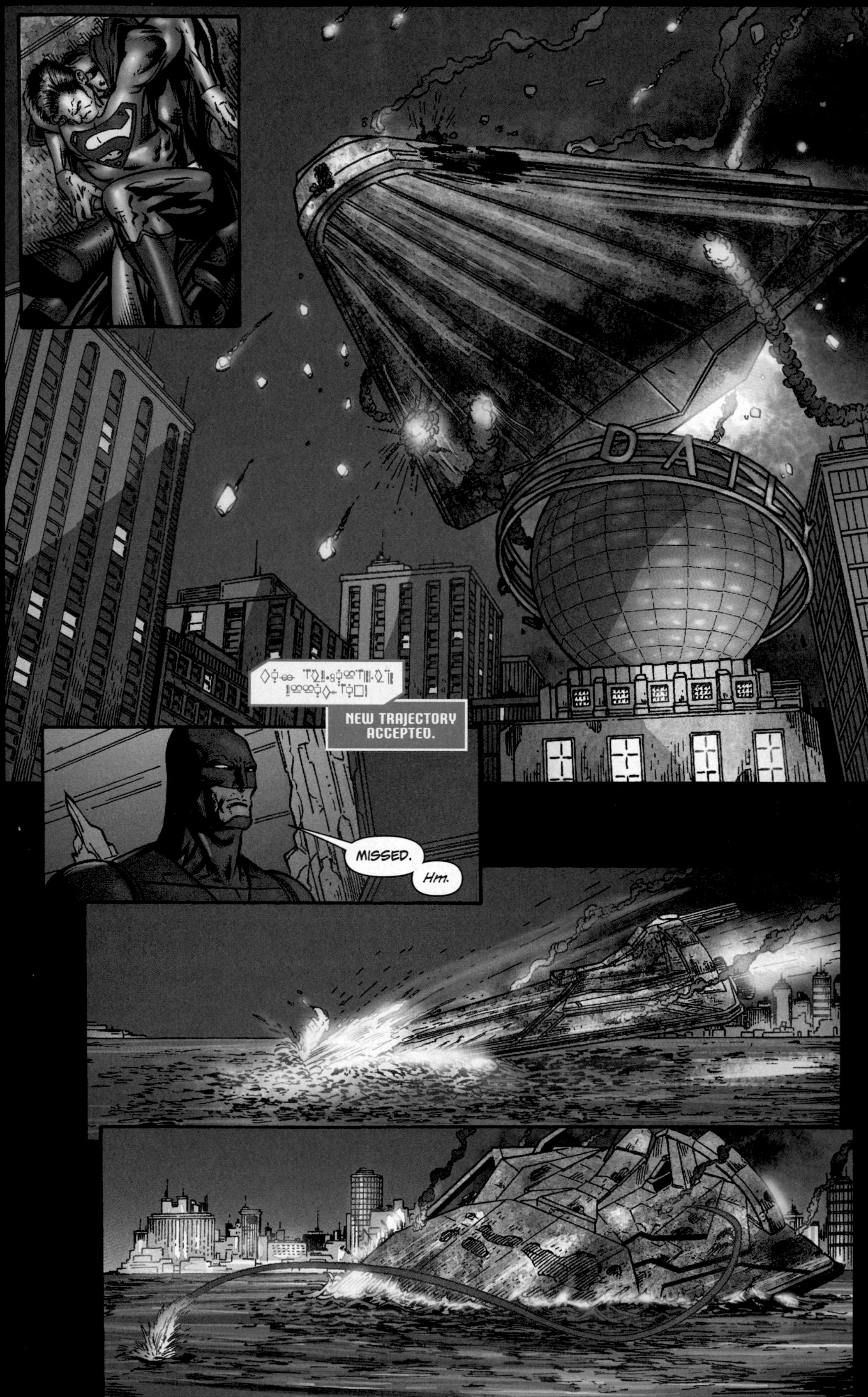

NEW TRAJECTORY ACCEPTED.
DAILY
MISSED.
Hm.

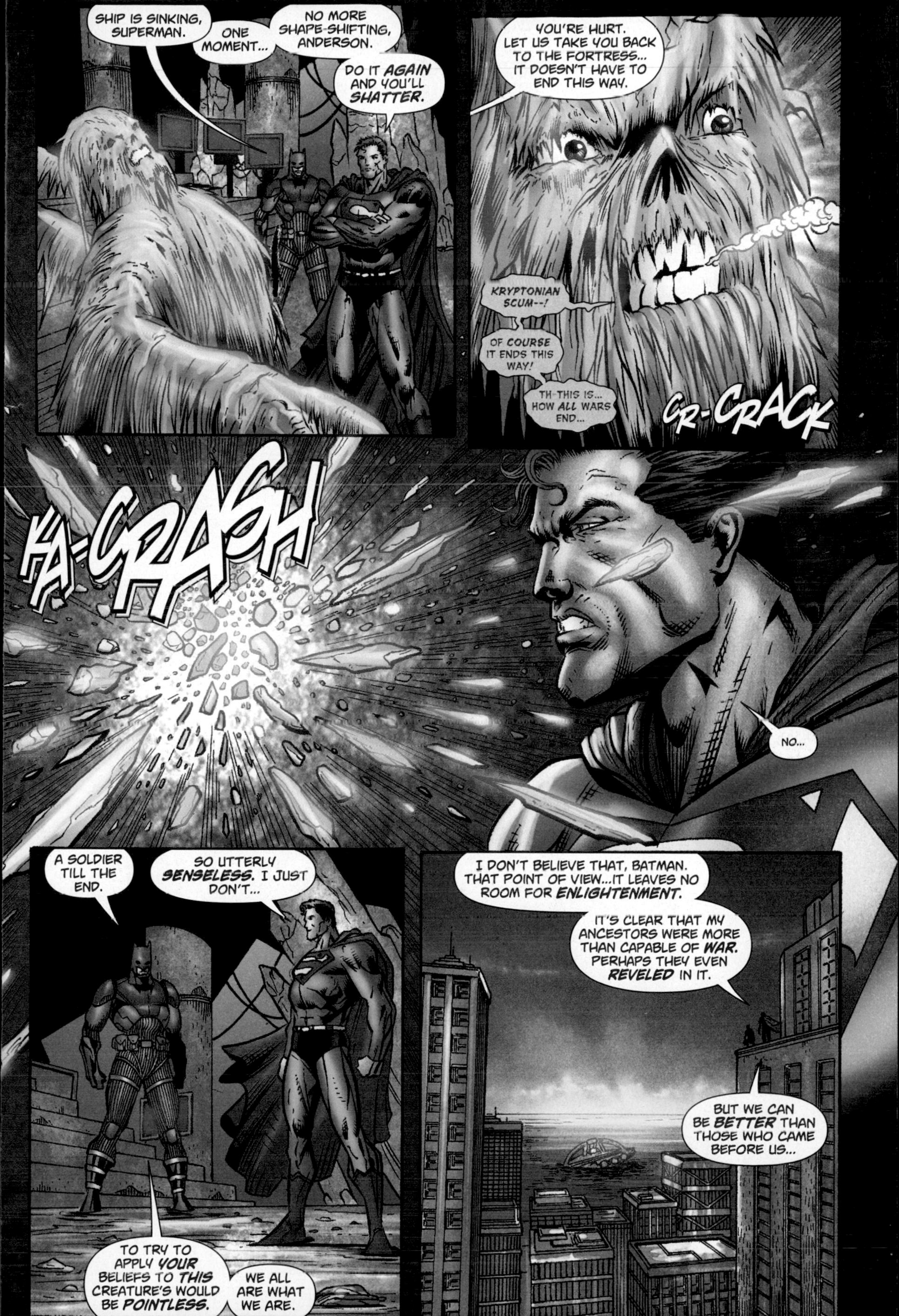

SHIP IS SINKING, SUPERMAN.
ONE MOMENT...
NO MORE SHAPE-SHIFTING, ANDERSON.
DO IT AGAIN AND YOU'LL SHATTER.
YOU'RE HURT. LET US TAKE YOU BACK TO THE FORTRESS... IT DOESN'T HAVE TO END THIS WAY.
KRYPTONIAN SCUM--!
OF COURSE IT ENDS THIS WAY!
TH-THIS IS... HOW ALL WARS END...
CR-CRACK
KA-CRASH
NO...
A SOLDIER TILL THE END.
SO UTTERLY SENSELESS. I JUST DON'T...
TO TRY TO APPLY YOUR BELIEFS TO THIS CREATURE'S WOULD BE POINTLESS.
WE ALL ARE WHAT WE ARE.
I DON'T BELIEVE THAT, BATMAN. THAT POINT OF VIEW...IT LEAVES NO ROOM FOR ENLIGHTENMENT.
IT'S CLEAR THAT MY ANCESTORS WERE MORE THAN CAPABLE OF WAR. PERHAPS THEY EVEN REVELED IN IT.
BUT WE CAN BE BETTER THAN THOSE WHO CAME BEFORE US...

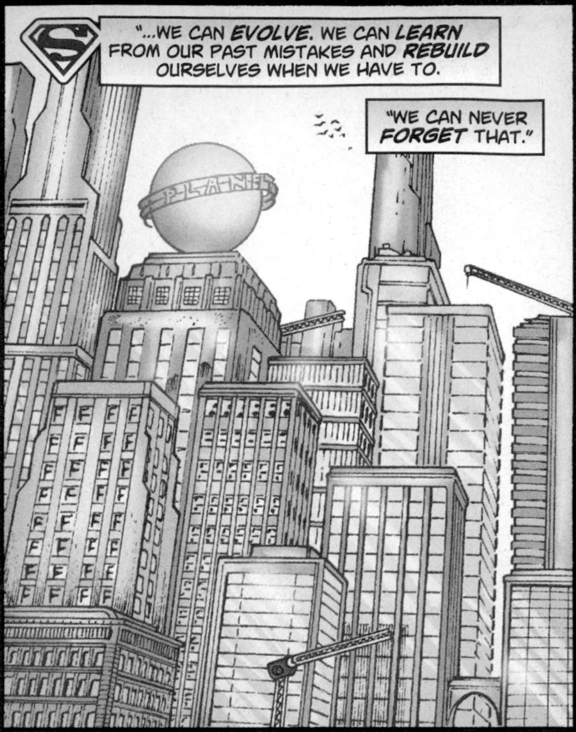
"...WE CAN EVOLVE. WE CAN LEARN FROM OUR PAST MISTAKES AND REBUILD OURSELVES WHEN WE HAVE TO.
"WE CAN NEVER FORGET THAT."

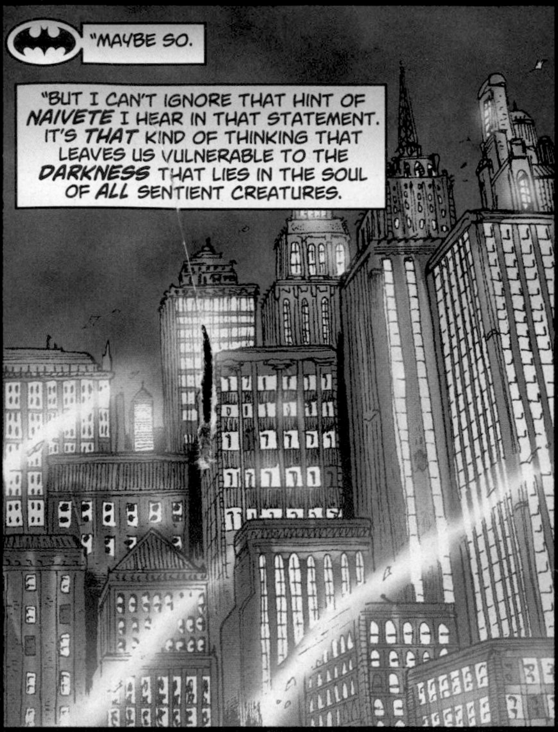
"MAYBE SO.
"BUT I CAN'T IGNORE THAT HINT OF NAIVETE I HEAR IN THAT STATEMENT. IT'S THAT KIND OF THINKING THAT LEAVES US VULNERABLE TO THE DARKNESS THAT LIES IN THE SOUL OF ALL SENTIENT CREATURES.

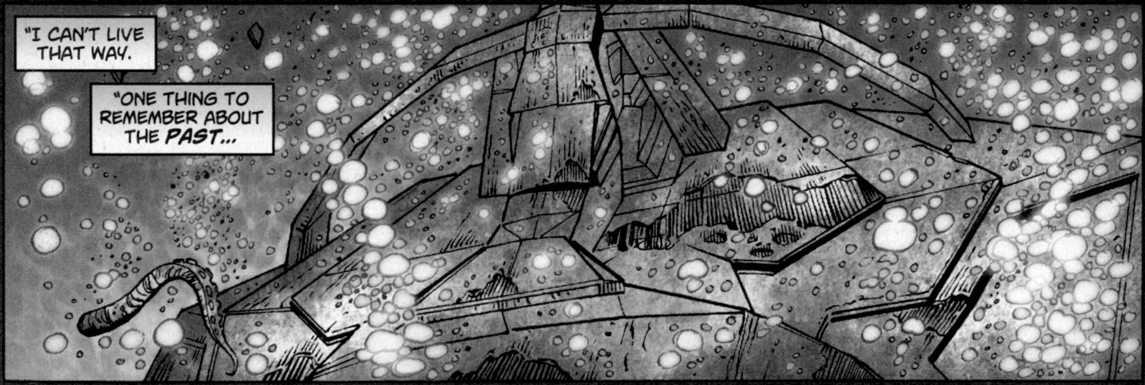
"I CAN'T LIVE THAT WAY.
"ONE THING TO REMEMBER ABOUT THE PAST...

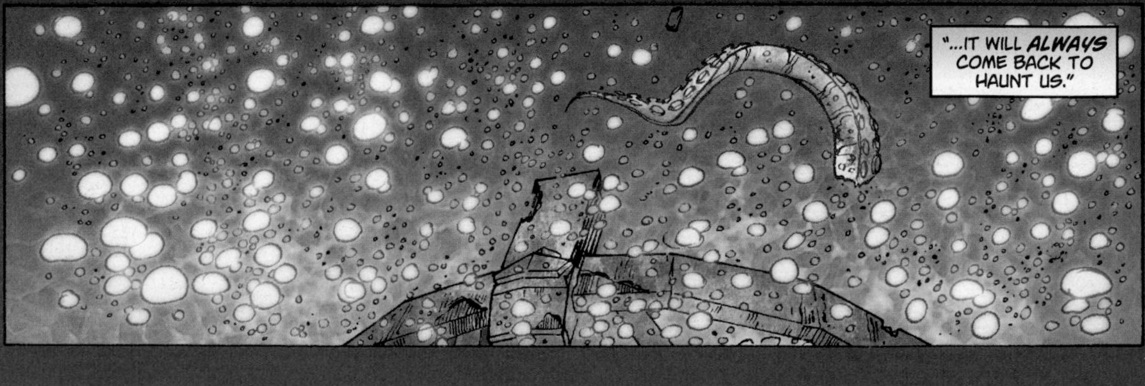
"...IT WILL ALWAYS COME BACK TO HAUNT US."

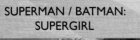

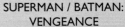

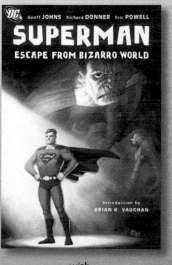

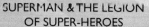

FROM THE WRITER OF
BATMAN: THE LONG HALLOWEEN

JEPH LOEB

with TIM SALE

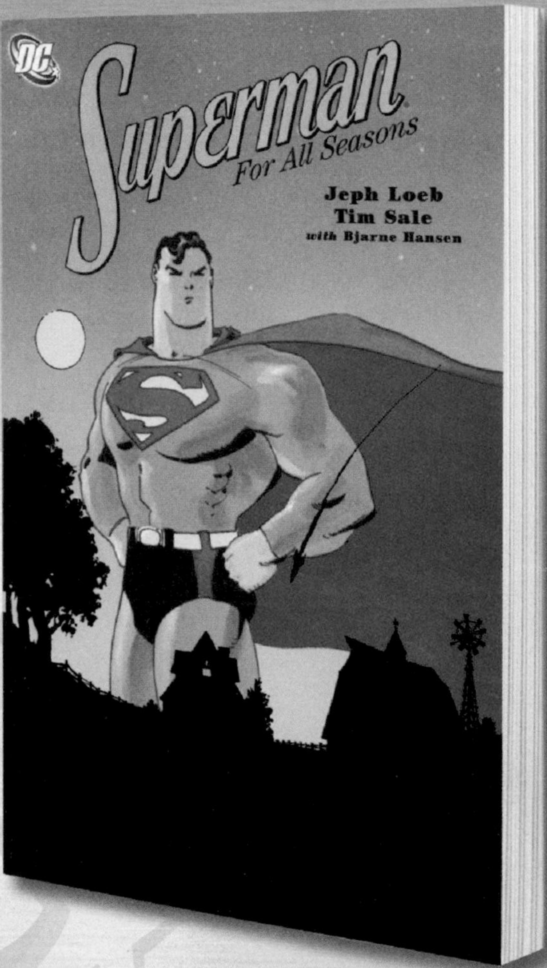
DC
Superman
For All Seasons
Jeph Loeb
Tim Sale
with Bjarne Hansen

This coming-of-age tale is an emotional and insightful examination of Clark Kent's transformation from a powerful boy into a heroic man. Told through the course of four seasons in the Man of Steel's adolescent life, it illustrates that it is the person, not the powers, that makes the Man of Steel a hero.

MORE CRITICALLY ACCLAIMED TALES OF THE MAN OF STEEL

SUPERMAN:
FOR TOMORROW VOL. 1

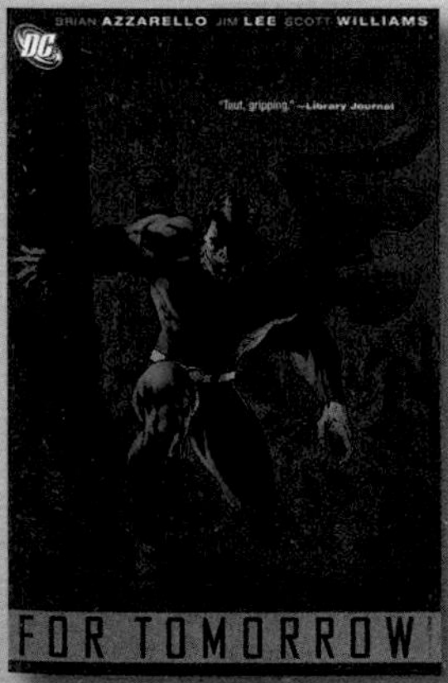
BRIAN AZZARELLO JIM LEE SCOTT WILLIAMS
DC
FOR TOMORROW

BRIAN AZZARELLO
JIM LEE

SUPERMAN:
FOR TOMORROW VOL. 2

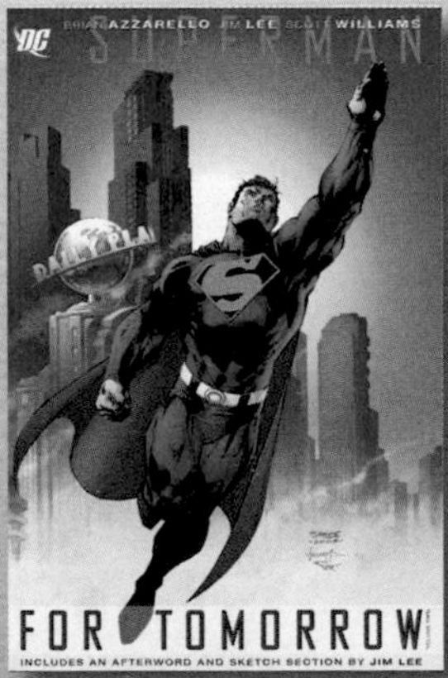
BRIAN AZZARELLO JIM LEE SCOTT WILLIAMS
DC
SUPERMAN
FOR TOMORROW
INCLUDES AN AFTERWORD AND SKETCH SECTION BY JIM LEE

BRIAN AZZARELLO
JIM LEE

THE DEATH
OF SUPERMAN

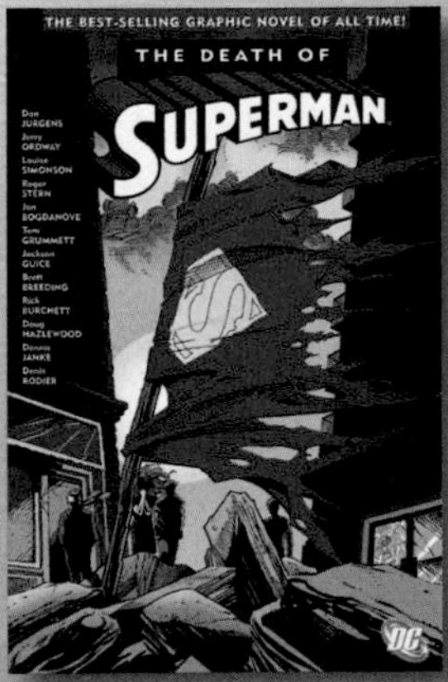
THE BEST-SELLING GRAPHIC NOVEL OF ALL TIME!
THE DEATH OF
SUPERMAN
DC

VARIOUS
WRITERS & ARTISTS

SEARCH THE GRAPHIC NOVELS SECTION OF
DCCOMICS.COM
FOR ART AND INFORMATION ON ALL OF OUR BOOKS!